BEAUTY DIPLOMACY

GLOBALIZATION
IN EVERYDAY LIFE

Beauty Diplomacy

Embodying an Emerging Nation

OLUWAKEMI M. BALOGUN

STANFORD UNIVERSITY PRESS
Stanford, California

STANFORD UNIVERSITY PRESS
Stanford, California

Printed in the United States of America on acid-free, archival-quality paper

Library of Congress Cataloging-in-Publication Data

Names: Balogun, Oluwakemi M., author.
Title: Beauty diplomacy : embodying an emerging nation / Oluwakemi M. Balogun.
Other titles: Globalization in everyday life.
Description: Stanford, California : Stanford University Press, 2020. | Series: Globalization in everyday life | Includes bibliographical references and index.
Identifiers: LCCN 2019019682 | ISBN 9781503608856 (cloth ; alk. paper) | ISBN 9781503610972 (pbk. ; alk. paper) | ISBN 9781503610989 (electronic)
Subjects: LCSH: Beauty contests—Political aspects—Nigeria. | Nationalism—Nigeria.
Classification: LCC HQ1220.N6 B35 2020 | DDC 791.6/609669—dc23
LC record available at https://lccn.loc.gov/2019019682

Text and cover design: Kevin Barrett Kane

Typeset by Westchester Publishing Services in 10/14.4 Minion Pro

To Kamil Ekungba, for the sacrifices

Contents

Figures

Acknowledgments

Books are long-haul projects and I have many people to thank for their help along the way. I have been tremendously blessed to have benefited from brilliant and thoughtful colleagues, friends, and interlocutors who helped shape this project.

First and foremost, I would like to thank the beauty pageant organizations for granting me access and for my respondents—contestants, organizers, opponents, and others—for opening up to me and sharing their stories. Without their valuable insights and perspectives, this book would not have been possible.

I am also deeply grateful to a number of people who mentored me. Raka Ray has championed this project from its early infancy. Through her generous support and thoughtful guidance, she inspired me to develop the emergent ideas in the book and laid the foundation for my trajectory as a scholar. Ann Swidler's careful engagement with my work from its early stages helped firm up many of the central points of this book, especially around Nigeria's reputational politics. Barrie Thorne's nuanced thinking made me reflect more deeply about questions of micro-macro connections and how to situate inherent tensions and contradictions more productively. Paola Bacchetta encouraged me to deepen my theoretical engagement by bringing in insights from transnational and postcolonial feminist theory to bear on sociological questions about gendered nationalism in Nigeria. Michael Watts pushed me to engage more precisely with the complexities of Nigeria's political economy, especially the state and contentious politics. I am greatly appreciative for all of these scholars since they have been critical to my intellectual growth.

I have benefited from many writing groups over the past decade who have read several drafts at various stages and kept me afloat emotionally. I thank Abigail Andrews, Ruha Benjamin, Jennifer Carlson, Dawn Dow, Katie Hasson, Kimberly Hoang, Jennifer Jones, Kate Maich, Katherine Mason, Jordanna Matlon, Sarah Anne Minkin, Jacqueline Mougoué, Heidy Sarabia, Nazanin Shahrokni, Stanley Thangaraj, and Gowri Vijayakumar for their penetrating feedback, which is imprinted throughout this book. Jane Jones, a fabulous developmental editor, was an invaluable sounding board throughout this process.

Talks at conferences and universities also enriched the key points of this book, especially the University of Cambridge's Politics of Beauty Conference and Mimi Nguyen's comments as a discussant, Washington State University's Women's Studies Lecture Series, and the University of Oregon's Introduction to African Studies Seminar, whose participants and audiences provided critical engagement.

At University of Oregon I was lucky to have amazing colleagues who read my work and provided immeasurable support. I especially thank Yvonne Braun, Charise Cheney, Lynn Fujiwara, Lisa Gilman, Sangita Gopal, Aaron Gullickson, Jocelyn Hollander, Ana Maurine Lara, Ernesto Martinez, Michelle McKinley, Isabel Millán, Josie Mulkins, Matthew Norton, Eileen Otis, CJ Pascoe, Julee Raiskin, Lizzie Reis, Margaret Rhee, Shoniqua Roach, Ellen Scott, Jiannbin Shiao, Carol Stabile, Lani Teves, Ed Wolf, Jessica Vasquez-Tokos, Priscilla Yamin, and Kristin Yarris. At Oregon I held a one-day book manuscript workshop where Yvonne Braun, Erynn Masi de Casanova, Maxine Craig, Ebenezer Obadare, and Oyèrónkẹ́ Oyěwùmí read the entire draft manuscript. I am grateful for their time and sharp insights that helped me clarify the key concepts in this book. A special thanks to Erynn, who read the entire manuscript twice and provided incisive feedback to further hone the book after the workshop.

Aside from the University of Oregon, I have also benefited from other institutional affiliations and generous support. While in Nigeria during fieldwork, I was an affiliate at the University of Lagos. I thank Lai Olurode, Funmi

Bammeke, and Adebowale Ayobade for their support of my work. At Pomona College, I was provided with the space to reconnect with former mentors who were formative to my thinking and to meet new colleagues. I thank Colin Beck, Jill Grigsby, Phyllis Jackson, Sidney Lemelle, Gilda Ochoa, Lynn Rappaport, and Hung Thai. Fellowships and grants from the University of California Berkeley, including the Designated Emphasis in Women, Gender, and Sexuality Studies Grant; Rocca African Studies Fellowship; and Sigma Xi's Grant-in-Aid of Research helped fund initial stages of the research. Funds from the University of Oregon's Center for the Study of Women in Society, College of Arts and Sciences, Oregon Humanities Center, and Women of Color Project assisted with images, indexing, and editing. External funding from a Woodrow Wilson Career Enhancement Fellowship and a West African Research Association Postdoctoral Fellowship provided resources for time off and financial support to complete the research and to write.

Research assistants have helped me at various stages in this project. I thank Hannah Argento-McCurdy, Gracia Dodds, Talon Kennedy, Gervais Marsh, and Sophie Murray for their organizational assistance and editing. In addition, I was lucky to have run into Joseph Ayodokun one afternoon at the National Archives in Ibadan. He helped me gather additional materials from the 1950s–1970s that informed my analysis in Chapter 2.

The editorial staff at Stanford has been a pleasure to work with. I am grateful for Marcela Maxfield's support and patience as I completed this project. The invaluable feedback made writing this book much less difficult than it otherwise would have been. Editorial assistant Sunna Juhn was also incredibly helpful with navigating the entire process and managing countless logistical issues efficiently. I thank series editors Rhacel Salazar Parreñas and Hung Cam Thai for their enthusiasm for my work. I have also benefited immensely from the comments of the anonymous reviewers who pushed this book to new heights. An earlier version of parts of Chapter 4 appeared in *Gender & Society* 26, no. 3 (2012), and a small portion of Chapter 5 appeared in *Sociological Perspectives* 61, no. 6 (2018).

My time in Nigeria was made possible by a large network of extended family and friends too numerous to name individually who provided me with contacts, logistical support, and housing and food. I especially want to express my gratitude to my in-laws, Chief and Mrs. Jamiu Ekungba, who opened up their home to me and my daughters and truly made Nigeria feel like my second home. Without their care, this book would have been impossible to complete. Other friends and kin also graciously assisted in myriad ways. I thank Olaitan Balogun, Amber Croyle, Mia Thornton, the Daughters of Africa, and the Sister Circle for their support. My mother, Bolanle Apaokagi Balogun, has tirelessly backed my education since childhood, and I am grateful for the persistence she instilled in me. Her grit has always inspired me. My siblings, Tunji Balogun, Bisola Esiemokhai, Tosin Balogun, and Tomi Balogun, have cheered me on from the start. I am thankful for their wit, care, and assistance over the years. To my partner, Kamil Ekungba, and my daughters, Nuraya and Rania, your loving spirits have sustained me.

BEAUTY DIPLOMACY

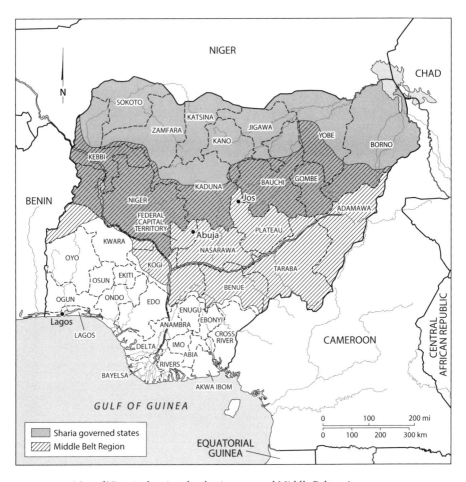

MAP 1. Map of Nigeria showing the sharia states and Middle Belt region.

1 | THE NIGERIAN FACTOR

A CROWNING MOMENT

On November 16, 2001, Agbani Darego, an eighteen-year-old computer science and mathematics major from Rivers State, Nigeria, won the Miss World Pageant held in Sun City, South Africa, making her the first Black African to achieve this feat in the international beauty contest's fifty-year run. Upon her return to Nigeria, public carnivals, receptions, and official state functions were held in her honor. Throngs of cheering well-wishers chased after her chauffeured car from the airport to her father's house in Port Harcourt, a major southeastern city. The National Assembly stalled legislative activities for a courtesy visit from the newly crowned beauty queen, and the federal government bestowed upon her the national honor of Member of the Order of the Federal Republic (MFR). A portrait of her was hung in the National Assembly. In addition, the *oba* (a traditional ruler) of Lagos, Adeyinka Oyekan, awarded her the high chieftaincy title of Omoge Agbe Wage Agbaiye (Lady who has lifted us worldwide).[1] The president at the time, Olusegun Obasanjo, hailed Darego's win as a source of national pride and a direct reversal of the dominant image of Nigeria mired in "the dark days of military rule [and] the number one haven for corruption and bad governance [to] number one in beauty and intellect."[2] Dele Alake, a Lagos state commissioner for information and strategy, concurred, declaring: "This young and gifted lady symbolises the new Nigeria and a democratic dividend. . . . [Her] victory has now opened doors to our youths to compete with the best in the world."³ Adokiye Young-Harry, chairman of the House Subcommittee on Oil and Gas, commented, "This is good public relations for Nigeria and we [the House of Representatives] want to set the pace in ensuring that this opportunity is recognised as such."⁴ In a welcome address for a reception held in Darego's honor at the National Centre for Women Development in Abuja, a representative for the Minister of Women's Affairs and Youth Development said, "Darego [has] become the greatest ambassador of Nigeria and of the continent. . . . Darego [will] have access to areas that even diplomats may not be able to reach."⁵

In these statements, politicians and government officials linked a single crowning moment—literally, of a woman's body—to Nigeria's trajectory as a nation, claiming it had successfully jettisoned its dismal past. Darego's Miss World title symbolized the promise of promoting continued development within the country as well as the prospect of launching Nigeria as a bona fide member of the international community due to a world-recognized competitive edge. It also solidified the country's long-standing desire to be a trailblazer for the African continent. Within the continent, there is a specific narrative about Nigerian exceptionalism in which, due to access to vast human and natural resources, it should be a worldwide success story of economic prosperity and political stability. However, a series of economic and political stumbling blocks stifled its potential, and it is often described by pundits, development specialists, and policy makers, through the lens of failure. By referencing Nigeria's return to democracy and the changing demands of the global economy, state officials viewed winning the Miss World competition as proof of the country's readiness to successfully engage in other types of competitions within political and economic arenas. Darego's crowning was not just a cultural triumph; state elites also viewed it as having reverberations for the nation's political economy. Agbani Darego's win served as a litmus test for and symbol of Nigeria's brighter future, repairing its stigmatized image. The elaborate meanings attached to this crowning moment, linked to issues of gender, nation, globalization, and embodiment, spark the underlying questions behind this book. How do beauty pageants link everyday aspirational identities to national and global politics? How are embodied discourses and bodily practices used to engage in nation building within the context of globalization? How are categories of gender, race, ethnicity, and class mobilized through these social processes?

These contests position Nigerian beauty queens as ideal role models to communicate specific narratives about femininity, respectability, and embodiment. Various stakeholders capitalize on contestants' embodied labor for specific political and economic ends. In *Beauty Diplomacy,* I examine how Nigerian beauty pageants are both shaped by and inform Nigeria's shifting position in the global economy, contentious cultural politics, and gendered power. As civic-cultural institutions—that share properties with cultural and creative industries like entertainment, performing arts, and tourism and civic organizations that foster engagement with citizens and champion the public good—these beauty competitions expose and conceal anxieties and aspirations of nationhood and subjectivity. In addition to their own self-interests, organizers, contestants, corporate sponsors, fans, and critics of beauty pageants all have agendas related to the Nigerian nation. Together, they transform them into institutions that highlight the complex relationship between culture, politics, and the economy. As the fastest-growing economy in Africa, pageant participants echo the sentiments of many Nigerians, that the country remains the inevitable leader to ensure a vibrant future for the region. However, they do so against an uneasy backdrop in which they must engage in repair work to redeem Nigeria's spoiled reputation. Well-known stories of turbulent politics, fraudulent business schemes, and communal conflict have marred Nigeria's image. Beauty queens view themselves as public figures who understand the high stakes involved in restoring an untarnished reputation.

I have coined the term *beauty diplomacy* to explain how different groups mobilize the strategic position of beauty contestants—young and upwardly mobile women—to stress goodwill, connect with Nigerians, cement relationships with others around the world, and gain worldwide recognition. Beauty diplomacy simultaneously contends with internal and external logics and politics. Through beauty pageants, women's bodies symbolize the aesthetic center of the nation by unifying an otherwise ethnically diverse country as well as signaling Nigeria's economic potential. Using Nigerian beauty pageants as a lens, this book documents attempts to rebuild national and individual credibility, visibility, and acceptability.

NIGERIA AS EMERGING NATION

Beauty, through the vehicle of pageants, is a site where national identities are managed in relation to a larger global landscape. In Nigeria, colonialism drew national boundaries around a region of considerable ethnoreligious diversity, which complicates the project of constructing national identity in Nigeria, as elsewhere. Nigeria's national borders are an inherited legacy of colonialism, when European powers negotiated and portioned national borders in oftentimes arbitrary ways, without regard for ethnic, religious, and linguistic differences. Splits between Christians and Muslims and among over 250 ethnic groups (with three main ethnic groups associated with specific regions in the country: Yoruba in the Southwest, Igbo in the Southeast, and Hausa in the North), in addition to a widening gulf between the super-rich and those facing crushing poverty, have led to contentious ethnopolitics and class divisions. This postcolonial history means that, in the Nigerian context, national identity has conventionally been thought of as fragile at best. Yet an ambition for self-determination, economic growth, and cooperation has helped position civic-cultural institutions like national beauty contests as moments to understand points of conflict and consensus surrounding the nation. I view Nigeria as an emerging nation to understand this budding process of how a country both comes to terms with itself as a nation, given incredible ethnoreligious diversity, class stratification, and shifting geopolitics, and also gains global traction as a prominent center for culture and capital.

Despite many obstacles, Nigeria aims to become one of the largest economies of the world as an emerging market. Emerging markets are countries that development scholars have identified as places undergoing rapid economic growth, which often outpace established economic hubs, and as being in the middle of a transition between developing and developed status.[6] The most well-known examples of countries that have made that transition are Brazil, Russia, India, and China, which as a group are known by the acronym BRIC.[7] Scholars consider them ripe for investment based on factors such as a burgeoning middle class, and believe they will be pivotal in reshaping the international political economy. According to the World Bank, between 2005 and 2015 Nigeria's gross domestic product (GDP) grew almost 6 percent, at a time when many other countries' economies were contracting.[8] Several international investment firms and information companies have dubbed Nigeria a frontier market and predicted it will be the next to join the BRIC nations.[9]

Demographers, economists, and cultural critics often point to Nigeria as leading the charge of a broader "Africa rising" narrative, capturing the high expectations for exponential growth in Africa. This narrative was expressed in the 2000s by development finance agencies, which recognized much of the African continent as an untapped market. These financial experts center their assertions on optimistic figures such as high GDP, low inflation, well-performing stock markets, increased consumer spending, leapfrogging technological advances, and a demographic dividend. Nigeria is the seventh most populous country in the world and the most populous nation in Africa. Demographic experts predict that by 2050, Nigeria's population size will come close to tying or surpassing the United States for third place. The population is not only predicted to continue to increase in size, but the makeup of this population explosion is expected to be increasingly younger and more middle-class.[10] These changes counteract dominant images of Africa as crisis-stricken and show the growing global importance of the African continent.

Beyond its economy, Nigeria is also experiencing a global cultural moment. A boom in literature by novelists like Chimamanda Ngozi Adichie and Nnedi Okorafor; lively Naija pop stars such as Tiwa Savage and D'banj, who, like several other popular Nigerian musicians, have inked 360 deals with major American recording labels; cutting-edge couture fashion lines such as Jewel by Lisa; and the influential Nollywood film industry have fueled what cultural critics have termed Nigeria's creative golden age. These cultural shifts point to a wider aspiration among many Nigerians to be seen as movers and shakers who shape international trends. These cultural industries focus on aesthetics to move and disrupt the global order.

The optimism about Africa's rising movement tempers the perennial "African crisis" narratives that hone in on autocratic kleptocracies, political uprisings, chronic disease, and famine; yet some critics have said that a focus on Africa rising is too hopeful. These "African realists" advocate for a more cautious perspective, which examines needed infrastructural changes to support demographic and economic changes. An African *rising-realist* approach frames the position I take in this book, in that I take seriously the work beauty pageants do to manage aspirational politics and mold emerging identities, while also being mindful of the structural realities that constrain this work. My approach recognizes three prisms through which an emerging nation is filtered: crisis politics, redemptive politics, and mirage politics.

Crisis Politics

Nigeria has been battling its negative reputation for decades. The country's poor image is due in large part to persistent corruption, best epitomized by advance-fee fraud schemes that originate in the country. Around the world, spam emails filled with misspellings, florid prose, and subject lines like "My Dearest One" and "Urgent Matter" sent by supposed members of Nigeria's royal family, officials from state agencies, or prospective romantic partners, have flooded inboxes. These emails promise a cut of large sums of money (typically several million dollars) once recipients send a few thousand dollars to release the funds and transfer the money out of the country. These Internet cons are typically perpetrated by everyday hustlers. On the other end of the spectrum, more established, high-ranking government officials are also riddled with corruption. The Nigerian populace has largely become accustomed to news accounts exposing public officials accepting bribes, skimming off the top of budgets, and maintaining undisclosed offshore bank accounts. For example, in 2017, the Economic and Financial Crimes Commission (EFCC), the government agency tasked with investigating and prosecuting money laundering and corruption, seized cash bundles in dollars, pounds sterling, and naira (₦) currencies totaling $43.4 million, £27,800, and ₦23.2 million from an unoccupied upscale Lagos apartment that was traced to a career diplomat, the then director of Nigeria's National Intelligence Agency.[11]

Visitors to Nigeria oftentimes directly confront corruption immediately upon entering the country. The US State Department has issued travel advisories on the country, sometimes targeting specific regions of Nigeria. From 1993 to 2000, travelers in US international airport terminals encountered warning signs posted by the US Federal Aviation Administration (FAA) advising passengers about security conditions at Lagos International Airport and cautioning that the airport failed to meet the minimum standards of the International Civil Aviation Organization. The airport was notorious for criminal activity, with federal customs and immigration officials routinely requesting bribes from travelers for entry into and exit out of the country.[12]

These scams, colloquially known as 419 after the section of the Nigerian criminal code that targets fraud, constitute part of the "Nigerian factor" that potential business investors, tourists, and diplomatic envoys input into their plans. Transparency International's Corruption Perceptions Index (CPI) measures citizens' public opinion of corruption based on their interactions with police, corporations, and the court system among other public institutions. When President Obasanjo made his remarks praising Darego for her 2001 Miss World win, the country was ranked the second most corrupt country in the world with a CPI score of 1.0 on a 10-point scale (with 10 being very "clean"). Recent figures give the country a score of 27 (under a new scale with 100 being "very clean" and 0 being "highly corrupt").[13] While there are ongoing efforts to clean up corruption, for example through the EFCC's whistleblowing policy, which rewards informants, conducts asset recovery of stolen public funds, and engages in the criminal prosecution of fraud, bleak figures like the CPI show that Nigeria's poor image both within and outside of the country rests on the widespread perception of corruption. Indeed, as anthropologist Daniel Jordan Smith points out, Nigerians express an ambivalent relationship to its pervasiveness by both condemning it yet perpetuating it through everyday acts of deception.[14] In Nigeria, persistent corruption remains part of the social backdrop, and increasingly public anti-corruption campaigns to target graft, bribes, and scams implicate both state officials and the general public (see Figure 1.1).

Nigeria's tumultuous political history also contributes to its bad image. After experiencing shifting military dictatorships and short-lived civilian administrations ever since securing independence from Great Britain in 1960, the country returned to democracy in 1999. Sani Abacha's 1993–98 military junta solidified the government's international status as a political pariah due to well-known cases of human rights abuses such as the execution of Ken Saro-Wiwa, an environmental activist who led the Movement for the Survival of the Ogoni People, a social movement focused on the ecological damage caused by crude oil extraction in the Niger Delta.[15] Ethnoreligious and regional conflicts within the country, such as activity by militants in the

FIGURE 1.1. Airport sign instructing travelers to report any instances of corruption. These types of official campaigns show how corruption remains central to Nigerian public discourse. *Source:* Photo by author.

Niger Delta, who have engaged in piracy and kidnapping to counter global oil corporations and the state's inequitable distribution of oil funds, sectarian violence in the Middle Belt regions, and the rise of Boko Haram, an insurgent jihadist group active primarily in the Northeast, were conflicts that largely gained momentum in the 1990s and 2000s as a result of political jostling for power and competition over economic resources.[16]

Nigeria's economy is heavily dependent on oil revenues, which account for an estimated 80 percent of government export earnings. As a rentier petro-state that derives the vast majority of its revenues from foreign sources through oil exportation, Nigeria appears to be a quintessential example of the "resource curse," in which nations with high levels of natural resources nonetheless face steep poverty rates and infrastructural problems.[17] "Resource curse" is a term used by development economists to explain the paradox of countries with abundant natural resources that nonetheless experience slow economic growth and are prone to autocratic governments and violent clashes. It can be likened to lottery winners who, after hitting the jackpot, squander their newfound wealth and usually end up in worse economic circumstances and with their personal lives in ruins. The most common explanations for the curse include volatile commodity pricing, lack of economic diversification, extractive exploitation from foreign powers, and political mismanagement. As evidence of Nigeria's resource curse, even though it is the eighth largest oil supplier in the world, there are often fuel shortages in the country, and it imports refined oil because it lacks the infrastructure to provide consistent gasoline to Nigerian consumers. The worldwide oil bust of the 1980s and 1990s caused Nigeria's economy to nosedive with a devaluation of its currency, the naira, high national debt, and soaring inflation rates. The state introduced a comprehensive Structural Adjustment Program (SAP) as a measure to rehabilitate the economy, but this reform effort only further plunged the country into economic crisis. The SAP was effectively dismantled at the end of Ibrahim Babangida's eight-year rule in 1993, with the approval of the 1994 budget.[18]

Redemptive Politics

While the conditions described here paint a poor picture of the country, Nigeria's image has not always been so terrible. In the oil-fueled wealth of the 1970s, astronomical economic growth and fast-developing state-sponsored infrastructure development certified its status as a poster child for economic progress.[19] During the 1970s, the naira was valued above the dollar at $1.60 and its GDP grew at close to 300 percent.[20] Rather than focus on Nigeria as stuck in a constant cycle of crisis, a redemptive logic emphasizes reclaiming the nation's potential through a strategic course correction.

Agbani Darego's pageant win seemed to momentarily suspend a barrage of critiques about the country—at least among some segments of the

Nigerian populace. The press, politicians, and pageant affiliates expressed hopefulness about a successful course realignment of Nigeria's image. In the lobby of the headquarters of one of the most widely circulating Nigerian newspapers, Mr. Marachi Omo,[21] a seasoned journalist, reminisced about Darego's homecoming, which included seismic crowds:

> In Nigeria, whether you liked beauty pageants or not, the fact that a Ni-
> gerian won the pageant, made them like it. Agbani beat almost 81 girls
> and won the crown. You should have seen it when she came back; every-
> body wanted to have pictures with her. You should have seen when we
> took her back to her [home] state; it was [like] a public holiday! Imagine,
> what millions of naira [Nigerian currency] could not do for Nigeria, an
> 18-year girl did it. You can put an article in the paper and spend millions
> of dollars on it; it didn't give Nigeria the goodwill [that] Nigeria got when
> Agbani won.

The "millions of dollars" spent on newspaper articles referred in part to high government expenditures poured into attempts to rehabilitate Nigeria's image through media blitzes. Mr. Omo emphasized that Darego's feat served to energize the public's national pride in a way that state-sponsored campaigns could not. Darego brought "goodwill" to Nigeria, he claimed; he compared the Miss World Pageant to the Olympics or the World Cup.

The Nigerian Tourism Development Corporation (NTDC), a parastatal (quasi-state-owned) board charged with regulating and promoting Nigeria's fledgling tourism industry, invited Darego to a series of international tourism exhibits in Berlin, London, the Netherlands, France, and the United States. The director of the agency at the time explained to me the underlying mo-tives for actively involving Darego in trade fairs and travel expos in 2002:

> I saw a reason to promote her all around the world when she became
> Miss World. The international community won't say anything good about
> Nigeria. . . . For three months [after her win] I never read or saw anything
> about her. Not in the papers or the television. Nothing! This is the first
> African to win Miss World and as I'm talking to you it hasn't happened
> again. The first African to win is a Nigerian and CNN is not talking about
> that. They are talking about our bad roads in Lagos, about Ajegunle [a
> densely populated slum in Lagos], about our dumpsites. As if they don't

FIGURE 1.2. Nigeria's 2002 booth at ITB Berlin, a leading travel trade show, which included large photographs of Agbani Darego. *Source:* TAG Nigeria. Reprinted with permission.

have dumpsites in New York! . . . Every country has a blend of the negative and the positive. I realized that if we don't tell our story, nobody will tell our story for us. . . . Agbani Darego became the brand for Nigeria to the international community.

The exhibitions displayed large life-size photographs of Darego posing with her Miss World title, crown, and sash prominently displayed against a backdrop of pictures from Nigerian tourist locations (see Figure 1.2). A news article described the effect of her attendance as "magnetic, as other exhibitors momentarily abandoned their stands to either have a glimpse of the most beautiful human being on earth, or to [have her] sign autographs, and most importantly, make enquiries about Nigeria and its tourism assets."[22] In a country better known for its Internet scams than its tourism industry, the NTDC thus sought to parlay Darego's win into a large-scale campaign to redeem Nigeria's poor image abroad and develop the country's tourism business. Thus, the win opened up venues of representation through which to reposition Nigeria in the global scene.[23]

FIGURE 1.3. ₦20 and ₦50 stamps issued in honor of Agbani Darego. *Source:* NIPOST. Reprinted with permission.

The state took an active part in using Darego's win to mold and advance a new image of Nigeria as a nation, long after her reign ended. In 2006, the Nigerian Postal Service (NIPOST), the nation's national postal carrier, sold ₦20 and ₦50 stamps honoring Darego's reign with an image of her wearing the Miss World crown (see Figure 1.3).[24] The state directly embraced Darego as a visual showpiece and as a spokeswoman for a newly democratic and internationally acclaimed nation. While the state's intention has had limited success at best, Darego's own career has flourished and she has risen to become a beauty icon. After her win, Darego, who is now a globetrotting entrepreneur based in Lagos, extended her fame through a modeling contract with Ford, a L'Oréal cosmetics campaign, a hosting gig on Stylogenic, a Pan-African style and fashion reality show, and a premium eponymous womenswear clothing line. In 2012, she reenrolled at New York University and earned a bachelor's degree in psychology. In 2010, during Nigeria's Golden Jubilee celebration, which marked the country's fifty years of independence, Darego was featured in a government-endorsed event titled "50@50—Nigerian Women: The Journey So Far," which commemorated the nation's fifty top women achievers.[25] A video montage celebrated Nigerian women's "strength and diversity" and how despite the "odds against her, [she] holds up her head to be counted." It heralded a long tradition of women's contribution to the nation from "antiquity to present-times," making mention of the "farmers, traders, and warriors of yesteryears" which paved the path for professionals in finance, law, medicine, business, education, the arts, and entertainment today. These examples showcase how women's visibility, status, and achievements are used to corroborate national advancement. Women's bodies and their labor symbolically stand in for the nation, elevating national profiles and materially integrating countries into the global economy.

Darego's victory revitalized hope in improving Nigeria's image, and also its beauty pageant industry, particularly the leading "Most Beautiful Girl in Nigeria" (MBGN) franchise, which is the national pageant, whose victor goes to the Miss World Pageant. From the late 1950s to the 1970s, the Miss Nigeria Pageant, Nigeria's first national pageant, which began in 1957, had earned the reputation as a respectable national institution, but it floundered in the mid-1980s due to the military governments' takeover of the *Daily Times Nigeria*, which was the contest's main sponsor. This steady decline provided an opening for MBGN to enter the industry, but to find participants, organizers relied heavily on personal contacts to convince women to attend small-scale auditions with a handful of aspiring models. According to pageant owners, in the year immediately following Agbani Darego's win, parents escorted their daughters to open screenings where hundreds flocked from all walks of life, clamoring for a chance to participate in the contest. Whereas public opinion toward beauty pageants had been largely ambivalent—driven by a perception that beauty pageant contestants were promiscuous dropouts—pageant insiders noted a palpable shift in which many people now saw beauty pageants as a viable platform for career advancement and national promotion.

To maintain the momentum behind Darego's win, Nigeria placed a bid to host the international Miss World competition in 2002, the year following Darego's victory. When I asked Mr. Uzoma Kalu, one of the organizers, why they had been determined for Nigeria to hold the contest, he stated:

> The first reason was to make history in Nigeria and about Nigeria. You remember, Agbani was the only Nigerian and Black African to win the Miss World contest. It is prestigious. Then, the idea of why can't Nigeria host it came up and the emotions of Agbani's success set in. In short, it was a logical thing to take it from there.

It seemed, to this organizer, to flow logically—if a Nigerian could meet and excel at the standards for world beauty, then surely Nigeria had arrived on the global stage sufficiently to host the pageant. While even this organizer himself was a little bemused by the idea of history being made through a beauty contest, he still regarded Darego's win as an important historical milestone that continued to hold cultural significance and political heft even when I interviewed him over eight years after the event. Nigerian organizers anticipated hosting the Miss World event as an opportunity to build the country's infrastructure, boost tourism, and attract global investment. They believed that by managing the logistics of an event scheduled to be broadcast worldwide, they would present Nigeria as ambitious, efficient, and worldly. Their expectations contained a twofold strategy of solidifying national consciousness and securing international legitimacy.

Yet as Nigerian organizers prepared to hold the contest, two dramatic sets of conflicts emerged simultaneously which led to the 2002 Miss World Pageant being moved to London. Nigeria found itself in the middle of a global public relations nightmare. Protestors, both within and outside Nigeria, used this moment to announce their political platforms. These conflicts were tied in part to religious differences among the country's almost evenly split Christian and Muslim populations, but they also involved broader political and economic dynamics.[26] The first conflict was international in scope. Citing the mistreatment of women under newly codified sharia law (Islamic legal doctrine) in Northern Nigeria, human rights organizations such as Amnesty International called for a boycott of the pageant. The Amina Lawal ruling, which sentenced a woman accused of committing adultery (*zina*) to death by stoning just a few months before the start of the pageant, captured international attention and increased tensions over issues of regional sovereignty. In the second conflict, riots and bloodshed erupted, largely in Kaduna city, a Northern Nigerian state capital. Nigerian organizers and opponents, most of them from Muslim religious groups, clashed due to an offensive news article about the Prophet Muhammad's likely approval of the beauty competition, published just a few days after delegates arrived for preliminary events. More than two hundred people in Kaduna died in the riots, with a thousand more injured and the homes of close to eight thousand people razed to the ground. Either one of these conflicts would have been enough to justify the pageant organizers' eventual decision to move it to London; together they constituted a perfect storm that thwarted organizers' hopes to recast Nigeria's image. Although they appeared to be separate protests, a newly emerging politicized conversation about gender, the nation-state, and international politics linked them. The Miss World crisis happened at a critical historical moment, which was rife with conflicts over sharia law and Nigeria's newly reinstated democracy. The hosting of the pageant became a heavily contested site for national representation. The events of 2001 and 2002—Darego's triumphant win and Nigeria's lost opportunity—bookend Nigeria's national narrative of exuberant promise and its crushing problems. The events set the context for how contemporary national pageants frame their efforts to gain a position as global leaders and assert national credibility.[27]

Mirage Politics

Nigeria's problems are real and attempts to rectify them are noteworthy, but there are limits to the aspirational hopes of nations and to individuals' dreams. The image work done to consciously remedy Nigeria's poor reputation through beauty pageants operates through a set of contradictions that I term *mirage politics* that develops from Nigeria's position as an emerging nation. The Nigerian factor that epitomizes this changing status is like an "it" or "X" factor—an unknown, hard-to-define but special quality that is as much about confronting the country's negative image as it is about what makes the nation valuable. Beauty pageants are an industry where image management and public relations are paramount. I learned over the course of my research to not always take things at face value. Mirage politics refer to the double meanings and sets of illusionary appearances that push us to rethink the lines between rhetoric and reality. The pageant industry is rife with ironies and inconsistencies and things are not always as they appear. This also means that some people are able to leverage these ambiguities to their benefit. Within Nigeria's political economy, endemic corruption is not only about a perpetual cycle of crisis but is also a possible creative response to pervasive socioeconomic inequalities in an unequal global system. Similarly, beauty diplomacy is an inventive reaction to realign global and national hierarchies, but one that might not always unfold smoothly. The perception that Nigerian beauty pageants facilitate social mobility and improve life chances exists in tandem with the idea that they manifest social ills and warp personal livelihoods. In a highly competitive and visibly public industry, which is well-attuned to projecting a glossy image, there also exist elements outside the purview of the general public, which are hidden to avoid spectacle and scandal.

Though I do not make a linear connection between the beauty diplomacy tactic and the turning around of Nigeria's negative image, I do outline the stakes involved as well as investments made into this strategy with respect to time, money, and energy. Beauty diplomacy as a tactic harnesses potential, and in this book, I show the material conditions that enable this tactic as well as how complex imaginings are projected onto these sets of perceptions about emerging nations and aspirational selfhoods. This approach unlocks new agendas that try to challenge common assumptions about power and politics in the world.

BEAUTY DIPLOMACY

Over the course of my fieldwork, pageant participants insisted that beauty contests serve as a means of promoting national culture and increasing the nation's standing in the world. In doing so, they pointed to the redemptive potential of the industry both in terms of the nation and also in raising the individual profiles of affiliates. Contemporary foreign commentary on Nigeria typically portrays it as a nation antithetical to beauty—a country mired in the ugliness of conflict, corruption, and chaos. Through performative entertainment, beauty pageants stress the positive attributes of Nigeria, such as order, progress, and reform, while also being used by pageant affiliates to cement relationships with other countries around the world.

Some critics of beauty pageants trivialize their importance. Yet it is because of its perception as an innocuous leisure site, in which contestants assume positions as innocent and respectable young women, that this deep cultural work to symbolically reconfigure the nation can continue. Nigerian beauty competitions may seem superficial to some, but like other pageants around the world, they provide an important link between the nation-state and the public. The beauty pageant industry works to symbolically restore the public face of the nation as well as to materially shift the private lives of its affiliates through potential economic opportunities. While beauty pageants around the world are commonly used to enhance national reputation,

Nigeria's especially poor international image, juxtaposed against the high hopes for a promising future, heighten the stakes. These redemptive strategies work to better Nigeria's position in the global political economy and cultural marketplace. These shifts occur within a framework of highlighting Nigeria's potential, caught between the high level of optimism about its future and pessimism about the lack of progress in fully living up to this promise.

I began fieldwork for this project in 2009, the same time frame in which Nigeria launched its "Good People, Great Nation" public relations campaign, which promoted a national conversation about "rebranding the nation" and measuring up to "international standards." The term "international standards" is a buzzword that permeates the Nigerian landscape as a set of benchmarks that influences everything from nongovernmental organizations (NGOs), financial systems, and cultural industries like fashion, movies, and beauty contests. The rebranding campaign served as an important backdrop for the way in which beauty pageant affiliates situated their work. This national image campaign, which was developed by Nigeria's Ministry of Information and Communications, sought to rehabilitate Nigeria's image abroad and energize domestic commitment to the country by urging the public to adjust their manners and etiquette in order to be better "global citizens" by, for example, being punctual and waiting their turn in line, bridging ethnic and religious differences, and purchasing Nigerian-made goods and services to support the local economy, thus counteracting a marketplace flooded with imports.[28]

Beauty diplomacy expresses sentiments of the promises many others felt about Nigeria as the "next frontier" of beauty, wealth, and innovation. Nonetheless, a narrative of a country mired in poverty, disease, and stagnation persists. Beauty queens and other pageant affiliates see themselves as key actors in turning this narrative around by providing a unique window into understanding the dual strategy of securing national solidarity and garnering international recognition. As the nation persists in its attempts to revive its weak reputation, it continues to revel in the reminders of its past glory as Africa's golden child. These tensions provide a broader context for understanding how Nigeria negotiates the dilemma of staking a claim in the global political economy while remaining attuned to its internal sensibilities.

Beauty pageant industry insiders often connected their goals to the broader government-sponsored rebranding campaign and saw themselves as best equipped and uniquely positioned to undertake this symbolic work. While the Nigerian beauty pageant industry has long been connected to national visions, the focus on repackaging Nigeria in a more favorable light is a more recent phenomenon. Beauty diplomacy is a strategy mobilized by different groups within and outside of the beauty pageant industry to navigate between state politics and mass culture. Conventional accounts of diplomacy focus on trained public officials who engage in formal correspondence between state representatives over conducting foreign policy, drafting resolutions, and negotiating treaties focused on trade, peacekeeping, and human rights. These trained diplomats engage with political elites at the highest levels of government, and through their connections to the state, they are responsible for retaining extensive knowledge of domestic affairs while deftly engaging in complex international relations. State diplomacy, however, does not only occur within the realm of officially sanctioned actions, but also through unofficial activities like backchannel communications, which can be essential to statecraft, foreign affairs, and international development.[29]

Moreover, nonstate actors like NGOs also contribute to diplomacy through cultural exchanges, the arts, and humanitarian aid. Experts in the field term these actions "civic diplomacy" to refer to the types of "soft power" meant to target the "hearts and minds" of citizens to gain influence, garner respect, and shape policies of national interest. These forms of civic diplomacy are meant to attract foreigners by advertising and showcasing the best attributes of the nation while mitigating possible conflict to foster cooperation between nations. Diplomacy also includes recognition by foreign entities to legitimize a nation's existence. Beauty diplomacy is a tool of statecraft and nation building, but from a middle-out rather than top-down perspective. That is, the industry views state bureaucracy and public officials as necessary to gain momentum for their endeavors, but also points to the ineptitude of the state. The industry aligns with the state at opportune moments, for example, to ingratiate themselves with prominent government representatives, but also seeks to bypass the baggage that comes with associating with the state.

Beauty diplomacy is an example of these broader types of civic di-plomacy, which have a loose relationship to the state but are not entirely state-sponsored. Through forms of ambassadorship that require in-depth knowledge of culture, history, and politics, beauty contestants skillfully man-age public affairs, which requires interpersonal skills such as tact, altruism, and finesse to help build alliances and serve as reliable representatives of the nation-state that communicate the needs and concerns of the general public. Through these diplomatic efforts, beauty pageant participants encourage dialogue between groups and develop personal relationships to influence public opinion and foster mutual understanding. Moreover, they serve as international relations liaisons, seeking to boost the nation's economic prosperity, maintain its political interests, and promote cultural values. In another vein, they advocate for diplomatic recognition—to have other coun-tries acknowledge their own as an eligible and rightful member of a broader "international community." Standard definitions of diplomacy are usually associated with masculinity, which colors how we understand politics and international relations. In the case of pageants, beauty becomes the central avenue through which the industry promotes diplomacy. By centering on beauty, and by extension, femininity, we can think more deeply about how gender, cultural politics, and the political economy matter to nation-states.

Beauty diplomacy operates at several different levels in ways that link macro nation building and global positioning to the everyday lives of people. Beauty pageant contestants, owners, and viewers navigate within this larger macro context, showing how globalization, nationalism, and ethnopolitics are made and disputed on the ground. Beauty queens saw one of their central tasks as presenting a positive image of Nigeria. The reemergence of Nigeria was thus mobilized through embodied gendered discourses—narratives that gain traction by centering bodies to serve specific ends—that relied on women's bodies as stand-ins for the nation. Beauty queens used their aesthetic labor in the service of building up Nigeria's credibility by stressing respect-ability, humanitarianism, and cultural ambassadorship. They also promoted diplomacy between nations through their travel to international events and interactions with people abroad, which they viewed as a form of cultural exchange. Likewise, pageant owners were invested in particular narratives about the nation's image that are bound up with the respective goals of their beauty competitions. These imaginings of the nation are connected to the anxiety about the direction of the country and the hopes of fostering a more favorable national reputation.

The Nigerian beauty pageant industry is also connected to collective motives through engaging in community work and promoting private enterprise. Beauty pageant affiliates justify their participation as serving a greater good and set of broader collective interests. Beauty queens are also hired to promote products and services in the private sector, while pageant owners boost the business culture of the country. Because of their public fame as beauty queens, contestants stressed that they were uniquely poised to occupy an intermediary position to reach out to ordinary Nigerians and represent their interests to political and economic elites. For their charity work, beauty queens must acquire resources either through the state or other stakeholders with power, and also keep in touch with those at the grass roots in order to push forward genuine and thoughtful agendas. Through competition, contestants and owners gain moral integrity, which they channel into their activities.

Taking on a pet project to promote social causes and ensuring productive business practices are not entirely altruistic platforms, as they also remain tied to individual career trajectories. For example, contestants are concerned about their future economic options. The beauty diplomacy narrative provides them with legitimacy, which they leverage into pushing for changes to their own livelihoods in terms of "getting ahead." Contestants linked changes in their own ability to secure upward mobility to the benefits offered through participating in pageants, such as having an authoritative voice and garnering needed social contacts, to this beauty diplomacy narrative. In a social context where personal contacts are key to getting ahead, strategic connections eased their transition to post-pageant careers. Organizers pushed for respectable entrepreneurship for themselves and the contestants. As such, their public platforms were directly connected to their career prospects.

However, the opportunities that the industry opens up are both enabled and constrained by domestic politics within the nation and Nigeria's place in the global political economy. Individuals on the ground navigate within this context, attempting to materially shift their own lives while advocating for the improvement of others. While beauty diplomacy emphasizes the favorable possibilities that the industry provides for both the nation and its people, it is important to point out that the options that beauty diplomacy offers are differentially shaped by structural realities. Specific requirements regarding social class, embodiment, and ethnoreligion limit the number of those who have access to these national representations. That is, only a narrow group of women enter the beauty pageant world, and of those just a select few win. Still, only a handful successfully achieve the stratospheric mobility that the industry promises. Moreover, shifting national narratives also entail external buy-in and validation from outside of the country.

Beauty Pageants: Power and Politics

I initially became interested in studying beauty pageants in Nigeria during preliminary visits to the country, when I noticed a seemingly ballooning industry, attached to a host of activities and part of the everyday social landscape of urban life. In the course of a two-day period, I was handed a leaflet about a pageant, saw a bill posted in the front window of a boutique at a shopping mall advertising a pageant, and caught a snippet of a beauty pageant on television. Pageants appeared to be everywhere. A few years after I wrapped up my fieldwork, my younger sister was heavily recruited to take part in a "Miss Kwara" state pageant during a visit to Nigeria, a "full circle" moment that seemed to clinch my original hunch about the ubiquity of these contests. In 2015, Basketmouth, a well-known Nigerian standup comedian, mocked the sheer number of beauty pageants in the country by posting the following to his millions of followers on Facebook:

> It started with Miss Nigeria and MBGN. Now we have the following:
> Miss Comely Queen Nigeria.
> Face of Unity Nigeria
> Miss Heritage Beauty Peagents [sic]
> Miss Tourism Nigeria
> Miss Earth Nigeria
> Miss Ideal
> Face of the Globe
> Miss teen world supermodel
> Miss Dazzle Nigeria

Queen of Aso Rock

Miss Grand Nigeria

Miss Vip Nigeria

Most Beautiful Face in Nigeria

Miss Ambassador for Peace Nigeria

Queen of trust beauty Nigeria

Face of Nigeria

Miss Global Beauty Peagent [sic]

Sisi Oge Beauty Peagent [sic]

Miss Esquisite [sic]

Miss Olokun

Miss Ecowas Peace Peagent [sic] . . . did I mention we have over
    1,000 now?

Very soon you'll hear of:

Miss Pretty feet Nigeria.

Miss Long Neck Peagent [sic].

Miss High Heels Nigeria.

Miss Fresh Lap Peagent [sic]

Miss No hair for leg Nigeria Peagent [sic].

Miss Pointed Boobs Nigeria.

Miss No Stretch Marks For Body . . . just watch.

While Basketmouth's post makes fun of the growing number of Nigerian beauty pageants, the Association of Beauty Pageants and Fashion Exhibition Organizations of Nigeria, a private regulatory board formed to monitor these events, claims that there are over one thousand beauty pageants in the country. Over the course of fieldwork in Nigeria, I encountered near daily coverage of beauty pageants in newspapers, social media, and advertisements, where these contests were used to plug everything from beauty products (Miss Delta Soap), specific industries and commercial enterprises (Miss Telcom, Miss Tourism, Glo Mobile's Miss Rock 'N Rule), religious institutions (Household of God Church's Queen Esther, a Nigerian Muslim won the 2013 Miss World Muslimah), state contests (Miss Oyo state), local government areas (counties) (Face of Njikoka, Anambra state), diasporic communities (Miss Nigeria in America, Miss Nigeria Ireland), universities (there are countless

campus contests like Miss Unilag as well as for specific university depart-
ments), community events (Bekwara New Yam Festival's Miss Ipiem Ihihe
and Carnival Calabar Queen in Cross Rivers State), and social causes (Face
of Amnesty, to promote peace for Niger Delta militants). While women's
beauty competitions dominate, there are also pageants for men (Mr. Macho,
Mr. Nigeria), some novelty contests like the Mother-Daughter Contest, and a
small number of child pageants for seven-to-ten-year-olds (Little Miss Nigeria). Beauty pageants are big business in Nigeria where they are youth-driven
urban affairs geared toward an audience of teeming adolescents and young
adults and gaining in importance, as 50 percent of the population now lives
in cities.[30] While the primary consumer base and main contestants are young
adults, pageant affiliates include a wider age range of organizers, production
specialists, and fans.

Much of the response I have gotten about my research tends to fall into
one of two camps: the first reaction typified the project as fun, cute, or, less
judiciously, silly; the second was a concern about beauty competitions as
prototypical sites of women's oppression and the commodification of Western
hegemony.[31] This pits binary understandings of women, as either victims of
patriarchy, global capitalism, and nationalist politics or heroines who actively
resist these forces, against each other. Western feminist criticism of beauty
pageants usually bookend their responses through perspectives that focus
on these contests as either oppressive or anachronistic. As African feminists
like Oyèrónké Oyěwùmí have shown, Western-centered definitions of gender and inequality give primacy to body-centered concepts that presume a
uniform, all-pervasive gendered subordination.[32] In fact, like many other
pageants around the world, Nigerian beauty pageants take up the mantle of
"women's empowerment" by showing how contestants can propel themselves
as self-made, upwardly mobile subjects who embrace new forms of leisure
and conspicuous consumption.[33] What does it mean when seemingly feminist
language is used to reproduce rather than critique gendered power relations?

Feminist scholars of body and embodiment have advanced particular
ideas about the relationship between body, inequality, and agency. One group
of scholars understand women's bodies as *reflective* of power inequalities. For
example, there is a long-standing feminist critique of beauty more broadly
and beauty pageants more specifically as oppressive for women and a means

of regulating their bodies by glorifying emphasized femininity in the form of unattainable bodily ideals in the societies where they take place.[34] Another group of scholars views women's bodies in their capacity as *resistant* forces through self-fashioning, pleasure, and identity.[35] For example, some see beauty contests as platforms for upward mobility through the opportunity to win cash prizes, scholarships, or celebrity status. The edited volume, *Beauty Queens on the Global Stage: Gender, Contests, and Power,* by anthropologists and folklorists Colleen Cohen, Richard Wilk, and Beverly Stoeltje, was a pioneering book that tackled "the beauty contest stage [as] where these identities and cultures can be—and frequently are—made public and visible."[36] Similarly, historian Michael Stanfield's work on Colombia describes beauty as a "powerful cultural mirror . . . that is crucial to the image and status of nations."[37] In describing new Black standards of beauty that arose at the cusp of the Civil Rights and Black Power social movements, sociologist Maxine Leeds Craig cautions that to underestimate the relevance of these pageants misses the "joyous, cultural victory experienced when dominant meaning is subverted and what was formerly ridiculed is finally celebrated."[38] My work bridges these reflective and resistant perspectives by positioning women's bodies as *constitutive* of social realities and cultural meanings. Beauty contests symbolically reproduce boundaries that are constrained by hierarchies of gender, class, sexuality, race, and ethnicity. Pageant affiliates have used women's bodies to assert new definitions of Nigeria that have strategically worked to destabilize global hierarchies and refashion ideas about ethnoreligious boundaries, but have eventually served to reinforce local hierarchies concerning gender and class. This book does not start or end with popular discussions of beauty pageants as either exploitative or empowering but rather focuses on how beauty pageants unravel the messy and complex demarcations of power, belonging, and difference.

Symbolic dimensions of the nation are always in flux and disputed. For example, Charles Ndubuisi, a freelance photographer, made a comment to this effect while gesturing toward a group of pageant contestants. He insisted, "If you want to feel the pulse of Nigeria, you won't find it here." He continued,

> Go to the BRT [Lagos's public transportation service], go to a market like
> Mile 12, or go to Surulere [a mostly working-class area located on the

Lagos mainland] and talk to people. They will tell you themselves that these people do not represent them. The connection between the pageant and everyday Nigerians is a very average one.

Charles's observation that the pageant world was weakly connected to the everyday experiences of ordinary Nigerians was a common refrain that I heard in many conversations throughout my fieldwork. His admonition that I venture into the hustle and bustle of Nigerian life to get a "real sense" of Nigeria's national identity was couched within a rejection and skepticism of pageants as a legitimate site of national representation based on class and culture. Yet I found that even those who trivialized these contests had an opinion about them, and I was often surprised by people who I first assumed did not care much about pageants but who I later discovered closely followed these events. There is a range of investment in the reception of Nigerian pageants from casual viewers, fans, and critics.

While beauty pageants have declined in popularity in countries in the Global North such as the United States,[39] they are becoming increasingly popular in many nations of the Global South such as India, Venezuela, and Nigeria,[40] where participation in international beauty contests is seen as an entry point into the global arena. Nigerian beauty pageants are a central node in the entertainment world, bringing booming creative industries like fashion, music, and modeling together. In interviews, proponents of the Nigerian beauty pageant industry often described the contests as allowing others around the globe who either knew nothing about the country or believed only the negative stories to see it in a more positive light. Contestants stressed how they served as positive role models for the large youth population, who are the group hardest hit by unemployment. Recent figures are grim, with youth unemployment (15–35 years old) hovering at over 20 percent.[41] While beauty pageants in places like the United States and the United Kingdom are portrayed as old-fashioned and kitschy, the Nigerian beauty pageant industry views its work as part of a larger project of announcing and advancing Nigeria's modernity. If anything, part of the opposition to these pageants stems from the viewpoint that Nigerian beauty pageants are *too* edgy and out of step with Nigeria's heritage.

FIGURE 1.4. Billboard promoting Nigeria's soccer team, the Super Eagles. *Source:* Photo by author.

Sporting Cultures as National Rivals

Many beauty pageant industry insiders viewed Nigerian football (soccer) as occupying an enviable position. Flush with cash from corporate sponsors, an entire branch of government dedicated to its promotion (the Ministry of Youth and Sports), and a general public obsession with the sport in particular, they often contrasted it with the relatively lowly status of beauty contests, which did not garner the same degree of accolades, funding, or position as a harbinger of national unity. They viewed themselves as doing the same kind of work as athletes in terms of national promotion but noted the stark contrast in how easily soccer players were legitimatized, their training was recognized, and they found it effortless to secure corporate funding and government backing. Pageant affiliates thought that when it came to men and their activities, they were garnered venerable adulation, a situation that was much less clear for women and their equivalent activities. In Nigeria, soccer is often brought up as one of the few examples of activities that bring Nigerians together across ethnic, class, and religious fault lines (see Figure 1.4).

When Nigeria hosted the FIFA (World Football Association) U-17 (under-17) World Cup in 2009 in eight cities around the country, much of the press focused on the excitement of showcasing the nation's world-class players as well as promoting tourism and investment opportunities. Though the hosting had to contend with threats from the Movement for the Emancipation of the Niger Delta (MEND), an armed militant group fighting for recognition of the exploitation of the oil-rich Niger Delta region of Nigeria, to disrupt the event, the government offered them amnesty in exchange for turning in their weapons. Though the specific contexts are not identical, this is in striking contrast to the government's sluggish response to the Miss World crisis. The U-17 tournament went off without a hitch, and the media capitalized on its success as part of propelling the country's ambitions.

Conceptually, major sports competitions, particularly soccer (the "world's game") and the Olympics, offer a parallel to beauty pageants. Peter Alegi's research on South African soccer establishes how sports can inform our ideas about national belonging, gender, and race/ethnicity, while also having deep political meaning. For example, soccer was a driving force in the international movement against apartheid in South Africa; many African nations, including countries like Nigeria that supported the movement, pressured FIFA to exclude South Africa from participating in the World Cup until apartheid ended.[42] Likewise, Toyin Raji was forced to exit the Miss World competition held in South Africa, due to political pressures from international human rights organizations protesting the military Abacha regime which had just executed Ken Saro-Wiwa, a prominent activist.

These large-scale sporting events are similar to beauty pageants since they garner substantial international attention through media coverage and audience viewership. When Nigeria's soccer team won the 1996 summer Olympics, the joining together of masculinity and nationalism narratives was clearly evident. Participating countries use these events to assert political aspirations, further private enterprise, and celebrate national culture.[43] These mega-events have high stakes as they are meant to raise their international profile and bring national prestige to the host countries, since successful hosting, which is contingent on careful preparation and proper infrastructure, will secure the nation-state's position as a serious player in the world's political economy.

Yet protests and boycotts often surround the decision to host.[44] The Olympics has been a major site of political protest. For example, the 2014 Sochi Winter Olympics, the most expensive Olympics in history, which cost $50 billion, was described as a "charm offensive" to help rectify Russia's image, but faced continued criticism because of the government's homophobic policies.[45] The 2008 Olympics, the second most expensive Olympic games, with a $40 billion price tag, was hosted in China and witnessed opposition from a wide variety of social movements, such as those opposed to the occupation of Tibet, groups that pointed out how China's economic policies helped support genocide in Darfur, and organizations highlighting China's poor domestic human rights record.[46]

Similarly, beauty pageants have garnered their own fair share of political protests, including feminists' protests of the Miss America Pageant in 1968 in Atlantic City, New Jersey,[47] student-run demonstrations against the El Salvadoran government's 1 million dollar payment to host the 1975 Miss World Pageant,[48] and India's 1996 protests against Miss World by feminists, Hindu nationalists, and labor organizations.[49] As with research on sporting bodies,[50] scholarship on beauty pageants emphasizes gendered nation building and embodiment but focuses on femininity as the central lens. The parallel work but differential respect that pageants have received relative to sports has often positioned sports as a foil to their arguments.

Personal Reflections: Methods and Strategic Positionality

As a married, overweight mother, in my late twenties when I started fieldwork in 2009, my background and body meant that I would be disqualified from most mainstream Nigerian pageants, who cater to young women between the ages of 18 and 26 who are slim, unmarried, and childless. Therefore, to study pageants I decided to work behind the scenes. From September 2009 to August 2010, I spent eleven months in Nigeria conducting fieldwork on the Nigerian beauty pageant industry, with one-to-three-month-long follow-up visits to conduct additional interviews and archival research in 2013, 2016, and 2018. For my ethnographic observations, I worked as an unpaid intern for six months for the Most Beautiful Girl in Nigeria (MBGN) contest and as a chaperone for the week-long training session leading up to the Queen Nigeria national competition along with an additional week traveling to state-level contests. While in some respects, I occupied a position of authority relative to contestants, in many ways this was short-lived. Contestants soon learned that I did not *really* work for MBGN or Queen Nigeria. Though I carried out instructions from organizers and owners, I had a fairly hands-off approach, which meant, in the busyness of pageant preparations and rehearsals, I often faded into the background. Because of tight scheduling and contestants' laser focus, I did not conduct interviews with them during the days leading up to the national finale, but instead tracked them down afterward. I found that follow-up interviews with contestants outside the confines of the pageant organization—for example, away from the corporate offices, after the show or official period of reign—yielded much more fruitful and candid interviews.

I selected these contests because of their contrasting organizational structures and divergent national discursive claims. Because I spent most of my fieldwork in Lagos, where MBGN is based, I came to know the organization much more intimately than Queen Nigeria. Queen Nigeria's organizers were split between Ibadan and Abuja and traveled throughout the country to organize state feeder contests for the national finale. It was also only in its second year of existence when I began the research. Though Lagos was my home base, I also traveled to Abuja, Benin, Port Harcourt, Jos, and Ibadan to conduct interviews and observe state pageants and auditions. For both contests I was granted access to observe the screening process of selecting contestants, rehearsals, preliminary competitions, and the show, and was permitted to accompany the winner during press interviews, photo shoots, public appearances, and courtesy visits. During fieldwork I kept jottings in my cell phone and wrote detailed daily field notes within twenty-four hours of observations.

I completed a total of sixty-five formal, in-depth, semi-structured interviews with a mix of owners, organizers, producers, corporate sponsors, contestants, judges, and critics. Interviews took place in a number of locations, including offices, coffee shops, eateries, homes, and a few times in cars. All interviews were conducted face to face, with the exception of two Skype interviews and two phone interviews. I tape recorded all interviews, excluding two participants who requested I not tape record. I transcribed interviews and used an inductive grounded theory approach to code and analyze emergent themes.[51] I was also able to conduct dozens of informal interviews with makeup artists, journalists, production crew, photographers, fashion designers, and fans. Though these interviews were unrecorded, I included them in my field notes. Formal interviews focused on questions related to experiences with beauty pageants in the context of participants' personal lives and professional careers, future goals and aspirations, perceptions about the role of the industry in Nigeria, and how Nigerian beauty pageants compared to others around the world. Though I used an interview guide, the exact order and phrasing of the questions shifted according to the context of each interview. Interviews lasted thirty minutes to about three hours and were on average an hour in length. All interviews were conducted in English, Nigeria's official language, though my knowledge of Yoruba helped me navigate Lagos, the main location for my research. I use pseudonyms for all participants for the sake of uniformity, except for cases where I rely on readily available information from newspapers and other public records. In some cases, I have changed minor identifiable details in order to protect the privacy of participants. Though nearly everyone I interviewed and interacted with are public figures, I decided to use pseudonyms to preserve their anonymity. Some of the sensitive information shared by some participants, particularly contestants, may jeopardize their reputations. I refer to some participants by their titles (e.g., Mr., Mrs., Dr.) to reflect my own positionality due to age conventions in Nigeria. Those I refer to by titles were in their forties and older. It was culturally inappropriate for me to call them by just their first names.

In addition to interviews and observations, I collected and analyzed hundreds of print and visual materials, such as newspaper clippings, and many hours of television broadcasts and video recordings. I scoured social media posts, and compiled advertisements, pamphlets, and websites about the Nigerian beauty pageant industry. Combining interviews, ethnographic data, and textual analysis of archival materials allowed me to delve into the embodied practices and symbolic politics surrounding Nigerian beauty competitions.

Sociologist Victoria Reyes uses the concept of "strategic positionality" to posit an intersectional perspective on reflexivity that acknowledges how multiple visible and invisible social identities influence access, rapport, and knowledge production in the research process.[52] As a Nigerian-American born and raised in the United States, I was simultaneously an insider and outsider. I often worked to play on my in-between status as appropriate, which sometimes made me feel like I was living a double life. For example, I would sometimes emphasize my American upbringing to have participants explain taken-for-granted points to me, and at other times I would emphasize my American educational credentials to help me access research sites as I discovered that participants often viewed it as a signal of international credibility. I also learned I could use my Yoruba background and surname tactically. Invariably people would ask me where I was from in order to trace my class status, religious identification, and family origins. Balogun is one of the most common names among the Yoruba ethnic group, which means that it was initially difficult for people to place me or make assumptions about my religious background because Yoruba people are both Muslims and Christians, while Igbos are assumed to be Christian and Hausas are presumed to be Muslim. I also had to absorb lessons on how to manage different aspects of my embodiment and background, including my accent, hair, and clothing, presenting them deliberately to facilitate my research and to gain further insight about the social expectations of those around me.

My parents' own immigrant story is tied to the rise and fall of Nigeria's political economy. They came to the United States for higher education in the early 1980s, right before the country's economic collapse, with the help of government-sponsored scholarships. Intending to complete their degrees and return, they reversed their plans after a two-year stint in Nigeria in the 1990s, which was a time of political and economic turmoil. I have heard countless conversations in both Nigeria and the United States about how the many hardships ordinary Nigerians encounter, such as traffic jams, an unpredictable electricity supply, and chronic corruption, are nonexistent in countries like the United States. Instances when I mentioned problems that Americans also face were largely dismissed and minimized. They had fallen into the trap of painting Nigeria and the continent at large as "fundamentally disordered" and places like the United States as wholly idyllic. Examples such as the lead poisoning of the water supply in Flint, Michigan, financial scandals like the Bernie Madoff pyramid investment schemes, and investigations into Russian interference in the 2016 presidential elections highlight how basic needs like accessible potable water or expectations that business deals and the election system are always above-board cannot be taken for granted, even in what are termed developed countries, like the United States. All countries face corruption, internal conflict, and moments of political instability. However, the constant juxtaposition of extremes makes social problems even more glaring in the Nigerian context. Indeed, most Nigerians remain hyper-aware about their place in the international political economy and prospects for national development.

BOOK OVERVIEW

Beauty Diplomacy focuses on four cases of beauty pageants held in Nigeria, three national and one international. The book relies primarily on intensive ethnographic fieldwork carried out in Nigeria during the 2009–10 cycles of two contemporary national beauty pageants (The Most Beautiful Girl in Nigeria and Queen Nigeria) and extensive archival research on the hosting of the 2002 Miss World contest in Nigeria and the Miss Nigeria beauty competition, Nigeria's oldest national beauty contest. I selected these pageants since they represent varied relationships between the state, market, and popular masses. While the three national pageants are adamant about their duty to represent the nation, they contend with the prism of internationalism, national solidarity, and cultural diversity in distinct ways. The book takes Nigeria's ethnoreligious fragmentation and tenuous position in the global political economy as a starting point to explore how beauty pageants as a civic-cultural institution seek to construct national cohesion in a time of major change. Four tension-filled case studies of beauty pageants illuminate this nation-building process. These realms are contentious but productive terrains for imagining the nation. By comparing these contests—their content, structure, and associated discourses—I theorize about nationalism as a multilayered process informed by local and global processes.

Chapter 2, "Snapshots of Nigerian Pageantry," begins with the history of the beauty pageant industry in Nigeria. Focusing primarily on the rise, the fall, and the subsequent return of the first national beauty pageant, Miss Nigeria, which was first held in 1957, I provide historical context for how beauty pageants became symbolic representations of the nation, detailing the origin and development of the Nigerian beauty pageant industry as linked to the trajectory of a postindependence nation. I detail the development of the Nigerian beauty pageant industry over the last six decades, as the nation changed from a country reveling in its postcolonial independence to an emerging nation self-consciously placed within the international political economy.

Chapter 3, "The Making of Beauty Diplomats," focuses on how Nigerian beauty queens embody specific ideals about class and sexual respectability, thereby positioning themselves against representations of other women. Contestants employ a type of aesthetic labor to pursue broader nationalist agendas. Through their bodies, and specifically their voice, walk, and smile, they present themselves as public figures—representatives of "ordinary people"—whose celebrity gives them access to elites they can lobby to promote their concerns in the national arena through a beauty diplomacy narrative. I also consider the financial incentives of contestants in their quest for upward mobility. They seek to bypass traditional venues of upward mobility by using the entertainment world as a means of getting ahead but face a set of structural and symbolic realities that constrain their aspirations.

Chapter 4, "Miss Cultural and Miss Cosmopolitan," draws from my ethnographic data on two national pageants to show how intranational dynamics like religion and ethnicity shape differing sets of skills, debates over appearance, and audience participation to embody distinct versions of gendered nationhood. The Queen Nigeria Pageant took an approach I call tactile. The object of adopting this approach was to focus on tangible cultural familiarity and stress unifying the nation by employing a "unity in diversity" mantra that actively sought to recognize specific cultural elements of each state through a federation model of the nation. The Most Beautiful Girl in Nigeria contest used a tactical approach, focused on cultural discovery, and emphasized globalizing the nation by focusing on securing its place as a "global leader" of internationally renowned pageants to express the nation's competitiveness on a world stage.

Chapter 5, "The Business of Beauty," examines how various stakeholders benefit financially from Nigerian beauty competitions. In Nigeria, owners of beauty pageants, most of them middle-aged male entrepreneurs, use these events to establish political access to key government officials and to attract investment in their organizations from a wide variety of corporations, from local business to multinationals. Through the relationships they develop with politicians and other business leaders, organizers recast their endeavors as engaging in "respectable entrepreneurship" that allows women to get ahead and gain a greater foothold in Nigeria's political economy, while also boosting the nation's business culture through economic reform efforts.

Chapter 6, "As Miss World Turns," analyzes the 2002 Miss World Pageant, an international beauty competition originally scheduled to be held in Nigeria, but ultimately moved to London due to protests both within Nigeria and globally. Hosting Miss World linked the pageant with political aspirations of strengthening Nigeria's fledgling status as an emerging nation. The 2002 pageant and the ensuing political crisis brought to the forefront underlying tensions that were based not just on religious divisions, but also on unresolved conflicts over secularism, region, and globalization. I show how debates about globalization and Nigeria's national trajectory played out through discourses surrounding the protection of women's bodies. The aspirations of Nigerian organizers to present a modern, rising Nigeria were ultimately crushed. Opponents within the country perceived the contest as an artifact of Western influence rather than a triumphant entry onto the global stage, and international NGOs focused on the controversy as further evidence of Nigeria's status as a conflict-ridden state.

In the concluding chapter, "After the Spotlight," I reinforce the argument that aesthetic economies and civic institutions like Nigeria's beauty pageant industry are not just sites of entertainment, but also a source that provides multiple ways of envisioning Nigeria. I discuss some of the changes to the Nigerian pageant industry and also how the concept of gendered diplomacy can be extended beyond beauty pageants to other arenas.

2 | SNAPSHOTS OF NIGERIAN PAGEANTRY

RISE, FALL, AND RETURN

Mrs. Bukky Ademola was one of the first people I met who worked in the Nigerian beauty pageant industry. This was early in my fieldwork, in October 2009. I arrived at the office building, located in the back of a large compound, at 12:10 P.M., ten minutes late for our scheduled meeting. As I entered the doorway, I heard Mrs. Ademola's voice conversing in Yoruba, one of Nigeria's three major languages, in the background. I greeted the receptionist sitting in the lobby room and introduced myself. The receptionist then slipped into another room to let Mrs. Ademola know I had arrived. She waved me into the room where she had been chatting with two men and asked me to take a seat. Mrs. Ademola, who was in her mid-forties but looked at least ten years younger, was dressed sharply in a black, pinstriped button-down shirt tucked into a gray knee-length skirt. Her short black hair was slicked back with gel and she wore minimal makeup. When she spoke, her voice had a slight British accent, which is typical of many middle-class Nigerians who travel frequently to the United Kingdom or who went to school there. She told me a little about her background. She had started a pageant four years ago after stepping down as manager of the Miss Nigeria Pageant. I took this reference as an entry point to start asking her more questions about her involvement in this, the country's first national pageant, which began in

1957, but was at the time on a six-year hiatus. When my line of questioning about Miss Nigeria started, her youthful face visibly soured, and she replied,

> I don't want to talk about them. They are still owing me back salary! I worked for them for too long without pay. They even recently contacted me about working with them again. But I laid out my terms. They have to pay back my owed salary and have a set budget. They can't meet my demands, so I'm not willing to go back. I don't even know what's going on with them now.

She then narrated Miss Nigeria's downfall, pointing to a new investor who had taken over the *Daily Times Nigeria* (*DTN*), the newspaper that ran the pageant, and who, no longer seeing the beauty competition as a priority, had allowed the contest to flounder. Mrs. Ademola then changed the subject back to her own pageant, Miss Green and Clean, which was coming up in two months, pointing out that while her pageant was focused on charity work, Miss Nigeria's restart was solely a business venture.

In the next few months of fieldwork, I heard rumors about the Miss Nigeria Pageant mounting a return under new management, but I admit I was skeptical. Mrs. Ademola's story about unpaid salary reflected several others' accounts of general economic mismanagement, with protracted layoffs, unpaid severance packages, salaries in arrears, and the overall disdain that plagued the pageant in the late 1990s and early 2000s, mostly due to its ties to the *Daily Times Nigeria*, whose reputation had shifted from that of a flagship newspaper to a flailing one. When I visited the *DTN* Lagos archives in 2010, which had been bought out from the federal government by Folio Communications Ltd. in 2004, I found it mostly in disarray. After paying a small fee to have the generators run so I could explore the *DTN* library, I discovered a bulletin board with the photos of previous Miss Nigerias posted on it, on the floor in a dark corner of the newspaper's library room. The photographs on the bulletin board, a couple of them torn and faded, seemed an apt metaphor for the descriptions of neglect that past Miss Nigeria affiliates had shared with me.

I first confirmed the return of the Miss Nigeria Pageant when I was in the Silverbird corporate offices, where I was wrapping up my work as an intern. Mr. Tim was sitting at the large glass conference room table, reading the daily newspaper. He showed me the ad for the Miss Nigeria Pageant with the tag-line, "One Nation, One People, One Nigeria, One Queen" (see Figure 2.1). "I'm not worried. The competition is healthy," he said with a smirk, and added, "No matter what, we are the only ones who hold the license to send contestants to Miss World and Miss Universe, so we will always be on top." Mr. Tim was the owner of the Most Beautiful Girl in Nigeria (MBGN), which had by then emerged as the premier national pageant, but once had had a bitter rivalry with the Miss Nigeria Pageant, which had included several lawsuits. While MBGN garnered the most national visibility at the time of my fieldwork, the Miss Nigeria Pageant was often described to me as a critical national institution and a must-watch event in its heyday in the 1960s and 1970s, and one that caught the attention of other West African countries. For instance, historian Jacqueline Mougoué discusses how, during the 1960s, political elites in Anglophone Cameroon looked to Nigeria as leading the way in pageantry and, as a result, pushed for the development of beauty pageants in their own country in order to stay abreast of continental trends.[1]

Contrary to my initial doubts, Miss Nigeria was relaunched as a scholarship program offering a full financial package to attend any university in the world in 2010, the same year as Nigeria's fiftieth year of independence, by the private events management firm AOE Events and Entertainment. When I met with four members of the new Miss Nigeria's organizing committee, they handed me slick marketing pamphlets and a DVD media package, which included a video montage of black-and-white photographs of previous Miss Nigeria winners. The organizers emphasized bringing back vintage Nigerian glamour. They discussed how in today's landscape, pageants had become "bastard-ized," tarnishing Miss Nigeria's reputation. Their perception was that the number of pageants now in the country was excessive. Auta Zamani, one of the pageant organizers, stated pointedly: "I remember when everyone in my family used to watch Miss Nigeria together. It was a family event. It was well-respected. We want to bring that back." The organizers' words and image selection in their marketing portfolios differed markedly from my observa-tions of the rhetoric from MBGN and Queen Nigeria, two national pageants whose organizers complained about their previous difficulty in organizing contests and the derision the general public had showed to the industry in the past. As the first national pageant in Nigeria, Miss Nigeria affiliates used

FIGURE 2.1. Miss Nigeria One Nation, One Queen ad. *Source:* Miss Nigeria Organization, Folio Media Group. Reprinted with permission.

nostalgic-nationalism, a strategy that glorified the contest's past history as a major national institution. Miss Nigeria once had a stronghold over the industry, tied in part to its cosponsor the *Daily Times Nigeria* newspaper, one of the most financially successful newspapers in Africa. By reclaiming their good name, Miss Nigeria affiliates sought to set an example for the rest of the industry. As the industry has grown exponentially, it has become increasingly privatized, but remains a key conduit for print and visual media and still navigates complex connections to the state. In the evolution of the industry, governing elites and leaders of private industry have alternatively endorsed, ignored, or actively advanced beauty competitions.

THE NATIONAL QUESTION

Since securing independence from Great Britain in 1960, Nigeria has witnessed profound changes due to market-oriented economic reforms, political instability, and heightened social divisions. A problem that has long plagued the country is "the national question," or the difficulty in forging a national consciousness. Nigeria's colonial history has meant that territorial lines drew together local ethnic communities that had never previously thought of themselves as one people. The notion of Nigeria as a "geographical expression," an idea conveyed by Chief Obafemi Awolowo, a Nigerian statesman and nationalist, refers to the point that although Nigeria may exist as a territorial designation,[2] it lacks a coherent national identity due to vast regional, religious, and ethnic divisions, which threaten its unity.

The question of whether Nigeria constitutes a nation at all persists today. Some suggest that Nigerians are much more likely to identify with ethnic or regional affiliations than national ones. Nigeria has over 250 ethnic groups, nearly all of which have their own language and dialects. Regional divisions between the North and South constitute another challenge that Nigeria faces. Although commentators often invoke regional religious splits between a "Muslim North" and a "Christian South" as a main source of political tension within Nigeria, these seemingly neat regional divides do not always map cleanly onto religious or ethnic divisions and do not fully capture the highly fragmented religious, ethnic, and regional differences in the multifaith and multiethnic country. This diversity is often animated along political fault lines in which voting alliances, political parties, and communal conflicts follow ethnic, religious, and regional affiliations. Further, the implementation of sharia law and the rise of Islamic fundamentalism, particularly in the Northern region, also poses a threat to Nigeria's national cohesion and global ambitions. Twelve of the nation's nineteen Northern states established sharia starting in 1999.[3] The formal application of sharia law in the North institutionalized regional divisions within the nation and further fused together ethnicity, religion, and politics.

The Nigerian state has long employed a conscious strategy of implementing image campaigns and national policies targeting reorientation of the nation in order to build solidarity and change civil society. These nation-branding projects are state-controlled political projects that shape citizens' national consciousness. Nigeria's first national image project, which was called the "Three R Program" ("R" stood for "reconciliation, rehabilitation, and reconstruction"), began in 1970, shortly at the end of the bloody three-year Biafran War. In 1984, Muhammadu Buhari's military government, which had seized power following a coup d'état, launched the "War Against Indiscipline," a program focused on routing out corruption and remedying the perceived lack of public morality. The 1990s military regime of Ibrahim Babangida implemented a political reform effort titled "Mass Mobilization for Self-Reliance, Social Justice, and Economic Recovery" (MAMSER). In 2005, the government of Olusegun Obasanjo launched the "Heart of Africa" image campaign, which was widely lampooned as wasteful and ineffective.[4] In 2009, the presidency of Umaru Musa Yar'Adua launched the "Good People, Great Nation" rebranding campaign. These image campaigns are examples of top-down citizenship that are as much about external image boosting as they are efforts to create compliant national subjects.

Nigeria has been seeking a secure footing on the international stage for decades. The nation has clear potential as a major global player economically and politically, and regional experts call it the "giant of Africa." Nigeria's military might, leadership in the region, and massive oil wealth have contributed to this designation. Yet this promise remains hampered by a reputation for political cronyism, severe poverty, and communal conflicts, with the result that terms such as "ailing" or "sleeping" often qualify the description "giant." These are major roadblocks to nation building and unity.[5] I use the term *emerging nation* to highlight both the simultaneous processes of making national unity visible and the ongoing international efforts to make Nigeria a prominent nation that has fully emerged onto the global stage. Given its ethnic and religious diversity, forging a strong and unified sense of Nigeria as a nation that can present itself in a coherent way to an international community remains a pressing issue.

National meanings are constructed within the context of larger global developments. Scholars have focused on the creation of national culture through widely shared symbols like food, public festivals, sports teams, monuments, and national literatures. A growing body of research on these cultural symbols and practices understands the formation of national identities as linked to the broader dynamics of the market, the state, and civil society.[6] Wendy Griswold and Lyn Spillman both identified two major frameworks for understanding national representations. One focuses on a "world cultural frame," which highlights how nations seek to position themselves as part of the "global community of nations." The other, an "internal integration frame," highlights the desire to unify diverse populations or emphasize national distinctiveness.[7] Classic scholarly accounts of nationalism tend to focus on how elites, such as political actors, the military, intellectuals, and merchants, use their influence to mobilize large-scale social movements, manage the state, and regulate the movement of capital.[8] Through these macro-level, primarily state-centered political projects, elites control nation building from above. Additional scholarship has placed greater emphasis on how people adopt and contest national identities through everyday cultural practices or discourses. They approach nationalism through the lens of routine, everyday micro-level actions that connect people to a broader "imagined community" from below.[9] My focus on beauty contests pivots toward understanding national image orientation projects through the lens of civic-cultural institutions like beauty pageants which involve interactions with state elites and ordinary Nigerian citizens. Symbolic shifts that involve macro-level connections to the state and micro-level ties to people on the ground play a role in political and economic developments in Nigeria.

EMBODIED NATIONALISM

Beauty pageants are not only institutions that center on culture, leisure, and entertainment, but are also embodied sites for the production and contestation of national identities. My work builds on the insights of post-colonial and transnational feminist scholars such as Nira Yuval-Davis, Anne McClintock, and Tamar Mayer, who have established how gendered bodies mark and destabilize boundaries of the nation through *embodied nationalism*.[10] I understand embodied nationalism as an overarching theoretical framework that uses gendered bodies to signal shifting ideas of the nation, as well as how fluctuating embodied ideals highlight the complex terrain of the nation. Beauty diplomacy is an embodied nationalist strategy. Some work has linked masculinity to the nation-state through the example of militarized masculinity, which draws on cultural proprieties and physical manifestations to argue that heroic warrior figures embody the strength and competition needed to shore up gendered national codes of citizenship, rights, and security.[11] I focus on idealized femininity as a public cultural construction that encodes specific expectations about physical appearance, corporeal lifestyles, and aesthetic morality. Popular Nigerian aphorisms and popular music provide some insights into how outer physical beauty and inner moral disposition have been packaged together in Nigerian culture. For example, in the song "Ina Ran" by Haruna Ishola, a maestro of *apala* music (a percussion-heavy genre featuring talking drums, which is associated with Yoruba Muslims), one stanza says, "If a woman is beautiful but has no morals, I would not marry her for half a penny, but if she has good morals and is beautiful, I can spend a thousand to marry her." Similarly, an Igbo proverb states, "*Agwa bu mma nwanyi. Ego bu mma nwoke,*" which translates as, "The beauty of a woman rests with her character. The handsomeness of a man rests with money." Timothy Burke, Jennifer Cole, Sanyu Mojola, and Lynn Thomas use the concept of consumptive femininity to show how using products such as cosmetics, soaps, and clothing mark idealized feminine norms that encode class-bound purchasing power. Staying abreast of and buying the latest status commodities—stylish clothes, smart phones, and chic makeup—asserts modern femininity, urban respectability, and aspirational desires for economic security.[12] Embodied notions of comportment, virtue, and commodity culture mark feminine ideals. Different groups in and outside the Nigerian beauty pageant industry mobilized these varied elements of idealized femininity in the service of nation building, ameliorating national conflicts, and making visible their oppositional claims. Modern urban tastes and virtuous femininity help proclaim the nation as both upstanding and on the rise.

In Nigeria, the mantra "No Woman, No Nation" has emerged as a political rallying call to signal the importance of women to the country in recognition of their economic contributions, fight for political rights, and targeted philanthropic efforts.[13] Women's active participation serves as a visible marker of their status in their respective societies and, by extension, the success and progress of a nation. Public visibility, however, also works hand in hand with prescribed gendered expectations for women's position in the nation that may be limiting or burdensome. For example, by positioning themselves as advocates for female-centered social transformation, the efforts of Nigerian beauty queens are a platform to boost nationalist and global politics. However, their roles as public figures are constrained by broader respectability politics which regulate the bounds of idealized femininity through codes of domesticity, chastity, and propriety. Anthropologist Alexander Edmonds notes that beauty "shapes a particular kind of modern subject with diverse aspirations for self-transformation, social mobility, and sexual pleasure and power."[14] Beauty is a public signal of national modernity. Transnational feminist scholars have advanced the woman-as-nation thesis to argue that women and their bodies serve as sites through which debates about the trajectory of a nation take form, shaped in part through shifts in the global economy, cultural globalization, and postcolonial trajectories. In the international political economy, women are positioned as ideal workers at the front line of integrating their nations into global markets through industries like factory work, microfinance, sex work, and the knowledge economy.[15] Beauty queens sustain this trend.

NOSTALGIC-NATIONALISM: MISS NIGERIA

The Miss Nigeria Pageant began in 1957. The *Daily Times Nigeria* held the license for the pageant, which initially started as a photo contest in which hopeful contestants sent their pictures to the newspaper headquarters. These pictures were published in the paper and selected finalists came to Lagos (the then capital) to compete in the nationwide competition. Sponsoring the Miss Nigeria beauty pageant served as a means of solidifying and growing its customer base.[16] The Miss Nigeria Pageant was regularly featured in the women's pages section of the *DTN* and in above-the-fold front-page head-lines. The *Daily Times Nigeria*, which was first printed in June 1926, was one of the earliest and highest circulated newspapers in Africa.[17] In 1947, the *Daily Times Mirror* Group in London bought the newspaper and brought foreign financial interests into the company. However, they maintained a policy of appointing and promoting Nigerian trainees, reporters, and managers. In 1963, *DTN* became a public company traded on the Nigerian Stock Exchange, and following a decade-long gradual transfer of ownership to Nigerians, by March 1974, *DTN* became a wholly Nigerian-owned company.[18] In 1975, the federal government acquired a 60 percent stake in *DTN*, which later increased to a 96.5 percent equity stake, marking its transition from a privately held company to a government-controlled enterprise. Circulation steadily declined over the next three decades. In 2004, *DTN* was bought by a private media company. Over the course of its history, *DTN* has changed hands from foreign to local owners and from private to government stakeholders, and back again. These changes undoubtedly shaped the trajectory of Miss Nigeria.[19]

The history of the Miss Nigeria Pageant, the country's original national pageant, has been a series of starts, stops, and revivals, punctuated by shifting moments in the nation-state from constitutional democracy and civil war to periods of military rule.[20] By examining shifting orientations within the Miss Nigeria Pageant and highlighting the economic, social, and political pressures that undergirded its development, I examine the trajectory of the contest through the lens of nostalgic-nationalism, focused on a longing for the lost glory of the past, but also a sense of the hopefulness about future possibility. I focus on thematic changes in the pageant's history, understanding them as consolidated within specific historical moments.

Modern Domesticity

The first Miss Nigeria Pageant was held in 1957, three years prior to Nigeria's independence from Great Britain, the same year in which Nigeria held its constitutional conference. In fact, the *Daily Times Nigeria* ran a news story on Miss Nigeria's recent trip to London directly opposite a photograph of Sir James Robertson, governor-general of Nigeria, and his wife about to board a plane to London to attend the Nigerian Constitutional Conference. The caption read: "He has expressed his faith in unity in Nigeria, and this unity is having its greatest trial at the conference. But he is still confident."[21] The start of the pageant in the final years of official colonial rule could be considered a prefiguring moment in which prior to formal independence, a gradual transition toward decolonization began. Symbolic events such as a national beauty competition legitimized the burgeoning nation-state both domestically and to the rest of the world and helped consolidate national unity in a time of transition.

In its inaugural national event, which was held in the hall of the exclusive Lagos Island Club, the Bobby Benson Band, a Nigerian highlife (a music genre popular in some parts of West Africa) musical group, entertained the crowd with its signature style of jazz horns and guitars. The winner that night was Grace Tinuke Oyelude, a twenty-four-year-old Yoruba salesclerk who grew up and lived in the Northern state of Kano. She later recalled her crowning moment: "On the day of the event, I dressed up in a native attire, tying my wrapper neatly. I was the only one dressed in iro [wrap skirt] and buba [blouse] that night." When asked what special qualities she possessed that allowed her to clinch the crown that night, Oyelude remarked: "Maybe the way I dressed. There was no make-up. Even the iro and buba I put on cannot reveal any statistics [her body measurements]."[22] Her choice of *aso oke*, a hand-loomed fabric typically worn for formal occasions and traditionally associated with the Yoruba ethnic group of southwestern Nigeria, was a way to promote Nigeria's cultural heritage through sartorial choices.

During the 1950s and 1960s, Miss Nigeria focused on modern domesticity to refer to public forms of feminine leisure, commodified class-based consumption, physical movement, and machinery through gadgets, new modes of transportation, and appliances. During this time period, the *DTN* launched *Modern Woman*, a woman's magazine, in 1963. Modern appeals to technology and leisure were juxtaposed against a connection to the home, entertaining guests, and well-being. For example, donated prizes for the finalists from Lagos firms included a Parker 51 fountain pen, watches, refrigerators, radios, autocycles, sewing machines, and a record player.[23] Many of the ads in the *DTN* included the reigning Nigerian beauty queen posed next to home appliances, health tonics, or drinks served when entertaining guests. For example, one ad featured Miss Nigeria with her arms outstretched as if

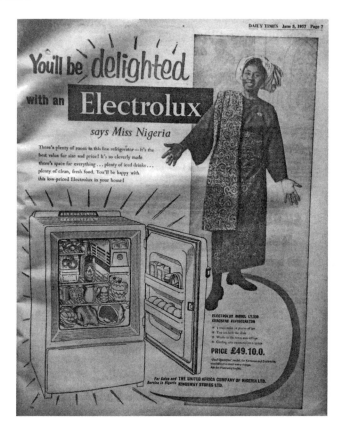

FIGURE 2.2. Miss Nigeria promoting Electrolux Fridge. *Source:* Miss Nigeria Organization, Folio Media Group. Reprinted with permission.

presenting something to an audience, with an Electrolux refrigerator in front of her, and a quote singing its praises (see Figure 2.2).

A 1957 ad with Oyelude holding a drink read: "Lovely Miss Nigeria says—Keep Fit with Krola! It's delicious, wholesome, healthy refreshment." Another advertisement, featuring Miss Nigeria 1959 dressed in *iro, buba*, and a headwrap and with a raised glass in her hand, stated:

> Miss Nigeria drinks Dubonnet. This picture shows the beautiful Miss Nigeria drinking Dubonnet at the great modern establishment where this, the finest of aperitives is produced. Her radiant smile reflects her pleasure when drinking this famous French wine. Her verdict? "It's

wonderful. I will always keep a bottle to offer my friends." We suggest you take Miss Nigeria's advice and always give Dubonnet, one of the world's most popular and health-giving drinks.[24]

Another 1959 ad states in part:

> Nigeria's beauty queen drinks Ovaltine for health and happiness. Beautiful Miss Nigeria knows that health is the secret of beauty and happiness! You too can build up your health and strength and stamina by taking Ovaltine daily. Nourishing, sustaining Ovaltine is a rich energy-giving food as well as delicious drink. It fortifies the body, soothes and calms the nerves and promotes sound, restful sleep at night. Ovaltine is world famous—there is nothing else so good.[25]

In these examples, advertisers linked consumptive femininity to beauty, health, and wellness through the iconography of Miss Nigeria, in which she stood in to provide expert advice, serve as an exemplar, and signal mass popularity.

An ad sponsored by Singer Sewing Machines in the form of a narrative retrospective on the recent Miss Nigeria Pageant stated:

> Singer also won on that night. Yes, Singer went away with a lovely prize: "Miss Cameroon" Suzan Abai [one of the finalists] has joined the Singer Sewing Machine Co. as embroidery teacher and she is waiting for the pleasure to teach you this wonderful new hobby that has become so popular in Nigeria: embroidery on a regular Sewing machine. Yes, she is there with her beautiful smile ready to welcome you, so here is your chance to have embroidery taught to you by none less than a beauty queen. After all, let us say again, it confirms what we have told you month after month: Singer means: the very best.[26]

The Singer Company used the beauty pageant as a way to promote their own equipment and sell its usefulness for a fashionable pastime. They called attention to the enticing beauty and welcoming hospitality of Miss Cameroon (Cameroon was a region of Nigeria at the time) as a way of drawing customers in and as confirmation of the high standard of their brand. In doing so, they used beauty queens as an asset to promote the company.

Miss Nigeria was also connected to technology. An advertisement including Oyelude smiling with drawings of three radio models, including a caption about their technical specifications, read:

> Grundig Radio—for perfect listening says beautiful Miss Nigeria. There's a whole world of pleasure waiting for you in a Grundig radio or radiogram. Wonderfully engineered and beautifully finished, Grundig receivers reach new heights of realism in radio and gramophone reproduction. Enjoy this thrilling experience in your own home.[27]

Anthropologist Brian Larkin's research on media infrastructure in Northern Nigeria highlights how the radio initially started as a public technology since radios were heard in the city streets through installed loudspeakers.[28] Given that context, the Grundig ad's emphasis on enjoying radio in the privacy of one's own home suggests a rising trend. This emphasis on domestic leisure, alongside the focus on world-class engineering and technological advancement, buttressed the national logic of modern domesticity.

As part of her prize package, Oyelude, as Miss Nigeria 1957, won a ten-day London excursion. News articles heavily spotlighted her jam-packed touring schedule. Her itinerary involved visits to Nigerian political officials, film studios, sightseeing, commercial firms, dinner parties, and fashion showrooms.[29] She flew on the first scheduled Lagos-London service on West African Airways Corporation, which was christened the *Stratocruiser International*, an aircraft with state-of-the-art features including both a main deck and lower deck for passengers and a pressurized cabin.[30] She was featured in an ad for the Vauxhall Victor, a large, just-launched, British-manufactured, family-styled car, one of the most exported British vehicles (see Figure 2.3). The ad included a full shot of Miss Nigeria and a photo of the car and an airplane in the background. It also included a first-hand account of Miss Nigeria's enthusiastic impressions that riding in the car was as "thrilling as flying." The ad goes on to state:

> "As I rode along, I saw all the wonderful sights through the big wide windows. The Victor is so comfortable, too, with soft, soft seats and wonderful springing that makes fast driving seem like flying! But best of all I like the Victor's lovely colors inside and out, and its big, modern look."

FIGURE 2.3. Miss Nigeria promoting UAC Motors's Vauxhall Victor car. *Source:* Miss Nigeria Organization, Folio Media Group. Reprinted with permission.

> Miss Nigeria is right! The Vauxhall Victor has wonderful style, comfort and economy. Let us arrange a demonstration drive for you, free of cost and obligation.[31]

Miss Nigeria's experience with these newly manufactured and launched modes of transportation were a means of social and economic positioning. For example, descriptions of the car focused on its modern look to appeal to newly forming Nigerian consumptive tastes, but also positioned Miss Nigeria as compatible with this stylish and fast-moving look. Moreover, using Miss Nigeria as a spokesperson for motor vehicles and planes portrayed her as a woman on the move.

The descriptions of her London trip also focused on domesticity through ideas of maternal instinct, cooking, and homemaking. For example, one news article stated, "What does 'Miss Nigeria', now back home, remember best about her UK visit? Not the tours of the commercial firms, the advertising stops, nor even the sight-seeing. It was surely the day she spent at Brighton with six-year old Janie and two-year-old Sharon." The article explained how her eyes immediately lit up when she ran into these two English children and that she instantly began to dote on them.[32] In her commentary, which was included in news accounts, Oyelude provided impressions about homes, furnishings, hospitality, standards of living, children's dispositions, and food. She commented that she disliked the way British people prepared their food since it was without flavor and undercooked. She commented, "Maybe we Nigerians should teach the British how to cook their own food," thus showing off her cooking skills and familiarity with British cuisine, in a selective embrace of colonialized culture but also a critique that the British had not mastered their own cuisine and Nigerians might have a thing or two to teach them. In her commentary, Oyelude counters a narrative of England as lively and modern and implicitly repositions Nigeria as the site of progress and growth. She also commented: "I grew up under the impression that all the houses in England were very bright and modern and that everything was on a very large and lavish scale. I now know different. As we were about to land at London airport we flew low over the houses there, and I was surprised to see that they were not only rather small, but sometimes rather unattractive and old." These impressions focused on modernity and commented on domestic things, but also placed Nigeria above "modern" England.[33] The great importance placed on this trip was reflected in an editorial signed by the "editress" of the women's page, in which she stated, "Tinuke's visit to London will be a real opportunity for her and she will have a valued experience which she can use in her own private life for the progress of the country. She is an ambassador of Nigeria's womanhood, which we will be proud to show to the world as much as our political progress."[34] This comment fused together public and private aspirations. It focused on the political progress of Nigeria as a nation tied to Oyelude's own success and placed her as worthy of the position of driving the progress of the nation. Oyelude also seemed keenly aware of this ambassadorship role, especially at this prime historical moment when Nigeria was on the verge of independence. She noted, "I must be careful to be a credit to my country and leave behind everywhere a good impression as Miss Nigeria since I represented my homeland in a very real way."[35]

Commercialized Wealth

In the 1970s the paper rose to prominence, reaching an unprecedented peak daily circulation of 275,000 copies and 400,000 for the *Sunday Times*,[36] and became known as one of the most successful companies in Africa. The newspaper dominated the publishing industry with a string of spin-off magazines and newspapers. In 1977, the Miss Nigeria Pageant returned after a five-year break.[37] Organizers attributed their commercial success to the rising reputation of *DTN*. Mrs. Sylvia Ndidi, a former organizer, explained:

> I think from our antecedents being the *Daily Times of Nigeria*, Nigeria's number one newspaper at that time, our reputation also took us a long way. It was the *Daily Times* organizing it. They would be sure that we are not going to go away. [If there was a problem,] *Daily Times* would always be there to be sued, not a company that would disappear overnight.

She talked about how their association with the *DTN* led to tangible benefits in the form of sponsors who took advantage of the newspaper's market share by branding the stage, cars, and product placement. Miss Nigeria contributed to the growth of the *DTN* subscription base, but the organization also further leveraged the newspaper's name to sustain itself as a business.

My interview with Mr. Seun Folarin, the organizer who revived Miss Nigeria in 1977 and served as the main organizer during most of the 1970s and early 1980s, centered on his motivations to shift the pageant's focus from a cultural form of entertainment to a commercial enterprise. The pageant was now organized under the auspices of the newly formed Times Leisure Services (later Times Ventures Ltd.), a subsidiary of the *DTN* formed to increase the newspaper's profits. This change was part of Nigeria's broader economic transition in the global marketplace, due in part to its unprecedented oil wealth in the 1970s. Explaining his rationale, Mr. Folarin described that he injected marketing and finances into the pageant by introducing appearance fees where they would charge others and divide the money between the Miss Nigeria organization and the queen. They reserved the queen's portion and gave it to her in full at the end of her reign. He also gave the winner a "good salary at the time" of ₦6,000 per annum (about $9,200 in 1977), and made sure that all winners received a car. In 1977, he was able to snag three cars and a chauffeur for the winner and first and second runners-up. He emphasized that in previous years no other Miss Nigeria had received a car during her reign, with the exception of Miss Nigeria 1960, who received a small Fiat from the Minister of Information to commemorate the country's independence. Mr. Folarin stressed that he felt it was imperative for the beauty queen to have a car as it signaled that she was independently financially comfortable and not reliant on a man for financial resources. He also made arrangements for the reigning 1977 Miss World to crown the new Miss Nigeria and for M. K. O. Abiola, a major political figure, to serve as chairman for the evening. When I asked him to describe what made Miss Nigeria unique, he replied:

> Because [we] reflect the national outlook, like MBGN is always Lagos. Let there be zonal [referring to the division of the country's thirty-six states into geopolitical zones based on region] [contests] so that people can feel it everywhere. It is laziness and all that [MBGN] is after is profit. Yes, we wanted profit, but it must reflect a national outlook. They [MBGN] just pick this one, Miss Sokoto and so on, and they're not even from that state most of the time. I don't believe in that. But our own, we do it in zonal, northern zone where states in the North will compete, Bendel Zone, places like Warri, Port Harcourt, East, places like Enugu, so we just pick a place in each zone.

Although the organizer of the 1977 pageant stressed that the pageant was after profit, he also insisted that the process of selecting contestants according to specific regional zones allowed for the development of a "national outlook." When I pressed him to clarify the zonal arrangement, he compared the process to the People's Democratic Party (Nigeria's then national ruling party) and its rotational power-sharing agreement based on the country's six geopolitical zones. He stressed that by alternating where the national finale was held and selecting finalists according to zones (the top three contestants in each zone participated in the national finale), the pageant could be "felt by everyone" in the nation. And while contestants were expected to wear the national attire that corresponded to a particular zone during the national show, he stressed how organizers used promotional considerations to choose the national wear worn by Nigerian queens at international pageants. Detailing the logic, he stated, "It [just] depends on what will sell Nigeria better; it does not matter whether it is Igbo, Hausa and Yoruba. If the girl is Igbo, we may give her aso oke [Yoruba hand-loomed cloth] because [we might] have a sponsor for aso oke." Mr. Folarin's remarks pointed to some flexibility in the positioning of ethnicity as reflecting national orientations. Forging pan-ethnic identities and shaping national sentiment through commodities like clothing points to the commingling of cultural and financial incentives.

Militarized Decline

By the mid-1980s there were two main national pageants in Nigeria: Miss Nigeria and the Most Beautiful Girl in Nigeria. Miss Nigeria organizers linked the demise of the *DTN,* and by extension their pageant, to military rule. Nigeria's military rule from 1983 to 1998 had a direct impact on the longevity of the Miss Nigeria Pageant.[38] This switch directly tied Miss Nigeria to the ebbs and flows of the state, integrating political actors into the pageant's national goals. The rise of MBGN and the fall of Miss Nigeria are also tied to privatization efforts within the country. Nigeria's economic crisis in the 1980s led to a privatization policy in 1986 that spurred the privatizing of state-owned industries like banking and communications. Miss Nigeria's close ties to the Nigerian government through its sponsorship by the *DTN* meant that the general public and corporate sponsors viewed the pageant as just another mouthpiece for an unpopular military regime. Mrs. Ndidi explained the impact of the takeover of the *DTN* by the military government in the 1990s, when it seized control as a majority shareholder in the company:

> The *Daily Times* had begun to lose its reputation. It was no longer as credible as it used to be. So, if you were organizing a beauty contest for instance and let's say that you went to a company, they would listen to you before. It was a heavyweight. I mean it was just enough to walk in and say, "I am from *Daily Times,* I want to talk to you." They would let you in because everybody knew *Daily Times.* But in the later years, *Daily Times* had lost it and that credibility had gone and therefore you could not just walk in and say, "I am from *Daily Times.*" That had been lost.

Without adequate sponsorship, Miss Nigeria eventually floundered. This allowed an opening for MBGN, owned by a private media company, to emerge as the dominant pageant in Nigeria. In the 1980s, MBGN acquired the rights to send candidates to the top international pageants, Miss World and Miss Universe, which the Miss Nigeria organization had previously done. Typically, the national contests pay yearly fees, which vary by country, to procure a license to be the official national franchisee to send contestants to international pageants. Records of these fees are not publicly available, but insiders estimate $10,000 to $100,000 for Miss Universe and $10,000 for Miss World. I heard differing accounts from various sources about why MBGN was able to secure the license; former Miss Nigeria owners speculated that MBGN bribed someone and stole it, while MBGN maintained that the rights were available since Miss Nigeria had allowed them to expire, and that they followed the proper procedures. Miss Nigeria filed a ₦10 million lawsuit against MBGN over its use of the "Miss Nigeria" moniker in international competitions (Miss World was also a named defendant) in 2002, which was later tossed out. Successive military coups hamstrung the pageant, and the precipitous decline in the state's standing tainted Miss Nigeria itself. Without sufficient economic capital, the competition could not effectively compete with MBGN, which was beginning to stage impressive shows with lighting effects and attractive staging.

The New Global Village

In 2010, the Miss Nigeria Pageant reemerged. It claimed it was the only national pageant and that the contest exuded the "virtues of womanhood."[39] The 2010 Miss Nigeria Pageant held zonal castings in four Nigerian states, covering the major regions in the country. They also included opportunities for Nigerians in the Diaspora to audition in New York and London. All of Nigeria's thirty-six states and the federal capital territory of Abuja were included in the 2010 pageant. Organizers sought the endorsement of not only the federal government, but also the three major traditional rulers in Nigeria. They announced that the new queen would not participate in any competitions abroad so that she could solely focus on national development through long-term charity work done in close coordination with the Ministries of Culture and Tourism, Health, and Women's Affairs, as well as exploring possibilities of working with international nongovernmental organizations (NGOs), like the World Health Organization and UNESCO.

The 2010 creative director of the Miss Nigeria Pageant, an ex-MBGN beauty queen, compared Nigerian pageants to those in other religious and conservative countries such as Indonesia and Cyprus, which have large Muslim and Christian populations where, she claimed, beauty competitions flourished, and explained that she aimed to strike a balance between "modern liberties and traditional values." Press coverage highlighted specific changes to the pageant's format, such as eliminating the swimwear segment and moving away from simply selecting tall, skinny, model types.[40] Their statements aimed to curtail the backlash against beauty competitions in Nigeria by dealing head-on with deep-seated cultural issues of pageants as potentially disgraceful, armoring themselves through the backing of traditional rulers, state officials, and comparisons to similar countries. These changes were packaged under a "global village" initiative, invoking a concept that understands the world as shrinking yet also expanding through accelerated interconnectedness, in which global actors compress the world's cultural diversity into a singular culture. Though they used the terminology of the global village, the new management team explained to me a slightly different perception of this concept. They emphasized bringing Nigeria's cultural values of respectability to the world through travel and charity work and by managing how beauty queens interacted with the global world—not by showing off their physical bodies but through self-sacrificing, virtuous womanhood.

Calling Miss Nigeria a historic project whose past contestants had been a witness to history, including one who was a guest of honor in the country's independence ceremonies in 1960, they positioned Miss Nigeria as the crown jewel of Nigeria's heritage. I understood their use of the global village terminology as speaking to larger anxieties about the country's position on the global stage through being purposeful about their engagement both domestically and internationally. Today, the *DTN* still oversees the contest, though the pageant has a separate management team. The newspaper restarted its print version in December 2014. It regularly features flashback retrospectives of headlines from the 1960s and 1970s, branding itself as Nigeria's oldest surviving newspaper, established in 1929, and seeks to return to its former position as the number one Nigerian media company. Like its media sponsor, Miss Nigeria's website refers prominently to its own establishment date of 1957. Through these specific tactics, the contest signals its proud past, harnessing it to claim its full potential in a rapidly shifting global and national landscape.

THE CONTEMPORARY LANDSCAPE OF BEAUTY PAGEANTS

Similar to the history of Miss Nigeria, both Queen Nigeria and the Most Beautiful Girl in Nigeria (MBGN) are plugged into the media industry, specifically through television networks. Not all beauty pageants in Nigeria are televised, but they are heavily featured in the gossip, entertainment, and celebrity sections of newspapers and magazines, and increasingly in blogs and social media. Benedict Anderson asserts that imagined communities—the socially constructed process by which diverse groups of people come to see themselves as a unified people through a shared vision of the nation—are institutionalized through media, providing key context for the importance of media's role in forging the nation through the pageant industry.[41] Political anthropologist Wale Adebanwi has documented how media (specifically the press) has been central to the struggle for collective identity in Nigeria in ways that provide insight into the postcolonial nation-state as "densely corporeal" yet "elusively spectral."[42] Queen Nigeria and MBGN's relationship with key media entrepreneurs provides them with a visual medium to craft a common vernacular of the nation—one that is both defended and disputed by their audiences.

The major groups in the Nigerian pageant world are owners, who own and control the operations through executive level positions in their pageants; organizers, who plan, manage, and direct these events; contestants, who are between the ages of eighteen and twenty-six (they are commonly referred to as girls though they are indeed young women); groomers, who are in-house or freelance coaches who drill contestants on how to walk, sit, eat, and interact with the public and sometimes choreograph dance numbers; production specialists, who do the behind-the-scenes work of coordinating lighting, staging, and filming; judges that are appointed by organizers, who use criteria focused on carriage, intellect, and physical attributes such as teeth, skin, and body type to assess contestants—they are typically celebrities, former beauty queens, philanthropists, fashion designers, political officials, and CEOs or managers of businesses, including sometimes sponsoring companies; sponsors, which includes major corporate sponsors who provide financial backing for the contest; individual personal sponsors, who directly and indirectly invest in contestants by helping them cover their costs; and supportive kin, who provide financial and logistical support for contestants; and support staff, which includes chaperones, assistants, and body laborers such as makeup artists, hair stylists, and fashion designers.

To enter, contestants fill out an entry form that costs ₦5,000 ($33), which they can pay at a local bank or at one of the drop-off sites.[43] On the form, they write their name and contact information and answer specific personal questions about their background, such as occupation, educational qualifications, career aspirations, and charity work experience. They must also attach a headshot and full-body photograph. All those who fill out a form are allowed to attend a screening exercise. Contestants sometimes set up social media pages on websites like Facebook to drum up support among the public and cultivate a fan following. Such efforts have become even larger with easier access to the Internet through smartphones. Some contestants employ handlers, managers, or agents to promote them or help them transition into other careers such as modeling and acting.

Examining beauty pageants throughout the world deepens the understanding of gendered boundaries, political contestation, economic conditions, and cultural membership, pinpointing moments of division and convergence. Popular international and national beauty contests typically include evening wear, an interview, talent, swimwear, and national costumes in their segments. Nigerian formats follow these segments to varying degrees. They typically all have evening wear, interview, and traditional attire segments, but the inclusion of the swimwear round is heavily disputed in the country. I understand the global beauty pageant industry as falling into three main camps: (1) fading establishments such as those in the United States and the United Kingdom, which still control the top two international pageants but whose own national franchises are seen as on the decline; (2) national treasures such as Venezuela that have record-breaking international title wins, and where the industry is booming and pageants are viewed as assets for the country;[44] and (3) emerging industries such as Nigeria, where pageants are rapidly growing, but have not gained full traction.

Race and ethnicity figure prominently in most pageants throughout the globe. Ideas about fixed physical appearance (most notably through socially constructed ideas of race and ethnicity) infuse national belonging and sustain the marginalization of specific groups. These assumptions about racial purity and national representation have rocked beauty pageants for decades and are linked to larger and shifting social contexts.[45] Within the United States, for instance, the crowning of racial minorities has been heralded as a signal of progress and equality throughout the country, even while formal and informal barriers to entry still display racial discrimination.[46] Within the context of Nigeria, debates about the degree to which ethnic membership maps onto state lines, about who can "rightfully" represent a state, and whether regional differences should be emphasized or obscured, play out through debates about cultural authenticity and national identity. As ideas about relationships between federalism and indigeneity transform, new narratives about ethnicity, culture, and the nation begin to emerge. Beauty pageants also highlight how gender boundaries are both tenuous and sturdy. Changing ideas about gendered representation within Nigerian beauty pageants signal Nigeria's place in the world. Studying these shifts on the ground as they remain tied to class, ethnicity, politics, and the economy helps illuminate the course that Nigeria's emergent nationalism is taking.

Cosmopolitan-Nationalism: The Most Beautiful Girl in Nigeria

The Most Beautiful Girl in Nigeria (MBGN) Pageant is run by the Silverbird Group, a private media conglomerate based in Lagos, Nigeria, with branches in Ghana and Kenya. The company is headed up by the Murray-Bruce family and has several divisions, with ventures in real estate holdings, shopping malls, several multiscreen Cineplex theaters, radio stations, a television network, and film distribution. The patron of the Murray-Bruce family, William Mullighan Murray-Bruce, started the Domino Group, a chain of grocery stores in Lagos, and has twelve children, many of whom now direct Silverbird's operations and continue to run the Domino Group. Silverbird was founded by media mogul–turned-senator Ben Murray-Bruce, who parlayed a ₦20,000 loan (about $2,000 in 1980) from his father into a multimillion-dollar business. He began by organizing live shows by 1970s musical groups such as Shalamar and Kool and the Gang and was listed in the *Guinness Book of World Records* for organizing the longest dance party, at 53 hours and 50 minutes, in the 2000s.

Because of the light-skinned looks, uncommon Anglophone names, and considerable ties to the United States of the Murray-Bruce family, the general public has raised questions about their family origins, mixed-race status, and citizenship eligibility. In eavesdropped conversations, I have heard the family referred to as *oyinbo* (foreign) Nigerians, "half-caste" (a term many Nigerians do not consider to be derogatory and use to refer to mixed-race peoples), or expatriates from Lebanon. They are natives of Bayelsa state, which is located in the coastal, oil-rich Niger-Delta region of the country, an area known for having a long history of interracial relationships due to interactions with sailors, traders, and businesspeople from Europe, Asia, and the Middle East. I found documentation that the paternal grandfather was Scottish,[47] but I was never able to get a definitive understanding of the origins of the Murray-Bruce family from their own mouths. One prominent member of the family casually mentioned that they had traced their genealogy to Great Britain, but his tentative tone and phrasing insinuated that their family origins were murky, even to them.

Before I headed to Nigeria to begin fieldwork, I had sent a message to Silverbird through the "Contact Us" section of their public website. I waited eagerly for weeks for an acknowledgment or reply, but did not receive one. About a week before I left, growing increasingly anxious about whether I would be granted research access, I sent a message through Facebook to Emeka Uche, one of Silverbird's top television personalities, briefly explaining to her that I was interested in observing MBGN. She invited me to meet with her at the STV office in Lekki one morning. The television network was behind a gate, manned by security guards. It was close to the beach, which gave the surroundings an airy vibe, but also made the area highly susceptible to flooding during the heavy rain season. I arrived fifteen minutes early for our appointment and waited in the green room while she wrapped up the live taping for her show. The waiting lounge was painted in two-tone pastel colors and plainly decorated with a small television with the show playing on it, perched on a low-standing cabinet with stacks of newspapers underneath it. After asking me to "hold tight" for forty more minutes, Emeka pulled me aside to a room next door so we could talk more privately. After I explained my research interests to her, she stated, "You can get tons of information through newspapers. Only certain people are authorized to talk on behalf of the company. You'll have to deal with the public relations spokesperson." It seemed to me that she first interacted with me as if I were a media representative, but when I pointed out that I was going to take an academic approach, her almond-shaped eyes lit up. "Remind me what university you're from again?" After responding with my university affiliation, a look of recognition flashed across her face and her demeanor seemed to soften. She earnestly explained:

> It's about time we got this kind of attention! I'm an intellectual too. The beauty pageant industry deserves attention because of the role they play

in developing countries. For example, Miss Congo is treated like a second first lady. But the Nigerian government is not really interested in getting involved and the level beauty pageants reach in each country is dependent upon the level of closeness between the pageant and the government. The government is not taking enough advantage of this platform because they do not see the value and the importance. These women are ambassadors for our country, but there seems to be more of a focus on women parading in bikinis or whatever. Ultimately it is a business! MBGN is the second largest beauty industry on the continent. We have a solid reputation. When other beauty pageants want to give other companies a licensing deal, they contact the Murray-Bruce brothers to see if they're legit. Our international reputation seems to be better than our Nigerian one, at least that's my perception.

I nodded attentively and then asked her what I should do next. She advised me to put together a formal proposal for my research and said she would present it to the company head. Two weeks later, I was granted access to work as an unpaid intern for Silverbird Productions. I shadowed Lola Olanrewaju, the newly hired pageant coordinator and a fellow "Americanah" (local slang for Nigerians who have spent a lot of time in the United States either due to birth or residence; sometimes used pejoratively to indicate Nigerian-Americans who put on airs or are too "Americanized"), who had recently moved back to Nigeria to live and work.

I quickly learned that Silverbird had a very tight-knit, family-controlled organizational culture. Some of the major sponsors, including the official makeup and retail fashion lines, are owned by other members of the Murray-Bruce clan. The executives at Silverbird are either family members, long-term employees, or childhood friends of the family. On several occasions people assumed that I was longtime friends with Lola, Emeka, or another Murray-Bruce relative, since that seemed to be the only logical way in which I would have gotten access. One interaction that solidified my understanding of the insularity and power behind the family was when I joined Lola at a club one late night for a "girl's night out" event. We were in a dark room upstairs in the VIP section of the nightclub. She was explaining to me how she had first gotten the job at Silverbird after a number of attempts to secure a job there.

She was eventually poached from her previous place of employment due to some media buzz that she had generated about her last employer. Lola was brought on to help "rebrand" the pageant. "They're like the mafia," she whispered, "They have their hands in everything. You definitely shouldn't cross them." The following day we were at the Silverbird-owned, bowling alley–themed restaurant sharing a smoothie. "You know how I said the family is like the mafia, right? Well last night R.J. said, 'Welcome to the family.' Yes! I'm in. There are certain people they have around that just can't be fired. Looks like I'm one of them now," she smiled gleefully. Months into my research, I was back at STV working on promotional videos for the upcoming show. The area around the television station was covered in knee-high water and my car barely managed to traverse it to make my meeting with Ronald, a video editor I was meeting for the first time. When he asked about what I was doing at Silverbird, I mentioned that I was researching MBGN. "Are you the one who sent us a message before saying you wanted to do a research?" "No," I replied, but then paused as I recalled the unanswered website messages that I had sent before starting my research.

I worked primarily with Silverbird Productions, which is the wing responsible for coordinating entertainment programming, live shows, and events. One of the main activities of the division is managing the Most Beautiful Girl in Nigeria Pageant (MBGN), one of the most visible beauty contests on the national scene, which sends contestants to top pageants in the world.[48] At the finale, MBGN selects five winners who go on to represent Nigeria at different beauty, modeling, and promotional contests within the country and around the world. The winner and first-runner up continue on to the British-based Miss World and United States–based Miss Universe Pageants, respectively. Additional runners-up have represented Nigeria in other competitions, such as Miss ECOWAS (Economic Community of West African States, a regional economic bloc of fifteen West African countries) and Miss Tourism International. Miss Universe and Miss World are the two most-watched pageants in the world. Along with Miss Earth and Miss International, they constitute the "Big Four" of top international beauty competitions in terms of their audience reach, number of participants, and longevity.[49] MBGN organizers consider Miss Universe to be more prestigious in the international pageant circuit, but see Miss World as more geared toward "developing countries."

Many international beauty pageant insiders think of Miss World as catering to the British commonwealth countries. As such, MBGN elevates Miss World above Miss Universe as the top prize as they estimate their chances of being more successful in a contest catered to countries like Nigeria. MBGN's claim to fame is producing the first Black African Miss World, Agbani Darego, in 2001.

The Most Beautiful Girl in Nigeria began in 1986 and grew out of Silverbird's initial attempts to organize Miss Nigeria Universe in 1983. The firm's earlier attempt to hold the Miss Nigeria Universe Pageant was panned as a failure by organizers since the winner was ultimately dethroned on the grounds that she was too demanding and difficult to manage, whereupon it decided to simply cut its losses and not send anyone to Miss Universe. To build up interest in MBGN, organizers started an international pageant called Miss Intercontinental (also known as Miss Africa World and Miss Africa International), which brought in between twelve and twenty-five delegates between 1986 and 1991 to compete in a Nigerian-owned international competition. Participants were mostly from Latin American and Caribbean countries, such as Bolivia, Colombia, and Jamaica, but also included other countries such as Austria, France, Gambia, Greece, and Singapore. Their organization of an international pageant in Lagos during the 1980s and 1990s shows the importance MBGN's owners placed on using international legitimacy to build their national reputation.

While the organizers are primarily Nigerian-based, MBGN also relies on grooming experts and production specialists from the United States and South Africa. For example, Gina Johnson, an African American choreographer and groomer, flies to Nigeria annually to help produce the show. Calvin Venter, a White South African technical production specialist, lives in Nigeria most of the time. These professionals are viewed as offering contestants a leg up in the Miss World and Miss Universe Pageants by giving MBGN more international credibility. The Silverbird Group has sponsored three different international pageants within Nigeria, which brought in delegates from throughout the world to compete: the Miss Intercontinental from 1986 to 1991, Miss World in 2002, and Miss Silverbird International in 2004. MBGN contestants were chosen at various cities throughout Nigeria, primarily in the southern part of the country (in 2010, Benin in South South Nigeria, Lagos in the Southwest, Port Harcourt in the South, and Abuja were the audition cities). Semifinalists selected from these screening venues then competed in Lagos, where thirty finalists were chosen to compete in the final show. The main show includes a swimwear segment, traditional wear, a modeling competition, and choreographed dance numbers.

I use the term *cosmopolitan-nationalism* to describe MBGN because it indicates how it remained invested in presenting the nation as worldly, urbane, and internationally oriented in ways that were not automatically equated with the West. On its face, combining cosmopolitanism and nationalism seems incompatible. Cosmopolitanism is usually defined as being a "citizen of the world," while national identity is associated with pride and allegiance to one's own country.[50] Moreover, cosmopolitanism is connected to the globetrotting international business class dominated by the West. For example, Eileen Otis's research on luxury hotels in China uses the concept of cosmopolitan capital to show how Chinese women service workers fashion themselves to cater to the needs of White Western businessmen, which facilitates these elites' movement across national borders without having to displace American-dominated culture.[51] Other scholars have used concepts like "vernacular cosmopolitanism" and "tactical cosmopolitanism" to understand how marginalized people make everyday sense of precarious and partial inclusion by claiming national membership but not being bound by it.[52] I use the term *cosmopolitan-nationalism* to highlight the process by which stakeholders promote cosmopolitan elements of Nigerian culture to elevate them as setting international trends for the rest of the world to take notice of. By positioning the country as part of the next crop of trailblazers on the global stage that forge new understandings of the country's cultural and political economy, it recognizes the nation's position on the fringes of global hierarchies but also exploits the country's unrealized future potential to make its mark.

Cultural-Nationalism: Queen Nigeria

My field notes are scattered with entries in which I was trying to decide whom to contact about the Queen Nigeria Pageant since it did not seem readily apparent to me who was in charge. I sent several texts to people who then referred me to someone else. I finally was able to get a hold of Lovett

Chidiebere, an employee of TV Enterprises (TVE), which is the commercial wing of the Nigerian Television Authority (NTA). She invited me to meet her at NTA in Victoria Island. I arrived forty-five minutes early and browsed online in the car with my smartphone until about ten minutes before our appointment. I then entered the reception room, which had a large white sign in reddish-orange lettering that stated, "TVE, a subsidiary of NTA," with a car rental sign below it. Lovett was running late and instructed one of her assistants to bring me upstairs to wait. About two and a half hours after our appointment, Lovett arrived, apologetic for her lateness. We headed downstairs so we could talk. She explained to me that Queen Nigeria had begun as a merger between a popular reality game show that incorporated mini–beauty contests, which had been going on for five years, and NTA's TVE, which evolved it into a national beauty pageant.

I asked her to give me more background on the pageant, which was only in its second year of existence when I started my fieldwork. The pageant has a spottier history because it has not been held consistently since it first started. "Well, unlike other pageants, contestants can actually lay some claim and connection to the states they represent, either through birth, living there, or being indigenes." Lovett's point was an obvious dig at the Most Beautiful Girl in Nigeria, which does not have such stringent requirements about state representation. She continued, "The pageant is linked to Nigeria as a brand because the queen serves as a brand ambassador and represents the ideal African woman. Queen Nigeria is a tool that can help the nation's rebranding efforts. NTA is a platform to broadcast this new brand throughout Nigeria and to the Diaspora since we have a station in each state and transmit on satellite." Lovett then assured me that I would get access to the pageant since I "came here to work." She warned that "it would be hectic," but on the upside I might even "shed some weight." Like Lovett, other Queen Nigeria affiliates viewed MBGN's dominance as a problematic representation of the country, since it did not center on a culturally "authentic" depiction of Nigeria. The organizers specifically brand Queen Nigeria as distinct from a Western-styled beauty pageant, claiming that it is a uniquely styled Nigerian contest in terms of fashion, talent, and social etiquette.

Lovett's description of the pageant sheds light on how I understand Queen Nigeria as representing *cultural-nationalism*, a national orientation focused on valuing Nigerian customs and unifying Nigeria's diverse population in the face of rapid globalization. Cultural sociologist Kristin Surak uses the concept of nation-work to explain varied parts of cultural nationalism: distinction to specify the uniqueness of a nation; specification to highlight how national membership is mediated by other social categories of gender, race, ethnicity, and class; and differentiation based on hierarchies that idealize and judge specific practices, events, and figures through, for example, debates about authenticity and morality.[53] These constitutive elements play out through cultural-nationalism in ways that bring globalization, ethnicity, and the nation together.

A couple of weeks after Lovett signed off on my research, I realized that I would have to go through yet another process of getting access through the head of their partner firm, Mr. Noah Gold (nicknamed "the Captain"), who ran a private events management firm, Silverstone Communications (not to be confused with Silverbird). Technically, Mr. Gold's company was tasked with organizing the state-level competitions, and Lovett and her team (with Mr. Gold and his assistants as backup) spearheaded the national finale. However, there was tension between the two partners and they did not always communicate effectively. Since the completion of my fieldwork, they have since dissolved their relationship and NTA has partnered with another entertainment firm to run Queen Nigeria. I ended up working as a chaperone for Queen Nigeria at the last minute because of an incident that showcases the lack of communication between TVE and Silverstone Communications (also known as Gotham City). Nneka Amaechi, a contestant who had participated in Queen Nigeria the previous year, had been appointed as a chaperone for the finale by Mr. Gold without Lovett's input or knowledge. The day before camp (the preshow training and rehearsal period) was scheduled to officially start, Lovett got wind of this plan and refused to let her take on the role. She felt that it would be inappropriate because Nneka was too close in age to the contestants and would not be impartial or enforce enough discipline. Since I had volunteered my time in exchange for access to observe the pageant, Lovett appointed me to take Nneka's place.

The Queen Nigeria Pageant began in 2008 as a joint venture between Silverstone and TVE. TVE, which cosponsored Queen Nigeria, launched in the same year as Queen Nigeria's inauguration. TVE is responsible for initiating business ventures such as organizing public lectures in Nigeria and the Diaspora about investment opportunities in Nigeria; hosting university soccer tournaments; consulting on broadcast equipment, editing, and recording; and providing car rental services. NTA is the largest broadcast television network in Sub-Saharan Africa, with about a hundred stations covering all the states in Nigeria, and includes international broadcasts to North America and Europe to target the Diaspora. The pageant is organized around a state tier system wherein contestants must first enter and win a state-level competition, but not all states participate. In 2009, state-level competitions were hosted in eighteen out of the thirty-six states and Abuja, the federal capital territory in Nigeria, with a vision of expanding to all states in the future. Winners from the various states then went on to compete in the national finale. All contestants must have a cultural tie to the state they represent, either through ethnic heritage (i.e., as an indigene who can trace her roots back to the original settlers of the community), birth, or residence. In addition to the judges, a group of invited elders and dignitaries was asked to certify the results of the contest at both the state and national levels. Queen Nigeria has two preliminary competitions, a cooking contest and a talent showcase. The main show includes traditional wear and evening gown (commonly called dinner gown) segments and a dance number in casual wear. The pageant appealed to cultural-nationalism by retaining unique contemporary cultural conventions to reflect a worldview that depicts the everyday lives of Nigeria's heterogeneous culture through a "unity in diversity" mantra in the face of rapid globalization.

CONCLUSION

Given Nigeria's tarnished national identity, these beauty contests engaged in reparative work to strategically improve the nation's image by positioning beauty queens as collective symbols rather than individual beings. Miss Nigeria's tumultuous past, which is characterized by fits and starts, looks backward to reclaim the best elements of its history in order to champion the country's glory days. Queen Nigeria uses Nigeria's rich contemporary culture to make a case for appreciating the nation's diversity. MBGN's long-standing global engagement through beauty contests aims to meet international standards of beauty and capitalize on the country's future potential as a major trendsetter that would catch the attention of the world stage. Though they relied on distinct narratives, all three Nigerian pageants positioned their contestants as ambassadors and role models who helped repair the nation's image through embodied work.

3 | THE MAKING OF BEAUTY DIPLOMATS

Doyin, Faith, and Ebun were taking a brief break at a training session. Their pageant coach, Noyo Okonkwo, a groomer much sought after by contestants and who offered a standard training package including catwalking, styling services, and diction lessons, had stepped aside to take a call. All of them were pageant veterans. I asked them about their plans for victory, and they quickly tried to outdo one another by rattling off a list of various charity ventures they hoped to pursue during their tenure. Doyin Taiwo, a recent high school graduate who had just competed in her first pageant and was gearing up to compete in another, explained that she participated in pageants because winning a prominent pageant would provide her with a platform in which "everybody will want to listen." Faith Agu and Ebun Moreira chimed in that beauty pageants had brought attention to Nigeria abroad while "awakening" an appreciation for Nigerian culture among its youth.

Doyin, in turn, made a direct link between her participation in beauty competitions and her newly acquired musical tastes. She confided that before she used to just listen to American hip-hop, but she now solely listened to Naija (Nigerian) music. By competing in pageants, she had learned to appreciate her "own culture." She emphasized that Nigeria had its own celebrities, who were not just popular in Nigeria but worldwide. Doyin continued,

"People around the world are listening to our music, watching our films, and wearing our designs." Faith interjected, "Pageantry is an important platform. It has to do with empowerment! Empowering the youth, creating awareness, drawing attention to Nigeria as a whole from the state to the national level to the international through pageantry."

As I listened to these three young women excitedly explain to me their motivations for partaking in pageants, a clearer picture of the aspirations projected onto Nigerian beauty contests came into focus. Many other contestants, like Faith, used the descriptor of a *platform* to situate the meanings they attached to the industry.[1] As a platform where entertainment and cultural promotion are celebrated, pageants elevate Nigeria as a country worthy of notice. They also lift up young women as faces to be seen and voices to be heard, where they stand up for public issues and initiate social action. Through selected *pet projects*, charitable endeavors that champion the common good, they serve as a liaison between those in power—political elites, affluent business people, and well-connected celebrities—and more vulnerable segments of Nigerian society, such as orphaned infants, indigent youth, and those who are elderly and infirm. Contestants position themselves as poised, ambitious young women who use their beauty, charm, and intellect to help others, and to also launch their careers and propel their mobility.

Beauty pageants are an aesthetic industry in which women accrue rewards based on their physical appearance and also their moral dispositions. In their complex roles as beauty diplomats, Nigerian beauty queens transformed their aesthetic capital—a total package of bodily, civic, and cultural assets that they worked hard to cultivate, refine, and deploy. By building their aesthetic capital, they hoped to capitalize on amassed social connections and enhance their economic mobility, activating a chain reaction that would ultimately culminate in financial success. Their good deeds, polished bodies, increased mobility, and other positive attributes were personally beneficial, but also meant to reflect well on the country as a whole. Understanding pageants as a platform, however, only skims the surface, since contestants also described their experiences as constrained by public scrutiny, high expectations, and pressure to navigate contradictory strains of respectability politics, which limited their aspirations. Contestants employed a number of strategies to walk a fine tightrope that fortified their drives to project an image of moral and upwardly mobile selves.

THE TOTAL PACKAGE

Social theorist Pierre Bourdieu conceived of social inequality as defined not just through differential access to economic resources but through other types of symbolic capital as well. He developed a theoretical framework focused on multiple forms of capital—economic, social, and cultural—that can be converted into mobility in various social fields. Economic capital refers to money, financial wealth, and material assets such as property. Social capital includes connections and relationships that offer support and influence. Cultural capital is defined as education, credentials, and knowledge such as speech, manners, and style that indicate social standing. His core concept of *habitus* describes the physical embodiment of dispositions, habits, and skills acquired through class positions that help or hinder social mobility. For Bourdieu, cultural capital relies on embodiment, commodified goods, and institutional recognition.[2] Chris Shilling extended Bourdieu's concept of cultural capital to develop an understanding of physical capital, which focused on the body as a form of capital in its own right. Shilling critiques Bourdieu's theory as too static and focused on social reproduction.[3] To address these concerns, I combine Bourdieu's insights with Anthony Giddens's work. Giddens uses the notion of reflexive selves to understand how people self-monitor, strategize, and make choices about social action.[4] Contestants embody and rework various forms of capital—which together form the "total package"—through engaging with beauty pageants as a reflexive aesthetic project. Contestants use their bodies as a resource to enhance their social mobility and cultivate moral selves.

Scholars have used the concept of aesthetic labor to pinpoint the modifications that individuals inflict on their own bodies in order to comply with the heightened expectations for specific forms of bodily presentation. Aesthetic labor focuses on the work involved in "looking good and sounding right" in the context of commercial enterprises.[5] This type of labor encompasses the work individuals perform on themselves in exchange for indirect or direct economic compensation. For example, in work settings like retail, service work, and the hospitality sector, many of the frontline workers strive to embody a company's image through the commodification of their corporeal bodies. These workers mold their bodies to exhibit specific types of accents, grooming, and gestures, which conform to organizational demands. Nigerian beauty queens not only put in the work to look good and sound right, but also aim to "do better" by engaging in civic work to present the nation in the best light.

Scholars have also focused on certain types of jobs where physical appearance remains a central job qualification. Ashley Mears and Catherine Connell argue that late capitalism has led to the prominence of a specific form of aesthetic labor, display work, which they define as the "primary exchange of bodily capital for the purpose of visual consumption. . . . The primary reason for their compensation is in *showing* their own bodies."[6] Display workers such as models, strippers, and beauty queens invest heavily in their appearance for the consumption of others.

As aesthetic laborers who engage in display work, Nigerian beauty queens stage their bodies in the service of national consumption while also pursuing their individual interests. They engage in body work, which Debra Gimlin theorizes as involving the labor individuals apply to their own bodies to modify their looks and the emotional management that accompanies these embodied processes.[7] They also rely on body laborers, who mold and produce ideal aesthetic looks for contestants. Through their body work and their interactions with body laborers, beauty queens groom themselves, with a focus on their voices, smiles, and carriage, to attain a sophisticated yet approachable air. Contestants seek to embody positive attributes such as charisma, intelligence, and being articulate. They also seek to promote their own voices and those of the general public in the national arena.

Tammy Anderson and her colleagues coined the term "aesthetic capital" to describe "traits of beauty that are perceived as assets capable of yielding privilege, opportunity, and wealth."[8] While this concept acknowledges that beauty produces a certain "halo effect," such that positive qualities, moral goodness, confidence, and authenticity are often associated with appearance, the concept gives primacy to physical attributes like physique, clothing, face, hair, and grooming habits.[9] Elizabeth Wissinger's research on modeling analyzes how forms of aesthetic labor center on physical bodies, as well as personality and image management, which require constant upkeep and vigilant emotion work, that can be used strategically but also constrained by social structures.[10] Nigerian beauty queens promote optimized lifestyles, engage in reputation management, and cultivate civic connections. Through their bodies, and specifically their voices, walks, and smiles, contestants view themselves as public figures—representatives of "ordinary people"—who, because of their celebrity, have access to elites whom they can lobby to promote their concerns in the national arena. They champion a perspective that stresses charity, social development, and goodwill in order to connect to everyday Nigerians. Through their aesthetic labor, these beauty queens work as cultural diplomats to promote unity domestically while advocating for the positive attributes of the country internationally, thus serving broader nationalist agendas.

I use the concept of aesthetic capital to understand both external physical capital through different bodily ideals as well as the internal qualities, such as a kind and warm disposition, that contestants seek to emulate. Aesthetic capital encapsulates the bundled bodily, civic, and cultural resources that contestants cultivate to convert into other forms of social and economic mobility.[11] Bodily capital includes posture, walk, and the refinement of physical features through makeup, clothing, and beauty treatments. Their cultural capital comprises their educational credentials, intellect, speech patterns, and knowledge of Nigerian current affairs and culture. Civic capital is developed through charitable work, communal obligations, and proper decorum through their position as role models. This form of capital depends on contestants being civic minded, by staying connected to the public and championing the common good through knowledge of social issues and exhibiting compassionate personalities. Critically, their cultivation of civic capital, which centers on Nigeria's success, contestants' dedication to community welfare, and a shift away from self-interest, serves as evidence that contestants have adequately built up enough aesthetic capital to shift their focus to their own aspirations. Through cultivating aesthetic capital, contestants position themselves as aesthetic reflexive selves: virtuous, responsible, upwardly mobile, and formidable young women.

To audition, aspiring contestants must buy a ₦5,000 ($33) form on which they list their hobbies, career ambitions, and body measurements. The form is often likened to buying a lottery ticket. For example, on one occasion after the forms had been available for sale for a few days, Mr. Tim, a Silverbird executive, remarked that the sales would start to pick up the following month in January when hopeful contestants realized that they were "broke," and that the process was "like a gamble" to them. Beauty contestants are seen as a financial investment since winning a pageant generates a prize package of ₦3 million for MBGN (about $20,000) and ₦1.5 million for Queen Nigeria (about $10,000) plus a brand-new car, along with the possibility of future lucrative endorsement deals that pay ₦450,000 ($3,000) and up per campaign along with lavish gifts such as free clothes, all-expenses-paid travel, and electronics. For comparison, entry-level civil service jobs pay about $2,500 per year for those with high school diplomas and $5,500 per year for those with a university degree.

To prepare for auditions, participate in camp (a five- to ten-day training and rehearsal period), and compete in the show, contestants purchased suitable attire, styled their hair, and wore appropriate makeup. Contestants cultivated a glamorous beauty queen look, which included impeccable makeup, manicured nails and polished toes, silky-long hair weaves worn in waist-length cascading waves or elaborate updos, trendy name-brand clothes and accessories such as luxury handbags and stilettos, and exclusive beauty treatments. In the 2009–10 cycle that I observed, Queen Nigeria and MBGN offered free makeup services and MBGN provided free hair styling for the finale. Contestants paid for optional enhanced beauty services such as manicures and false eyelashes out of pocket. MBGN provided them with coordinating violet metallic swimsuits and matching costumes for the dance number, a halter-style *ankara* (cotton fabric with vibrant patterns) minidress with a neckline made of beads and ruffles at the hem in assorted bright peacock-colored fabrics in yellow, red, purple, blue, and pink and accessorized with large ruffle hairclips. Queen Nigeria provided matching yellow-and-green *adire* (indigo-dyed cloth) outfits—scoop-neck tank tops and capri pants—for their choreographed dance. To participate, contestants purchased, rented, or borrowed dinner gowns (evening wear), cocktail dresses, stiletto heels, purses, traditional costumes, and other outfits that fit a smart casual dress code. Gowns alone can cost between ₦10,000 and ₦35,000 to rent or between ₦30,000 and ₦250,000 to buy, depending on the quality and amount of customization. In total, the cost of gowns, beauty treatments, outfits, and transportation cost as much as ₦150,000 ($1,000) to ₦450,000 ($3,000) at the highest levels, but contestants typically spent about ₦25,000–₦75,000 ($166–$500). This is an astronomical sum for most families. Even for middle-class Nigerians, these expenses are cost prohibitive. The average monthly salary for those in the middle class is between ₦75,000 and ₦100,000 ($500–$666).[12] Contestants faced additional financial hurdles because most had not started on their own career path, as they were current students, recent graduates, waiting for college admission, or had irregular jobs. Thus, they had to rely on others to lend them items or give them money to afford the costs.

MBGN's winner earned a clothing allowance for events and a year's worth of complimentary styling services, which included hair styling, manicures, facials, and waxing. However, the crowned queen still paid out of pocket for certain regular upkeep costs like bundles of hair weaves and wigs, accessories, and makeup, which can run ₦45,000–₦75,000 ($300–$500) per month. Premium human hair from India, Peru, and Brazil (which is considered preferable to cheaper, poor-quality synthetic hair, which is available for as little as $20) and custom wigs eat up the bulk of their expenses. The hair extensions needed to achieve the desired full and bouncy look vary from $300 to $800 and can be reused two or three times with proper care. Through their participation in MBGN, contestants were put in touch with high-end hair stylists, couture fashion houses, top makeup artists, and groomers, on whom they relied heavily for expert advice to perfect their looks.

Some hopefuls independently hired groomers (beauty coaches), who charged up to ₦150,000 ($1,000) for a standard two-week training package and drilled contestants on the proper ways to walk, sit, smile, and enhance their looks. Contestants worked with groomers prior to auditions or starting camp in order to prepare for the competition. Grooming contestants focused on making changes in both demeanor and physical embodiment.[13] Groomers offered professional tips, giving styling advice, etiquette instruction, and help with diction. I was introduced to one groomer, Noyo, on a windy and uncharacteristically chilly late December evening through Raul Erasmus, a pageant promoter based in Lagos who had helped with a state-level Queen Nigeria beauty contest. After an impromptu interview, Noyo invited me to observe his work grooming three contestants for their upcoming contests. The following day I arrived at noon, to find Ebun, Faith, and Doyin's lessons already well underway. Noyo had taken over an area behind a school sports stadium, where we sat on wood benches, notebooks in hand, so we could fully absorb his advice and instructions. He handed over a typed sheet of paper titled, "A Lady's Expectations: Poise and Charm," which served as our guide for the day's session. He explained that he had adapted these tips from a British etiquette handbook, yellowed with age, that had been passed down in his family over four generations. Having not seen this precious family heirloom myself, I took this depiction as just another part of Noyo's penchant for over-the-top flourishes. In the day's session, Noyo expounded that a lady was not necessarily someone already from a wealthy background or born into nobility but was a quality "of the heart" that radiated how "classy" you were. Noyo believed that to be classy meant attracting attention, exhibiting impeccable taste, and acquiring a standout and pulled-together style. As Noyo reeled off his lesson plans in a clipped English accent, I dutifully took note of such gems as providing "habitual courtesy to all that cross your path," and building "self-control" to tamp down an irritable mood. As a groomer, Noyo invested in the notion that "classy" contestants could be coached to exhibit these characteristics, embracing a "fake-it-till-you-make-it" maxim to assert that such lessons would drive the contestants' success.

I learned firsthand about Noyo's skills not just through observation, but also as I gradually realized that he was working on my own body in the hopes of making me over. I had read enough about feminist methodology to know that my own positionality would figure into my fieldwork, but I greatly underestimated the extent to which others' perception of me would influence my access and rapport with some of the participants. For our first lesson, I was wearing an outfit that was typical for me: a pair of ill-fitting jeans, a loose blouse, and a scarf wrapped around my head. I was not wearing a stitch of makeup on my face. As the etiquette lesson wound down, Noyo turned to Doyin and asked her about her typical diet. She responded that she ate "*eba* (cassava flour), Indomie (a brand of instant noodles), *suya* (spicy skewered meat), and tea." Noyo instructed her to "eat more to add to her behind." One of Noyo's friends interrupted with a comment, nodding quickly and saying, with a grin on his face, that Noyo's advice suggested a "more African style." Noyo then turned to me and asked me what I ate. Taken aback that his sights were now set on me, I sheepishly replied, "I usually eat spaghetti, chicken, *amala* (yam flour), beans, and rice." Noyo nodded and pointed to a woman in the distance who was overweight like me but was wearing a pair of black slacks, a white button-down shirt, and a black vest. He explained that although she was "big, she still looked good," and that with the right clothes I could improve my own appearance. I learned that while my overweight body was seen as excessive, Doyin's instruction to "add to her behind" meant that it was possible to have weight, but only in the right places. He next admitted that he did not like my scarf, pointing to it, and asking, "Are you an S.U.?" I asked for clarification, since I was utterly confused about what he was saying. Everyone else laughed and explained that he was asking me if I was a religious sister (a nun). I was embarrassed, flustered, and becoming increasingly self-conscious. Noyo explained to me that "Nigerians are snobs. You have to have the total package. To have a car, a good accent, but then to not dress well and to be big, means you have content with no nice cover page." Noyo was referring to my Toyota 4Runner, a preowned SUV I had purchased and shipped to Nigeria to help me get around for fieldwork, and my American accent as elements of "good content," but my overweight body and shabby clothes constituted major hurdles to achieving the perfect combination that unlocked the potential to be a "classy girl" who had the total package.

Noyo then announced that he was going to style me just like the others. Over the next few days I got a crash course on how contestants prepare for their pageants. Noyo introduced me to a personal trainer, took me to a hair salon to get my hair "fixed" with extensions in a long, straight style with blunt bangs (my first-ever hair weave), and took me shopping for a new outfit at a local fast-fashion retail shop: straight-leg brown pants, a sheer chiffon top, a brown shrug, and maroon patent-leather heels (a pair that had a familiar "Ross Price" sticker from the American off-price chain store still affixed to it); he also gave me lessons on how to walk properly in heels. After we wrapped up our final walking lesson, Noyo, pleased with his work, looked me up and down and smugly declared that I now looked "like a boss." Bodily laborers like Noyo can boost contestants' aesthetic capital, amplifying their value in competitive markets.[14]

Most contestants did not use groomers prior to participating in pageants, but rather counted on more experienced friends, learned the ropes as they went along, or just winged it. This was the case for Kamdi Ugwonali, a bubbly contestant with an infectious smile whom I interviewed a few days after she had competed in her first, and what would be her only, pageant. We sat in my car, parked with the air conditioner on full blast, in a shopping mall lot to offset the humid air outside. Kamdi grew up in a city in Southeast Nigeria and was raised by relatives while her parents worked abroad to provide for the family. A self-described "people person," she had won a year-long endorsement deal through the pageant on the basis of her outgoing personality and "approachable" look. Kamdi decided to participate in MBGN almost on a whim. Her university was on strike for three months, and some close friends had read about it in a magazine and urged her to enter. In Nigerian higher education, labor strikes are commonplace and may halt instruction for long, unpredictable stretches of time. Thus, by providing an opportunity to bypass traditional venues of upward mobility, pageants offer an appealing alternative. After one of her friends kept pestering her, she finally bought an entry form with her own pocket money. In her final year of university, she had recently paused her college plans and relocated to Lagos, Nigeria's commercial hub, with initial plans to pursue a career in broadcast television. Without much experience or many contacts in the industry, she viewed MBGN as a platform to help her reach her goals. Kamdi worked to reshape her body in preparation of the pageant by dropping 35 pounds, going from 178 to 143 pounds on an all-fruit diet. To feel more comfortable in front of the camera and large crowds of people staring at her, perfect her walk, and increase her confidence by "owning the stage," she signed with a modeling agency and was thrilled to have booked a few runway gigs and hosting events prior to her MBGN audition, including one that paid her ₦300,000 ($2,000), the most money she had ever made at one time. Though her father was initially uncomfortable with her participating in pageants, he warmed up to the idea after some gentle prodding from her supportive mother. Gathering money from friends and family, who "saw the victory in [her] and that [she] could make it," she bought some clothes and other needed items for the pageant.

Although she did not win the pageant, she viewed it as providing her with what she called the "total package" by teaching her how to "act like a queen" through her gait, speech patterns, and smile. These skills would allow her to be taken seriously both in her career aspirations and in doing the kind of lobbying work she wanted to do. She mused that pageants were "a kind of spring[board] to what I want to be in life [; they] will give me a voice in this country [and] will help me achieve my dreams in an easier way." Kamdi was determined to "touch people's hearts," and her use of the term *springboard* illustrates the multiple meanings attached to beauty contests as platforms since it spoke to her desire to work for social issues in the country while also securing her own aspirations. She linked her dreams of helping others to her ambitions of making a mark in the world. Kamdi viewed MBGN as providing an opportunity to "gain something" by offering millions of naira and an opportunity to "get popular" and meet new people. Speaking at a rapid-fire pace, Kamdi acknowledged that she was not yet "super-popular" but shared her lofty goals of being so well known and making such a big social impact that schoolchildren would sing songs about her in school assemblies and her face would appear on a newly introduced ₦5,000 banknote. Kamdi had intentions to make herself known by "attending credible events," assembling a top-notch management team, and interacting with media. She had already made some inroads through scoring a few media mentions, some published interviews, and a nomination for the most promising brand ambassador of the year award.

All contestants are expected to pick a specific cause and engage in charity work and acts of social responsibility, which are referred to as pet projects. Kamdi had settled on hers even before she had auditioned for the contest: working as an ambassador for the government-sponsored "rebrand Nigeria" campaign. When I asked her to tell me more about why she chose this issue, she explained:

> I am passionate about the image of this country and how we are represented, how we are spoken about outside [of Nigeria]. People don't really believe you can live in a beautiful house comfortably, have a nice family, that people can come into this country to invest without anything happening to them. They will rather have this picture that if you stepped out with money in your hands, you [would be] robbed, raped, kidnapped. But that is not who we are, we are beautiful people, we are very warm and welcoming. . . . I want to give a better image, a better projection of who we are but you have to start at home, you have to work with the people here.

She named specific examples of "starting at home" such as not littering, ignoring traffic signals, or interrupting conversations, forms of social etiquette meant to improve the country's image internally. She was enthusiastic about using her newfound name recognition to connect to the government's "Good People, Great Nation" national rebranding efforts and was adamant that she could help, stating, "I have a voice at least, even if I don't have so much money." Like other contestants, she insisted that they could use the attention garnered through pageants as a tool to magnify their voices, make a difference in the country, and reach for their goals. She told a story about meeting an American man who was in Nigeria on a business trip. Others had discouraged him from making the visit. She had acted as his tour guide, showing him around the city, and she told me that his initial skepticism had worn off and he planned on returning to the country with his friends. She directly connected the positive image of Nigeria to the possibility of boosting investment and tourism in the country. She saw her role as facilitating these changes through her hospitality, charm, and beauty. Though she admitted that she didn't have much money, she felt her voice had a certain currency that could impact the nation's youth, as they would be drawn to listening to her, especially those frustrated by the lack of opportunities in the country:

> Some people can't even afford to go to school, that is why they would rather do 419 [Nigeria slang for scams]. If we could just have a little bit of charity given to people and while you give [it to] them, you are telling [them,] "We love you and we want you to love yourselves." With that I think we can get to a point in helping repackage this country.

After participating in the pageant, Kamdi started an NGO focused on political advocacy. This focus on having a voice was a common theme throughout my interviews with contestants, who felt that without their pageant experience, getting others in power to listen to them and take them seriously was nearly impossible.

Faceless Hangers Versus Vocal Queens

One of the strategies beauty contestants used to emphasize their roles as public figures and the specific forms of aesthetic capital they cultivated was to distinguish themselves from models. Though both industries feature display workers who rely on their bodies and personalities, pageant contestants emphasized that the looks and skills demanded of their respective industries were distinct. As sociologist and former model Ashley Mears highlights, the modeling industry's tastemakers promote a "hanger-body" as an ideal.[15] During castings, models are expected to have a bare face with minimal makeup, their hair pulled back, and simple clothing to serve as a blank canvas for clients and bookers. To underscore the important work of beauty queens, Nigerian contestants described models as "hangers," "faceless," "mannequins," and "fine book covers without content." Some were pursuing modeling careers themselves but nonetheless described beauty queens as superior to models.[16] They derided models as being valued only for their physical appearance, while beauty contests involved public awareness campaigns, employing their looks for a different type of labor, which is tied to service, advocacy, and civic engagement. In applying this narrative, Nneka, who had worked off and on as a commercial model for a couple of years, described the difference between the two fields thus:

> Basically, [models] are just all hangers and they walk. They have [that] blank expression on their face and they just show basically the clothes. They are not doing anything. They just walk, come out, walk, come out, that is just what they do. But for pageantry, pageantry is you, your beauty, intelligence, creativity, boldness, communication, it is basically you, showcasing you and what you have got.

In contrast to the blank stares of models, beauty queens are expected to be expressive, smiling at all times, showing off their assets, and being socially engaged.

Contestants connected with ordinary Nigerians to promote their own voices and those of the public in the national arena. They referenced specific public concerns to highlight nationally and the positive attention they would bring to Nigeria. Indeed, pageant victors do craft special platforms to address public issues such as the welfare of women and children, chronic illnesses such as sickle cell anemia, poverty, and the environment, and also to perform charity work. They groom themselves as worldly citizens through their travel and participation in major international contests. Contestants stressed their role in highlighting the good elements of Nigerian society, both domestically and to the broader global community. Many start nonprofit organizations and maintain them after their reign. These contestants must navigate a complex process to represent and propel their country's progress to a global society through such activities.

Contestants were aware of their country's poor image abroad and sought to remedy it. Faith likened beauty pageants to football (soccer) and Nollywood (Nigeria's film industry)—they were just another cultural product that could be exported to other countries to cement relationships:

> Pageantry is another means of promoting the good side and nature of Nigeria. In other words, it means getting the attention of other countries down here to Nigeria, showing them how peaceful, hospitable we are here in Nigeria. You know, create a relationship with other countries. Pageantry is one of the ways that can be achieved.

Faith saw herself and other contestants as cultural ambassadors who could use their beauty, charm and hospitality to gain attention for Nigeria and maintain ties to other countries around the world. They also perceived pageants as a vehicle to counteract negative perceptions of their country. Penelope Eze noted how pageants could address foreigners' views of women's issues in Nigeria, saying:

> Number one, we are telling people that here in Africa, women are also given a sense of responsibility, and pageantry has been able to say that. There is a whole lot of misconception about women in Africa, in Nigeria: [that] they are treated badly, in terms of widowhood, sex education, and all of that. So pageantry has been able to break that barrier. . . . Pageantry has really done well; it has been able to not just help Nigeria but her citizens.

Beyond their work as cultural diplomats who sought to rectify the negative image of Nigeria and build connections to other nations, contestants also said that beauty queens needed to reach out to the community (especially the youth) and use their titles to gain access to political leaders in order to serve as liaisons between the general public and the state.

Contestants pointed out that while all beauty queens are expected to perform such work, not all used their title and office effectively. They admitted that some are merely after fame and fortune. Many contestants rejected "picture queens," who were just focused on attending events, posing for the camera, and showcasing their physical beauty. Doyin explained:

> We've had many beauty queens that we never knew existed. They didn't make an impact; they just carried the crown and they didn't use the crown efficiently. So when you have the crown, it's like an open door for you, so it is left to you to keep the door open. It is left to you to carry on the legacy and show them that I'm actually capable, I'm beautiful, I've got the crown, I've got brains. With the crown, you could enter the National Assembly, you could go to visit the governor, he'll give you a listening ear, he will say, "Oh yes, she is a beauty queen and she has something she is doing."

Similarly, Nneka noted:

> I always say that pageants give you a voice and then you speak. . . . If you decide to be a picture queen, you remain that, you'll just be taking pictures at events and that's it. But if you know that you have a voice to speak, this is what makes you a great woman in this time. Because for me it is not just about the pageant . . . it is about how she's helping the country, how can she take the message [forward], how is she using that crown on top [of] her head? It gives you a voice to speak for the people.

Through these statements both Doyin and Nneka emphasized the additional work needed to become a successful beauty queen. Like the differences noted between beauty queens and models, the term *picture queens* served as another distancing maneuverer, which positioned some beauty queens as vapid, opportunistic, and shirking their responsibilities. Doyin and Nneka did not view a beauty queen's work as automatic, but rather as a public role that required purpose, thoughtfulness, and dedication. According to contestants like these two, the proper way to be a beauty queen was through consistently engaging in humanitarian activities, giving motivational speeches, and exuding warmth toward the general public.

Their superiority over models also depended in part on "speaking well," in contestants' minds. Beauty queens were expected to maintain a high intellectual standard, which was directly tested in prejudging and the interview segment during the show (called the IQ or Q&A period). The IQ portion of the pageant is a highly anticipated segment for viewers since misguided or flubbed answers are regularly aired as bloopers on television. Contestants were scored on accuracy in answering questions such as how they would address illiteracy and what were the country's top natural resources, and in speaking ability. They believed that having a voice—the ability to speak up not just for themselves but for others in more vulnerable positions—would encourage the politicians and others in power to listen and have a social impact. Contestants stressed that speaking well allowed them to be taken seriously in a male-dominated society because they were effectively "speaking for the people," serving as a source of empowerment, and becoming agents for social change. Speaking ability was yet another way contestants separated themselves from models. For example, according to Ogechi Udo:

> They are not talking about Nigeria when they interview some models. [The models] can't even speak good English! In modeling you don't have to talk, but in pageantry you can't escape that, you have to talk; the camera will always get you.

Contestants continually stressed the need for beauty queens to have an excellent speaking ability in order to represent the nation. During the auditions, onlookers laughed and mocked aspiring contestants for their speech patterns, including their accents, grammar, and pronunciation. For example, one woman introduced herself by stating, "My names are" and said that she was studying English. "I thought it was 'My name is,'" Octavia Dike, a pageant coordinator, interjected, watching from the side lines. "And she says she is studying English?" she asked incredulously, sneering. In Nigeria, English is the official language used in formal schooling, official government business, and the media, but pidgin English and indigenous languages such as Yoruba, Igbo, and Hausa are commonly used in everyday interactions and informal conversations.

Organizers stressed speaking ability as well, and when I asked why the pageant emphasized it so regularly, Frankie Davies said:

> Specifically, their English must be good. You know the funny thing, when girls go for the Miss Universe and Miss World, the ones who can't speak

in English speak their local languages and you have the translator and that shows that it doesn't matter there. But in Nigeria you must be able to speak English well. You can't come on stage and start to speak in Hausa, Igbo or Yoruba [Nigerian languages], and translators will now have to translate again. It doesn't work here. It's strange isn't it?

Frankie's rhetorical question referenced the strangeness of English as an internal marker of class status, which shifted meaning on global stages. Contestants strived to develop a British or American lilt to their voices, which they viewed not as a sign of imitating people in the West, but rather as a status symbol, since it highlighted their education and experiences traveling abroad.[17] Noyo's pageant coaching included accent lessons; one of his qualifications was that he had taken English lessons at the British Council in Nigeria as part of his training as a broadcaster. As Faith prepared to begin one of his lessons, composing herself after rushing in late, she said to me and some other trainees who had gathered to await him, "It's time to act poshy now" in an affected accent that copied the subtle speech instructions we had learned the day before. She crossed her legs in a deliberate, prissy way. This "act" highlights some of the body work in which contestants engaged. Contestants used their physical appearance, walk, smiles, and speech to connect to ordinary Nigerians while also emphasizing their rising social status through drastic changes in their embodiment.

The Nigerian contestants I interviewed saw even the way they walked as reflecting their public role: while models walked in a manner that showed them as merely "fashion billboards," contestants learned to adopt a more pedestrian, but refined, gait. Using fashion models as a point of comparison, Ebun described how beauty queens had to interact with the public:

As a model you can decide to be saucy or snooty. You can decide to walk anyhow you want, just do anything because no one cares about what you are doing. But once you are a beauty queen, you are a public figure, people want to know everything you do. You have to comport yourself. It makes you a better person, but when you are a model you can do anything you feel in public. As a queen, you can't talk anyhow, eat anyhow, act anyhow you want in public. The paparazzi is there. Because she is well known, everybody is watching her, anything she does, any little mistake she does, you see it in the paper.

Beauty queens had to engage in deliberate emotional work by acting polite, pleasant, and well mannered. Their speech patterns, dining etiquette, and walks were a physical embodiment of some of this labor. In anthropologist Marcia Ochoa's book on Venezuelan beauty queens, she makes similar observations about the differences between modeling and pageantry by detailing the differences between catwalking on the fashion runway versus on the pageant stage.[18] Nigerian contestants not only learned how to catwalk, but also learned how to walk in public through maintaining a ramrod posture, polished gait, and refined gestures. For example, one of Noyo's grooming lessons included showing contestants how to act on the red carpet and in photographs. Ebun and Faith practiced walking at an event and posing for pictures while putting on sunglasses, flipping their hair, arching their feet, carrying their handbags, and shaking people's hands. Noyo stressed that subtle movements would make them look great in press photos and while interacting with others in public and showed them how to use their eyes in expressive ways by squinting, widening them, and batting their eyelashes. Through the body work of their walks, smiles, and voices, beauty contestants sought to establish the aesthetic capital needed to be successful in the pageant world, and the broader world as well. By making comparisons to "picture queens" and "faceless hangers," contestants also stressed the additional work done to give their labor the veneer of respectability. As sociologist Erynn Masi de Casanova argues, debates about physical beauty ideals can be complemented by judgments about internal qualities like politeness, sincerity, and modesty, which can signal a polished, well-groomed style.[19] For Nigerian beauty queens, accentuating positive internal qualities such as compassion, integrity, and dedication showed that they had paid their dues and eased their entrance into new social circles.

GETTING ACCESS

Contestants participated in pageants to build their social capital in order to fast-track their careers, and they also relied on social capital—namely, their connections to family, friends, and personal sponsors—in order to fund their pageant participation. One of the first hurdles some contestants had to clear was gaining the approval of family members. Many contestants dealt with having to convince unsupportive family members, a few going as far as hiding their participation until the eleventh hour, right before the contest was set to air on television, when they knew their cover would be blown. Faith vowed this would be her final pageant after competing in three others. The financial toil was starting to get to her. Despite her efforts at putting her best foot forward at each competition, she had garnered little success, having only snagged one title to date. She described how she was initially afraid of her strict father's reaction to her involvement in pageants since he viewed them as "sinful, carnal, and lustful." However, she rationalized her participation to her evangelical pastor father by pointing out that Esther, a biblical figure, had also participated in pageants. In the story of Esther, King Xerxes banished Queen Vashti after she refused to appear before the king and his guests to showcase her beauty. A beauty pageant was held to find a replacement queen, and Esther's youthfulness and attractiveness quickly caught the king's attention, who bestowed the royal crown on her. Following instructions from her cousin, Esther hid her Jewish background until she learned of a plot that endangered her people. With a strong wit and resolute grit, Esther successfully spared her community and persuaded the king to pass a decree to protect the Jews. By referencing Esther's story, Faith centered on how celebrating the flesh rather than entirely denouncing it could serve greater spiritual ends that ultimately glorified God and community. In doing so, Faith moralized her participation in beauty contests to emphasize her sustained compatibility with respectable public behavior and a solid ethical compass. She was quick to point to the charity work that pageants allowed her to pursue by giving her a platform, agenda, and political clout.[20]

Aside from seeking their approval, contestants also relied on family members to help them financially with the costs needed to participate. This sometimes meant collecting small sums of money from a number of relatives or hitting up well-off family members. Part of the process of converting skeptical family members involved letting them understand that pageants would help their professional careers and should not be something they looked down on as frivolous, but rather as genuine charitable ventures, as Faith pointed out, and as possibly lucrative. Victoria Biboye, a former contestant who now worked as a promoter for a string of pageants, discussed hounding her uncle until he finally forked over $1,000 (in dollars) to subsidize her pageant ambitions. With her own pageant days behind her, Victoria described how the current crop of contestants was "hungry for the crown and will do anything for it," scowling while miming placing an imaginary crown on her head. She seemed to miss the irony of her statement, brushing aside her own last-ditch efforts of calling her uncle several times a day to secure enough money for her own pageant crown.

Many contestants were recruited by friends encouraging them to participate. Lota Nebolisa grew up as an only child in a major city in Eastern Nigeria with a doting mother and distant father. In her first year of college, she bowed to peer pressure to audition for MBGN. A group of schoolmates had pooled their pocket money and bought a bunch of forms to dole out to the friends in their tight-knit circle. She "freaked out" and got cold feet at the last minute as they were preparing to make the over-eight-hour trip to Lagos on public transportation. After her friends threatened her with having to pay them back if she did not go, Lota did some mental math, calculating that even if she did not win, a consolation prize could pay for a full year of schooling the following year, easing the financial burden on her mother. Lota described herself as a rough-around-the-edges rebellious queen, who used to feel much more comfortable in a pair of flip-flops and a hoodie than high heels and an evening gown. She sailed through the rigorous screening process and returned to Lagos two weeks later to participate in the finale. Utterly ill-prepared for camp, with the exception of a pair of new high-heeled shoes, she pieced together a wardrobe by borrowing clothes from her college friends and a sympathetic roommate at the pageant.

I met up with Lota several years after her contestant days were over. Wearing a black bustier top under a black cardigan over jeans, with her hair styled in a large afro puff and light makeup, she had just come from one photo shoot and was about to hop straight into another one with her photographer-friend Tayo Ajewole, who had quickly built up a name for himself as the go-to portrait photographer. Tayo had turned the downstairs of his home into a studio with umbrella lighting kits, backdrops, and expensive camera equipment. While we waited for her to arrive, Tayo remarked that he refused to photograph beauty queens anymore since they expected to get "everything for free and then don't put you out there." Tayo's remarks belied an unspoken understanding that beauty queens were supposed to use their celebrity status and connections to generate publicity for the free or discounted services they often receive. Having been burned one too many times, Tayo felt he had paid his dues and no longer needed to hand out such freebies. But since Lota was a close friend, he was putting together this photo shoot to update her portfolio and waiving his typical ₦400,000 (about $1,110) half-day rate.[21]

Lota and I chatted upstairs where Tayo's captivating still portraits hung on the walls. Recounting her beauty queen days, she emphasized that beauty competitions "get you access, you meet all these people. You don't even know what to do with it. You get complimentary [business] cards like they're [out] passing flyers on the street. You get access, you meet all these people!" Lota described being thrust into a new social circle, where meeting "high-level" people was routine but was littered with the trifecta of temptations, "sex, drugs, and alcohol," which had placed her in some dicey situations due to overindulging. She conceded that "politics" entered into pageantry since those with connections tried to pull strings to win and that the rumor mill churned with stories about beauty queens sleeping their way to the top. Lota, however, credited the contacts she had made with keeping her in the public eye and giving her a career as a triple-threat entertainer who dabbled in acting, singing, and modeling. Contestants attend private cocktail events with high-rolling executives, hobnob with celebrities, and have courtesy visits with politicians. Beauty queens, who differ from contestants by being titleholders, get even more access to elite social circles under the guise of elevating their pet projects but also to propel their own career aspirations.

This access did not come without risk. Feeling compelled to help other aspiring beauty queens avoid the pitfalls of the industry, Lota had taken a few under her wing, responding to their direct messages on social media and providing tips on how to be successful. Handing over her cell phone so I could read a recent message from a hopeful contestant, she explained why she felt a need to provide such advice. Lota said, "I noticed the girls don't know what they're getting into. They're not prepared. And they will do whatever to get to this place that they don't know anything about." The promises of elevating their social capital tempted many aspiring contestants, and Lota was determined to inform them that the elevation in embodied lifestyles, tastes, and dispositions sometimes came with a cost.

The poor perception of beauty pageants is supported in part by the open secret that some contestants rely on male personal sponsors to help finance the costs of competing. Although most contestants opened up to me about the reality of personal sponsors, I initially had to read between the lines to grasp the full scope of the issue. While not all contestants rely on male sponsors, it was a recurring theme in interviews, either in distancing themselves from the expectation or emphasizing the financial constraints that made personal sponsors necessary. Since most contestants do not yet have stable careers before participating in pageants, they often have to depend on others financially. These personal sponsors are sometimes romantic partners, but other times it is more of a business relationship. Nonetheless, personal sponsors who are not relatives or friends are mostly older men who have the financial means to support aspiring contestants.

I met Iris Edegbe at a Chinese restaurant, where an action movie blared in the background, for lunch with one of her business partners. Iris, who was dressed in white jeans, with a white top under a long, bejeweled teal caftan and had a Louis Vuitton handbag perched on the edge of the table, now owns a high-end real estate firm, which she credits her pageant connections with helping get off the ground. She described sponsors as connected, rich, powerful men who not only help contestants financially, but also do a lot of backdoor manipulating to help contestants win, either through paying money directly to pageant owners or through their social influence. She said she was annoyed at the "bad eggs" who engage in predatory behavior (she used the term "point and kill") to take advantage of contestants by expecting sexual favors with nothing in return, and she characterized relationships with sponsors as mutually beneficial, stating, "It's a good thing to have a sponsor. It makes things better for you—it means they are investing in your brand. When your brand takes off, they have you on a platter of gold." Though Iris acknowledged the potential for exploitation, she concluded that when personal sponsorships worked well, they provided tangible benefits. Part of her perceptions, however, rested on the false assumption that sponsors and contestants were always on level playing fields. But contestants were often subject to the whims of sponsors.

Ebun met her businessman sponsor after she won her state-level pageant. He was in the audience and approached her after the show. Attracted to her reserved personality and determination, he offered to help her out, footing the ₦150,000 bill for Noyo's services to get ready for her national show. Ebun scoffed at the suggestion that he might have romantic intentions, insisting that there were some sponsors who helped contestants out of kindness and to inspire them to do better. According to Ebun, the most he might expect would be a return on his investment in the form of marketing products for his business and splitting any prizes she might win with him, based on a handshake agreement that he would get 40 percent and she would keep the rest. On a day when Ebun was running late for the lesson, Noyo was on the phone making arrangements for Ebun's sponsor to pay him for his services. Noyo mentioned that he had another very promising trainee, whom he felt the sponsor should invest in. He handed the phone to Doyin and she made a pitch to convince the sponsor to also help her out financially. The sponsor decided to divert some of his money to help her, taking Noyo's word that she would be a sure bet on the pageant circuit. Even if the sponsor did not expect sex in return for his financial help, it was clear to me that his quick diversion of funds to Doyin, which left Ebun a bit in the lurch, debunked the framing of his assistance as purely benevolent.

Sanyu Mojola's work on intimate relationships in the context of high rates of HIV infection in Kenya highlights the importance of transactional relationships in the form of "non-commercial, non-marital sexual relationships involving the exchange of money and gifts" in the lives of young women who define modern femininity through consumption.[22] She distinguishes these relationships from "survival sex," which are sexual relationships to get basic needs like food, and "commercial sex," in which sex is a means of securing a livelihood for women through direct monetary exchanges. As Mojola notes, transactional relationships are more prominent among economically mobile women since they enable the purchase of consumer goods. For pageant contestants, sponsors not only provided access to goods needed to be successful in the pageant, but also eased their entrance into elite social circles and helped them secure access.

Contestants stressed that beauty pageants are not a career in and of themselves, but instead described beauty contests as a "launching pad" to "secure their futures" in order to pursue lucrative careers in entertainment, business, or even politics. Many of the contestants use the social contacts they develop through the contest as a platform to pursue their careers in entertainment fields such as modeling or acting, or reinvest their prize money in starting their own businesses. It's not uncommon for contestants to participate in many different pageants, or even participate more than once in the same pageant over multiple years to maximize their chances of winning a title. In fact, repeat contestants are often mocked as "professional contestants," silently disparaged for being too desperate and not making the most of their previous attempts, since all finalists have the opportunity to make significant contacts as a result of their participation in the contest. Doyin explained that participation in the pageant was like a "ladder" that would provide her with a winning advantage. She noted, "Many of us youth want to go into a variety of things. Aside from modeling, we want to do movies, to be musicians and presenters, and, we think, pageantry is the only opportunity to achieve all these. The moment you enter for the contest, everything changes for you." Another contestant observed that participation in pageants

> makes you a better person. You have an opportunity to have the best and also improve. . . . [Y]ou meet a lot of better people, you have an opportunity to achieve something. If there is anything that you want to do, but you don't have an opportunity, it's just going to pave a way for you to do anything that you want to do, any positive thing that you want to do.

When I asked how she felt MBGN helped her achieve her professional goals, Joy Ijeoma said, "I made fantastic contacts. That was one major thing. People I don't know before, the movers and shakers, who can help you in life. I met them, and they were like, oh you are the new girl." Joy's position among the newest crop of winning beauty queens provided entrance into the social worlds of business leaders and politicians, allowing her to make the transition into a career in the oil and gas industry. Contestants saw the pageant as an alternative to traditional routes of higher education, climbing the corporate ladder, and relying on state-sponsored civil servant positions to ensure upward mobility. The time in the spotlight was short-lived, however, and contestants had to swiftly capitalize on their time in the limelight, when their chances of augmenting their social capital was at its highest.

THE FRUITS OF AESTHETIC LABOR

Selling the Dream

In commercials advertising the ₦5,000 ($33) entry forms enticing contestants to audition for MBGN, the concluding tagline invites hopefuls to "make all your wishes come true." On the afternoon of Children's Day, a day on which Silverbird's television network invites children to serve as substitute hosts for the regular presenters on certain programs, I observed the effects of this dream narrative on schoolgirls. A group of four girls dressed in matching burgundy school uniforms, white knee socks, and black flats stood inside the lobby during a break from a tour of the studios. They gazed at the rows of framed pictures of past MBGN winners on the wall. "Did you know Regina Askia [a former Nollywood actress] was one of them?" one girl asked the others. "There's Toyin Raji," another girl said, naming another actress. "I will [be in a] contest one day," one girl announced. "I will compete right now," another joked as she pretended to run toward the door of the CEO's office.

Askia and Raji had won the pageant before these girls were even born. Their continuing fame highlights the fact that some beauty queens have been able to become household names. While just as many Nigerian beauty queens fade into obscurity, beauty pageants offer contestants an opportunity, and some do succeed. By banking on the dreams and hopes of young women, beauty contests like MBGN hope to portray the image of being open to all. However, beauty competitions are winner-take-all markets, in which only one woman will be crowned in the end.

The use of beauty pageants as stepping stones is a familiar theme in the global pageant world.[23] However, Nigerian organizers stressed the role of high poverty rates in making beauty contests increasingly popular in the Global South. One marketing director asked me, "What do you think would happen if I plastered a call for a beauty pageant outside right now? Girls would flood this building out of desperation." Mr. Abe, one of Silverbird's top executives introduced me and Lola, the main pageant coordinator, to a young woman who had just relocated to Lagos from the eastern part of the country. She was interested in getting into the entertainment industry, and Mr. Abe was hoping Lola would "mentor her." Lola encouraged the young woman to purchase an entry form for the MBGN pageant. As Lola browsed through the young woman's modeling portfolio, making specific critiques and giving her beauty and fitness tips, Mr. Abe pulled me aside, leaned over, and whispered:

> You see her? She wants to be famous. The whole beauty pageant thing is just born out of necessity. How else would people here get famous? In Europe and the U.S. you don't need such things. But here there is poverty. . . . Here it's about limited circumstances. Poverty limits people. In the U.S. and Europe you have opportunities.

As he walked away to return to his office, he called to Lola: "Make her famous!" In a subsequent interview, Mr. Abe compared beauty queens to other creative people in the arts and sporting worlds who, according to him, typically come from "poor homes":

> Let me tell you, poverty is a good thing, poverty creates opportunity, it creates entertainment, it creates excitement and it creates creativity. Poverty is why we are successful today. . . . Beauty queens are usually from poor homes no matter where they come from in the world. Society looks down on them but when they become successful, they take them in. That's the irony of life.

Mr. Abe was partially right: Nigeria's comparatively blocked economic system has forced its youth to pursue more unconventional pathways for mobility, but the United States and Europe also have blocked mobility. Nigeria faces high levels of unemployment, especially among its youth. In a survey based on people who graduated from college between 2010 and 2016, 36 percent of university graduates were unemployed.[24] Nigeria is a highly stratified country. Though 50 percent of Nigerians live in poverty, between 2000 and 2010 the number of millionaires nearly doubled.[25] In a highly unequal society, in which the country's middle class is considered fragile or nonexistent by some, pageants offer attractive opportunities to bypass traditional modes of upward mobility to get ahead.

However, Mr. Abe's comments rested on the erroneous sentiment shared by many other MBGN organizers that the vast majority of contestants come from "humble backgrounds." They pointed out that those from wealthier backgrounds might not be in need or as appreciative of the respect, the invitations to special functions, and the business opportunities that might result from their participation. The reality is that those living in poverty would not have sufficient means to even buy an entry form, let alone develop the social networks or means to afford other associated costs. It was unlikely that those from the poorest echelons of Nigeria had even heard of beauty contests like MBGN. Based on my own interviews with beauty pageant contestants, they came from a range of class backgrounds, but mostly from the working class and middle classes. At the minimum, contestants have a secondary school education or some college experience, as required by MBGN and Queen Nigeria, respectively. Part of the reason MBGN organizers in particular insisted that contestants came from poverty was to take credit for the rapid upward trajectory of contestants' class status after the pageant.

Mechanics of Mobility and Embodied Lifestyles

Beauty queens described themselves as professional women who would use their newfound fame to strive for economic mobility. As a whole, they worked to associate themselves with royalty and first ladies and dissociate themselves from prostitutes and market women. Observers often noted that beauty queens were dramatically transformed from "bush girls" to "cultured beauties" and "cosmo girls." Both contests molded a specific classed version of their participants. Queen Nigeria made class distinctions based on local references, which promoted a cultured, middle-class Nigerian woman. Queen Nigeria's classed ideals presumed a settled and established middle-class identity that their participation in the pageant further polished. In contrast, MBGN focused on the rapid upward trajectory of their contestants who, through winning or even just participating in the pageant, gain entrance into an otherwise impermeable jet-setter echelon of Nigerian society, which is aligned with transnational capital and culture.

Cultured Beauties

Queen Nigeria organizers specifically targeted college students as ideal candidates and treated college courses as an unwritten prerequisite for entry. Getting a postsecondary degree in the country is often an uphill battle. College admissions in Nigeria are highly competitive due to the inadequate number of slots available in the tertiary education system. In 2010, 30 percent of applicants gained college admission. From 2013 to 2015, according to the

Joint Admissions Matriculation Board (JAMB), which oversees national standardized tests, every year an average of about 1.6 million students take the compulsory entrance exams, with only 600,000 seats available at accredited universities. This means that there are nearly a million qualified applicants without access to higher education. Of those who enroll, only about 40 percent are women (though this figure differs considerably from state to state, with some, such as Imo and Anambra in the Southeast, enrolling more women than men).[26]

Queen Nigeria also invoked specific, negative images of "market women" to create an implicit class distinction between the contestants and other women. This was evident when, late one evening during dance rehearsals, Will Orji, the choreographer, asked the contestants to walk one by one to form two lines for the opening sequence of the dance number. As one gawky contestant with gangly arms and a gap-toothed smile walked by, he bellowed, pointing at her, "You! Why are you walking like that? You look like a woman carrying firewood on her head. Start over!" Throughout the rehearsal he scolded, "You are all dancing like market women!" These terms evoked women living in rural villages or working in poor, urban environments. Market women have a long history of trading in Nigeria and other areas of West Africa, and serve as a recognizable symbolic figure.[27] In the context of beauty pageants, market women were imagined as rough and brash—characteristics that beauty queens should not exhibit. Market women were seen as lower class and out of place in public in ways that were out of sync with the expectations of beauty queens. Rather than include the sharp, multirhythmic movements with big jumps and leaps that often characterize West African dance, Will taught flowing movements that incorporated twirls and stylized walks. Contestants were expected to maintain a refined beauty queen stance, maintaining an excellent posture in high stilettos, even while dancing.

Jet-Setters

While the emphasis on humble backgrounds might reflect a tendency to see the contestants as innocent, organizers and other members of the production crew spoke disparagingly of them at times. They talked about how they often struggled to make decisions about finalists based on "very slim pickings" since the "most beautiful ones never come out." It seemed clear that appraisals of beauty were tied in part to social class. The MBGN audition process was designed to sift through the countless hopefuls to find the diamonds in the rough. During our sit-down interview, when I asked Octavia how the pageant had changed in recent years, she pointed out that auditions in the past couple of years were yielding higher-caliber contestants, whom she described as "classy girls," as distinguished from "local girls." Asking for further explanation, she stated:

> Remember that haggard girl in Port Harcourt that came in to contest [compete]? [She was referring to someone who had auditioned and whom she and others openly mocked due to her hair and accent.] She really had no business being there. Compare her to someone like [Penelope]. With the way she dressed and everything. I think she is a local girl to me. I might be wrong anyway, but you know appearance means a lot. I'm not saying [Penelope] is like [international pop star] Rihanna but you can't compare her with those girls. She looks far better. . . . If you bring a village girl to town [e.g., a city like Lagos] and she stays in the town but still surrounded by her village people, how do you think that girl is going to behave if she comes for MBGN and then comes to Lagos?

Pageant affiliates like Octavia used terms such as "local," "bush," and "village" to indicate the types of contestants who would not be welcomed at MBGN. As in the Queen Nigeria Pageant, this was a distancing maneuver that relied on class and divisions between urban and rural life. "Local girls" served as an ominous figure. Contestants were not "local" girls, but needed further refinement in order to fulfill their potential as "classy girls."

Octavia positioned Lagos as an obvious location where "classy girls" should reside and would thrive. However, other organizers mocked Lagos in other terms. A few days before the audition in Lagos, Mr. Tim noted: "In Lagos there will be a high turnout. But you will have more losers too. You will see house girls [servants] that managed to get ₦5,000 show up." By imposing an application fee of ₦5,000, organizers hoped to keep most of the poorest at bay, noting that this financial restriction was necessary to prevent just anyone from auditioning. Chibuzor Golibe, a marketing executive, pointed out the distinction between Lagos and other major cities. He felt contestants in Lagos were overly ambitious social climbers. He commented, "For the Lagos girls, MGBN is a platform to become big [influential] girls. But in the regions [cities outside of Lagos], MBGN is an inspirational competition." Remarking that pageants were once a "high society" event, he noted that "I learned that this year no girl bought the form who was from Ikoyi or VI [Victoria Island; both are affluent Lagos suburbs]; the ones from Lagos are from the outskirts." While pageants might have been an occasion that attracted attendees from the crème de la crème of society, contestants from Nigeria's most privileged class have been the exception rather than the rule. In the 1950s and 1960s, contestants were educated, urban-dwelling young women who worked as seamstresses, nurses, school teachers, shop clerks, and clerical assistants. They were certainly upwardly mobile, but not from the upper-crust sectors of Nigerian society. Mr. Abe, who began working in the pageant world in the 1980s, reminisced about the struggle to find contestants. He recalled having to conduct home visits and practically beg people to participate. Those from wealthier families simply refused to take part. Chibuzor's comments echoed rhetoric I came across in newspapers from the 1960s, where the same debates about Nigerian beauty pageants not selecting the most appropriate contestants and lament about the industry as already being on the decline were also evident. I interpret these comments as part of a broader social anxiety about class, gender, and nation at play.

MBGN organizers focused on picking the "right kinds of girls," noting that while they were able to avoid choosing those considered to be at the bottom of the barrel, they rarely had access to those considered the cream of the crop. Though the general public assumes that all MBGN contestants come from wealthy families, those from upper-class backgrounds largely view pageants as a downgrade because of their perception as an upward mobility strategy.

Throughout the rehearsals, organizers constantly questioned how they managed to select some of the women as finalists, even speculating that there had been some logistical glitch that mixed up the final tallies. After the prejudging, in which contestants would be whittled down to the final fifteen, I asked Mrs. Ellen, the wife of one of the executives, what she thought of the contestants. She complained: "Some of these girls have behinds bigger than me. Some of them have been gaining [weight]." Calvin, the producer, nodded his head in agreement. "I think there might have been a mistake with some of them. Like maybe their numbers didn't match up properly. Some of the girls, I don't even know how we picked them." Mrs. Ellen responded: "It's the buffet. It's a killer. Most of them haven't seen as much food all in one place at once before." Some pageant affiliates remarked that contestants were motivated to participate since they knew they would get decadent meals three times a day. Others speculated that the girls had starved themselves for the auditions and then stuffed themselves with food once they had secured a spot as a finalist. On the first day of camp, Omar Gowon, one of the MBGN reality show hosts, said to me, shaking his head: "These girls. They're no good. I expect them to be more polished. They're shallow and tacky. Our kind of girl wouldn't go for this kind of thing. They think this platform is too easy. These are just regular girls." Expressions of class bias such as these were frequent.

Yet the "rags to riches" storyline served a purpose for MBGN organizers. When one of the executives learned that a former beauty queen, married to a high-ranking executive in agribusiness, had refused the complimentary VIP tickets and insisted that she would only attend if she was granted the more exclusive VVIP ("very very important person") tickets, he roared: "We made [her]! We wiped [her] out from poverty. She was living in a *face me face you* [a tiny apartment that faces another]! Her mother was selling *akara* [bean fritters] on the streets! Who does she think she is!" Though this particular ex–beauty queen did come from very modest means, she was also a college student at the time of the pageant, highlighting the economic headway she was making. Positioning contestants as coming from poor, humble backgrounds allowed MBGN to take credit for the elevated lifestyles that beauty queens enjoyed after the contest and to also create an understanding that contestants should feel indebted to the organization.

Deriding contestants' backgrounds stood alongside the constant focus on their rapid transformation over the course of camp. I was chatting with one of the chaperones, Ada Ibe, as the contestants were having their photographs taken for the brochure. She motioned toward the group of contestants gathered outside the pool of the five-star hotel that served as host for camp. She said: "They will all change. You'll see them next year and you won't even recognize them." Toward the tail end of camp, Omar echoed Ada's comments. He discussed one of the contestants whom we both saw leaving in a heavy downpour after the Benin audition as we rode back to the hotel together. We were riding in a black, bulletproof armored luxury SUV with tinted windows, while she was riding on an *okada* (motorbike).[28] "Remember that girl we saw in Benin? She is not even the same girl anymore! She has really changed. Now she acts so different." Frankie talked about a previous queen who, after winning, hired a personal assistant to carry her designer bag, describing it as an example of how contestants change after they win. Cracking up with laughter, he recalled how everyone burst into a fit of giggles when the beauty queen did that. He then proclaimed, "They change after they've won, their presentation and everything changes."

With access to hairstylists, makeup artists, and some of the top Nigerian fashion designers, contestants' physical embodiment was expected to change over the course of the contest and beyond. They were expected to own the latest smartphones, designer handbags, heels, and clothing. Joy, the reigning queen, entered the room wearing strappy heeled sandals and a black sequined dress, with her crown nestled inside a large silver makeup case. A photographer and reporter had come to see her for a magazine article. The photographer introduced himself to her: "We have met before [but] I don't know if you remember me. Wow! You've really changed," he remarked, looking her up and down. "Silverbird's money has changed me," Joy responded cheerfully, with a broad smile.

During the audition process, a couple of the chaperones pointed out a woman who had auditioned for the past two cycles of MBGN. While she had made the cut in the past, she did not go on to win the crown. "Each year she comes back cleaner and cleaner," said one. When I asked the chaperone what she meant, she responded that each time this woman returned to audition, her skin looked lighter. This observation was one of many describing physical changes in contestants' bodies as a result of participating in the pageant. In this case the changes came from access to exclusive skin and makeup treatments. Contestants worked to achieve vibrant, even-toned skin that was free of blemishes, and eliminate black patches on their elbows and knees. The focus on lighter, spotless skin secured and verified economic mobility.[29]

Planes, Homes, and Automobiles

Mobility was defined, not just through the consumption of luxury goods such as handbags and physical changes in appearance, but also through access to cars, preferably chauffeured, for transportation; new housing accommodations in ritzy neighborhoods; airfare for first-class flights; and the opportunity to work, study, and live abroad. It is very common for Nigerian beauty competitions to present winners with a new car wrapped with signage and branding for the pageant. For many beauty queens, this is their first car. When I reconnected with Kamdi over seven years later, we caught up by phone while she was on a year-long medical esthetics training program in the United States. Kamdi's voice had audibly hardened from the chirpy tone I recalled, which I took as a sign of both maturity and navigating dashed hopes over the years. Reluctant to give much credit to MBGN for her career trajectory, she begrudgingly admitted that the pageant had put her in the spotlight and opened some doors for her, but added that the pressure had overwhelmed her. She said, "You go from a regular girl— going places in buses or taxi[s—]and overnight people expect you to not be that girl anymore. They expect that you wake up with so much money. You have to have your own car, fly first class to Paris." Kamdi revealed that there had been a five-month gap between when she signed her endorsement deal and when she was finally paid, meaning that while everyone expected her to "spin around immediately" into this sudden (she repeated this word numerous times for emphasis) jet-setting lifestyle, she did not immediately have the funds to back up those expectations. She recalled that her whole village (typically Nigerians, even if they live in the city, have extended family members who live in smaller, more rural communities) called her mother, believing that "this means life is good. This means life is perfect," and that she heard rumors that she had just bought a new home in Ikoyi, a tony neighborhood in Nigeria.

She repeatedly described herself as "just a regular girl" who had previously only owned one designer item, but that she faced skyrocketing expectations. Because she ran the risk of being smeared in the tabloids for riding an *okada* (motorbike), *danfo* (large passenger buses that carry between sixteen and eighteen passengers), or taxi since they were not considered suitable means of transportation for beauty queens, it dawned on her that "I can't take *danfo* and the money I have is only [enough] money for the bus, so I have to stay home, while every other girl is out there. I couldn't afford it." She got bombarded with calls from family and friends asking for financial help, and she had to string them along for months. Not wanting to burden or worry her parents, she hid out for a month in her home, refusing to attend any events. After MBGN, she completed an MBA abroad, got a job in a luxury travel agency that afforded her the opportunity to travel around the world, and then opened up her own medical aesthetics clinic in Lagos, which was funded through a combination of savings and investments by her parents. She viewed this new business endeavor as a way of continuing her goals of rebranding Nigeria, but now through beauty entrepreneurship and integrating a vision of corporate social responsibility by working against childhood poverty for people living in the slums.

Marrying Well

"Marrying well" was viewed as another element of mobility. Pageant contestants had direct access to some of the nation's most powerful political officials, elite businessmen, and acclaimed celebrities. I stood in the corner, watching the contestants run through dress rehearsals the day before the finale. Mr. James Oke, a longtime staff member at Silverbird, commented:

> I'm always scared of these girls. They are powerful. That's why I'm always nice to them. They're all going to dump their boyfriends after this is over. You'd be surprised, one of them might be the future wife to a [government] minister; [he snaps his fingers and adds,] they might just be the one to make that phone call to make or destroy a deal.

I was initially taken aback by Mr. Oke's characterization of these young women, who were twenty years his junior and who mostly did not have a regularly paying job like he did, as powerful. However, I did notice the subtle shift from derision to deference in how he and others interacted with the contestants as the finale drew closer. Part of what Mr. Oke's words signaled was that in the future, these contestants would likely be in a relationship with an influential man more financially successful and politically connected than he was. Leaving a bad impression with a contestant could come back to bite him later. Mr. Oke's words related a familiar narrative arc that many other pageant affiliates shared. Beauty queens were expected to find a rich man to marry, have children, and pursue an entrepreneurial endeavor or professional career. As Mr. Oke explained to me, contestants' newly acquired positions allowed them access to elite social circles with political access, financial capital, and social status.

Lota, who was now in her thirties, had bucked the pressure to marry. She discussed the expectation that contestants use pageants to find a "baller" (wealthy man). Lota's love life was often cause for speculation in gossip magazines. She shared that married women looked down on her because she was unmarried. However, she valued her financial independence and happiness, and derided others who had chosen the path of "marrying well" as overly dependent on men, remarking that "they can't even take a taxi without their husband paying for it." Resisting pressures to be married was a way of retaining control and self-respect.

FALL FROM GRACE

As beauty diplomats, Nigerian beauty queens command respect and attention. However, they also navigate a context in which this admiration must be built up and constantly protected. They walk a fine tightrope in which the expectations of expressed femininity are both concealed and revealed. On the one hand, beauty queens should be sexy, titillating, and alluring, while on the other, they should also be demure, chaste, and innocent. They must both fit the expectation of the male gaze, but also subvert it by asserting their voice, to be seen as successful. This double bind, which places beauty queens within a complex set of contradictions, uncovers more nuanced ways of thinking about power. As Marcia Ochoa notes in her book on beauty queens in Venezuela, scandal is inherent in the pageant form.[30] While one of the ways in which scandals enter pageants is through judging decisions that taint the pageant through associations with the political gears of the state or Nigeria's notoriously murky private business environment, there are other ways in which the specter of scandal figures into Nigerian beauty pageants. Ochoa describes these routine scandals as a "falling out of order" that allows us to see the inner workings of stakeholders' motivations, expectations, and decision-making processes.[31]

In Nigeria, the threat of public spectacle through scandal, primarily around contestants' sexuality, means that pageant contestants must carefully toe the line between projecting desirability while maintaining a wholesome image as role models who project and perform class and sexual respectability for other Nigerian girls and women. Those who veer off course are deeply stigmatized. Over the years, the most high-profile scandals in the Nigerian beauty pageant industry have involved sex and accusations of falsifying age and school certificate records, marking the bounds of respectability that beauty queens should embody. Ochoa's "falling out of order" concept pushes us to consider how a perceived falling apart of morality at the level of subjectivity, industry, and the nation are rectified through respectability politics which position Nigerian beauty pageants as propelling individual gains through economic mobility, collective benefits through charity work, and national advancement through positive recognition.

I witnessed the defense mechanisms and corrective order that Queen Nigeria and MBGN put in place to ensure "scandal-free" reigns. Pageant organizers constantly emphasized that beauty queens were under intense and constant public surveillance. After the semifinal wrapped up in Lagos, Mr. Tim, MBGN's national director, stood up to speak to the thirty finalists who would go on to compete in the national finals.

> You will all become nationally famous now. Nothing you do will escape the camera. Big Brother, or rather Big Sister [referring to the female chaperones who constantly monitor the contestants], is always watching you. There are rules and regulations here. No boyfriends, no "uncles" [a slang term used to refer to male patrons who informally sponsor contestants]. There will be no visitors and no outings except for supervised visits made by appointment. The only men you are allowed to associate with are those that work for the Silverbird crew.

During camp, contestants had to be accompanied everywhere during the scheduled trainings and rehearsals, even to the restroom. MBGN's strict chaperone policy is not uncommon in the global pageant industry. Throughout the course of the competition and during her subsequent reign, a beauty contestant's sexuality is carefully protected and projected as "pure." Without "purity," contestants cannot be recognized as suitable role models of charity, progress, and goodwill.

In an interview with Mr. Omo, a reporter, Joy, the reigning beauty queen, let slip that she had a boyfriend in response to his question. Hoping to trap her, Mr. Omo had asked her if her boyfriend was in the audience when she won the pageant. Joy replied, "Yes," in a matter-of-fact tone and Mr. Omo responded gleefully with, "Oh, I got you!" Joy played off his reaction, candidly stating, "I'm open about it. Let's be real." He responded, "You're not supposed to have a boyfriend, or you'll be dethroned." Joy replied, "Mr. Tim already met my boyfriend. Everyone knows." As this conversation was unfolding between Joy and the reporter, Lola kicked me hard under the table to signal her displeasure, quickly shushed Joy, and instructed Mr. Omo not to include that tidbit in his feature on Joy, though he did anyway. Later on, Lola scolded Joy for being so public about her love life. Reporters almost always ask beauty queens about their relationship status. A couple of weeks later, when I asked Mr. Omo why the boyfriend issue was such a big deal, he explained:

> It's just the Nigerian factor. Internationally it is accepted that you can have a boyfriend, you can't expect a twenty-year-old girl not to have a boyfriend, but the issue is downplayed here so that it does not take the shine away. It is a form of distraction because they might try to use you. If you have a boyfriend, you have to choose between the crown and the guy. That is why it is not allowed in Nigeria.

He further explained that beauty queens now had access to millions of naira, which required them to keep a low profile. I interpreted "taking the shine away" as potentially sullying the reputation of beauty queens, which would dim the spotlight on them. On one of the first official events for the newly crowned queen, Penelope, we were sitting in the back of her new car, driving to a magazine shoot and press interview. Lola firmly reminded Penelope, "If they ask, you do not have a boyfriend!" In the contract that MBGN beauty queens sign, they have to let Silverbird know about their relationship status, and there is an unwritten rule that they are not allowed to have boyfriends, at least not publicly. These measures counteract a specific stereotype of beauty queens as sexually promiscuous dropouts with dysfunctional family backgrounds. Organizers appeal to distinct narratives to craft an image of a respectable beauty queen who represents the nation in a wholesome manner.

In other instances, I saw how potentially unruly contestants were weeded out early on as part of a larger vetting process to ensure that crowned queens would not be disruptive. As we were window-shopping at the family-owned Silverbird boutique, Lola and Danielle, the daughter of one of Silverbird's executives, asked me about the status of my research. Holding up a strapless black jumper that she was thinking about buying, Lola offered a possible interview lead, stating, "You should interview Adanna Metu." "It will just go to her head," Danielle interjected. "Who is Adanna?" I asked. Danielle responded,

> She contested [competed] for MBGN before. She didn't win, didn't even make top 10. But if you saw the way she was acting in camp! She had a major attitude. She came in telling girls that she was going to win, and that they shouldn't even bother with the competition. Imagine if she acted like that in camp, how would she act if she won. She was the prettiest girl there, but her attitude lost it for her.

Through the prejudging portion of the MBGN competition, organizers pull a lot of weight in determining the top fifteen and can thus pluck out likely mischief-makers. After losing the competition, Adanna booked a couple of commercials, which by chance happened to be playing as we wrapped up our shopping trip. Lola and Danielle pointed her out to me. I realized I had seen Adanna before, hanging out at the Silverbird offices and mall. Adanna's name came up a few more times during my fieldwork, as a counterexample of a queen whom organizers could trust to follow rules, not be pretentious, and remain compliant. Similarly, during Queen Nigeria's camp, I discovered that a contestant had been kicked out of the competition before the start of the national finale because she had bad-mouthed the organizers to the press. Through these tactics, organizers weeded out potential troublemakers as soon as they could.

The reality of the pressures to maintain a particular lifestyle drove some contestants into relationships with older men after the contest. After a heated conversation in which Ebun, Faith, and Doyin aired their frustration with beauty queens being associated with sexual promiscuity, Noyo interrupted to point out that beauty queens had to be "more slutty" after they win a competition because they now have a car, which elevated the expectations about their social status. According to Noyo, beauty queens needed to have relationships with men in order to maintain their new lifestyle. An example that illustrates Noyo's point was Rose's story. Rose Pepples recounted how she had broken up with her boyfriend, who had helped her out with occasional bills, but that mounting financial pressures had pushed her into having an affair with a married man. She described this ordeal as a low point in her life, adding that she left the relationship once she was able to get on her own two feet and felt a sense of relief once it was over.

Yinka Olugbode was one of the most candid contestants I met. She detailed the pressures she felt to rely on personal sponsors to help provide the resources needed after she had won the state-level Queen Nigeria competition. To participate in the national-level competition, she was able to borrow clothes and got some financial assistance from the general manager of the state-level NTA television network. But Yinka described how, after failing to win the national pageant, she faced increasing financial burdens upon her return as a state titleholder. She did not own a car and could not buy expensive clothes, elements that were considered essential for beauty queens. Yinka, who was a college student at the time and still very much financially dependent on her parents, described herself as "too trusting," and had hired a manager to help her during her reign who had stolen close to ₦250,000 ($1,666) in scholarship money from her, including selling prizes that she had won and pocketing the money. The manager increasingly badgered her to secure a personal sponsor to help generate funds, but she refused, stating that she had decided to take a different but more difficult path of striking out on her own.

Sexual harassment is insidious in the pageant industry. In one of the more egregious stories I heard, Susan Martins, a contestant who was pursuing a degree in information technology, recalled an encounter she had with a man who invited her to his hotel room one afternoon. When she entered his room, she found him naked and he requested that she give him a massage. She managed to find a way to leave, but just days later had to attend an event at his home with his family in tow as part of her expected duties. She noted that when she greeted him, he hugged her and then whispered in her ear, "You can run, but you can't hide." When she told me her story, a chill ran up my spine, but her story was unfortunately not too surprising to me. After this incident, she refused to participate in any further pageant activities and cut herself off from the organization. As her story illustrates, one potential option to fend off the sexual harassment in the industry was to disappear, though that sometimes meant cutting off social contacts.

Beauty contestants often discussed dashed hopes, feeling like pawns used to benefit others, and the desires others had to control the way they acted. Lota used a vivid image to help illustrate how beauty contestants had to navigate the industry. She discussed how "your life is not your own," and enumerated the various pressures that beauty queens face: constant gossip, the need to fit a mold that organizers create, and the inability to openly complain. Stating the need to build a thick skin, Lota explained, "The beauty queen hides everything in the smile. Because once you get out there, you are putting on a mask. When you get out there in front of the world. You have to be able to separate that from your real self." She used this metaphor of the mask to show how beauty queens had to put forward a certain face in ways that paradoxically let their true self shine, painted a picture of perfection, and distanced themselves from public scrutiny.

As we ended our phone chat, I asked Kamdi, "Was it worth it?" Even after she had described all the false promises, intense pressures, and need to increasingly distance herself from the "beauty queen" title as she grew older, she still described her time in the pageant "as the best moment of my life."

> KAMDI: I can't completely discredit that it was a good thing for me. It was a courageous thing for me to do. It felt really empowering at the time for you to wake up and you never understood how you got there overnight.
>
> OB: Why do you describe it as being courageous and empowering? What's that about?
>
> KAMDI: First of all, it was a competition with probably thousands of girls across the nation. You feel, "Wow." That is another massive step. It puts it in your mind like, "I can do this." In the course of it, you get a lot of girls telling you how much they want to be like you, how much you inspire them. You can actually have a voice. So, it is empowering as a woman in Nigeria.

Like others, Kamdi asserted a sense of empowerment, reflecting on how their attractive bodies were applauded on stage, their voices lauded in public, and their style admired. Feeling powerful meant recognition, validation, moral authority, and mobility actualized through reflexive self-projects. While they often felt empowered on stage and through their charity work, they felt constrained by the public scrutiny and the unsavory aspects of navigating the behind-the-scenes world of beauty pageants. Some took advantage of these contradictions, developing entrepreneurial and intimate relationships with powerful men to garner economic and social capital. Others folded under the pressure. Kamdi ended our conversation on a decidedly optimistic note. Despite all the pitfalls, viewing pageants as a platform—that honed her body, provided her with social contacts, and gave her a voice—was still an appealing narrative to her. These stories tell complex narratives of how women navigate the industry to access power, sometimes with unpredictable and grim consequences, but always with a focus on standing up for themselves and their country.

CONCLUSION

Through their aesthetic labor, beauty contestants seek to establish themselves as reputable and effective diplomats whose own attractive attributes serve to support a more positive image of the Nigerian nation. Contestants focus on projecting their voices, refining their walks, and perfecting their smiles in order to connect to the general public and advocate for social causes. They define beauty queens' work as extending beyond perfecting physical appearance. They connect markers of external beauty to additional internal qualities of altruism, kindness, and virtue. Their public image exists in tension with their private ambitions to use the pageant as a means of gaining economic mobility and catapulting their careers to the next level. Those whom I interviewed at both the Queen Nigeria and MBGN Pageants noted a shift in embodiment for contestants, who started out as "regular" and then transformed into cultured beauties and "cosmo" (cosmopolitan) girls. While Queen Nigeria engaged in class-based distancing maneuvers, MBGN went a step further by focusing on the rapid upward trajectory of contestants who, through the consumption of luxury goods, access to chauffeured cars, and posh accommodations, embodied jet-setter lifestyles. However, these mobility prospects were constrained by the intense public pressures, the need to maintain a constant cash flow, and navigating false promises, realities that most contestants had to contend with.

4 | MISS CULTURE AND MISS COSMOPOLITAN

THE 2009 EDITION of the front cover of Queen Nigeria's program was splashed with shades of green and white, Nigeria's national colors, and the pageant's logo, a silhouette of a beauty queen with a green head wrap, a crown, and a green sash across her torso (see Figure 4.1). When I asked Mr. Gold, one of Queen Nigeria's main organizers, to describe the pageant's vision, he stated, "[Queen Nigeria] is someone Nigerians can easily relate to and identify with in terms of how she is. . . . She has the core values of our people, our culture and our orientation. [Queen Nigeria] is who we are." In contrast, the brochure of the Most Beautiful Girl in Nigeria Pageant (MBGN) featured the headshot of the reigning beauty queen in a sequined gown with a pair of gossamer angel wings superimposed behind her, an image that seemed to hint at the Victoria's Secret Angels campaign (see Figure 4.2). Xavier (who went by his mononym moniker), a haute couturier who has designed custom fashion pieces for MBGN contestants, described these beauty queens as "Cosmo girls . . . someone who is trendy, passes time in the U.S. and the UK. . . . Very fashion-forward."

These two contrasting images, which the pageant affiliates' comments also typify, highlight the different versions of idealized femininity and the distinct nationalist claims these beauty contests exemplified. I find that these claims to represent beauty, nation, and cultural diversity show the complicated,

m1ER 4

FIGURE 4.1. Front page of Queen Nigeria program. *Source:* NTA/TVE. Reprinted with permission.

and sometimes contradictory, process of constructing the feminine national body. This chapter describes how each pageant understood cultural and state representation in the pageant, the level of audience participation, the meaning behind the traditional segment and its placement in the show, and how the pageants grappled with ethnic, religious, and regional differences, especially in regard to the northern part of the country. Queen Nigeria took an approach I call *tactile,* which was focused on rootedness and familiarity, sought to accommodate differences within the nation, and promoted a sense of unity. Meanwhile, MBGN used a *tactical* approach, which was motivated

FIGURE 4.2. Front page of Most Beautiful Girl in Nigeria program. *Source:* Silverbird. Reprinted with permission.

by strategy and discovery in addition to securing international competitiveness. Although these two narratives seem diametrically opposed, they both navigate within a global-African framework.

GLOBAL-AFRICAN VORTEX

In 2017, former 2005 MBGN beauty queen Omowunmi Akinnifesi, who has remained a fixture on the socialite circuit since her win, worked as an environmental ambassador for Lagos state, and now owns her own fashion line, starred in a Nivea ad promoting a product for "visibly lighter skin" that made her "feel younger." The ad ignited a firestorm across the world. Critics rightfully condemned the ad as supporting colorism, racism, and Eurocentrism. The ad campaign and the outrage it sparked are a prime example of discussions surrounding global beauty ideals that are conventionally conceptualized through the lens of hegemonic Western norms. In places such as Nigeria, preferences for light skin, bodies with low body mass, extraordinary height, and the promulgation of Eurocentric features such as light-colored eyes and narrow nose bridges are seen as an intrusion of rigid foreign influences that has spread rapidly across the globe to erode local cultures, fuel racial self-hatred, and ignite a fascination with the West.[1] I find that this focus on uniform hegemonic Westernization, which centers on Whiteness, reifies our understandings of embodiment. In line with other emerging postcolonial feminist scholars such as Grace Adeniyi Ogunyankin and Simidele Dosekun, I adopt a "multiple modernities" framework to decenter the West as the starting point for globalization, recognize diverse global centers outside the West, and recognize the multidirectional flows of culture between the Global South and Global North.[2] Ayu Saraswati, for example, analyzes ads for skin-lightening creams in Indonesia alongside ads for tanning lotions in the United States to conceptualize "cosmopolitan whiteness," as a virtual quality that is not equated with Caucasian Whiteness as a racial category, but rather as tied to consumption, mobility, and leisure.[3]

Skin lightening is a common practice in Nigeria, with estimates that 77 percent of Nigerians, mostly women, use skin-lightening creams.[4] Those within and outside of the pageant world explained the preference for light skin was in part because darker skin tones are more common in Nigeria, and light skin is constructed as unique and thus highly valued. Nigerians, however, come in a variety of skin tones yet light skin is disproportionately—but not uniformly—represented in the media. People, including pageant participants, often used the euphemism of "skin toning" to discuss how their goal was to even their skin rather than lighten it. Unlike in Susan Dewey's analysis of the Miss India Pageant, which details a one-month preparation schedule that included the regimented use of skin-lightening creams through the services of in-house dermatologists and estheticians, I did not witness this same pageant-directed routine in Nigeria.[5] Though some contestants did use skin-lightening creams, they tended to use the "toning" language described here. Though there is criticism, especially of MBGN, as preferring light-skinned winners, as I will detail later, skin color is commodified in much more complex ways in Nigerian pageants.

The dominant bodily ideals in Nigerian beauty pageantry emphasized slimness, height, and striking facial features like high cheekbones, straight teeth, and smooth skin texture. It also required a type of physical appearance that has been described by others as a form of "spectacular femininity" through the use of cascading hair weaves and wigs, heavy makeup, consumption of luxury accessories, and towering stilettos.[6] While much of this look required constant upkeep and maintenance, Nigerian contestants often noted that they differed from other competitors at international pageants because they were "natural." While cosmetic surgery is common among pageant contestants in places such as Venezuela and Puerto Rico, it is not common among beauty contestants in Nigeria. For example, during a media interview, Joy, the reigning MGBN beauty queen, was asked point-blank if she had been intimidated by South American contestants during the recent Miss World competition. In response, she complained that those contestants "weren't real" and expressed shock at the rise of "enhancements" in pageantry. She revealed that Miss World was the first place she had encountered someone who had had plastic surgery and lamented that these procedures displaced "natural beauty." During the time I did the bulk of my fieldwork, none of the contestants admitted to having had any plastic surgery and, as Joy's remarks show, it was generally frowned upon as distracting from claims of projecting "natural beauty." While I did hear rumors of ex–beauty queens undergoing cosmetic procedures after their reigns, it was not a common practice in Nigeria when I started this research. In fact, during this time period, Nigerians had to travel abroad to get cosmetic surgery because in Nigeria they could only get reconstructive surgeries and only in public teaching hospitals, which many Nigerians are distrustful of due to their poor facilities. In 2001, an entrepreneur did open a cosmetic consultancy that flew in American-based cosmetic surgeons once or twice a year to perform surgeries. But these limited options made getting plastic surgery logistically difficult and prohibitively expensive for contestants. However, since about 2012 there have been private local plastic surgery clinics springing up in major cities like Lagos and Abuja and a rising popularity of minimally invasive procedures such as laser skin resurfacing and body contouring, which some Nigerian beauty queens are starting to pursue. Within Nigeria more broadly, plastic surgery is becoming more socially accepted and readily available for those who can afford it.

Flipping through popular Nigerian magazines in which beauty queens commonly appear, readers will find spreads with African American celebrities such as Beyoncé, Rihanna, and Tyra Banks, who are labeled international icons, alongside features on Nigerian celebrities such as actress Genevieve Nnaji and singer Tiwa Savage, who are known not just in Nigeria, but throughout Africa and the world due to the country's thriving Nollywood film and Afropop music industries. Prominent magazine distributers such as Condé Nast and Hearst have introduced South African editions of *Elle*, *Marie Claire*, *Glamour*, and *Cosmopolitan* over the past two decades, while shying away from other African markets, including Nigeria. However, homegrown Nigerian magazines such as *Today's Woman*, *Genevieve*, and *Arise* have established high-end glossies that emphasize Africa's "international style"; generate global advertising from luxury brands such as Yves Saint Laurent, Ralph Lauren, and L'Oréal; include editorials with African designers from Nigeria, Tanzania, and Ghana; feature Black international models such as Alek Wek, Liya Kebede, and Oluchi Onweagba; and have well-known Nigerian actresses, beauty queens, and singers on their covers. They have distribution networks in Nigeria, other African countries, Europe, and North America.[7] Nigerian fashion labels, women's lifestyle magazines, and beauty brands use buzzwords such as "Afropolitan" and "Afro-chic" to signal the importance of African aesthetics and their rising relevance to the entire world. These discourses and media images were part of the social landscape that contestants sought to emulate.

By far the celebrity that most contestants looked up to was Agbani Darego, the winner of the 2001 Miss World Pageant. Many of them viewed her as an international beauty icon, and several contestants were encouraged to initially audition for pageants because someone mentioned that they "look just like Agbani," pointing to her stature, slim body, and gracious personality as ideal characteristics for beauty queens. Mr. Omo, a journalist who covered Agbani Darego's victory extensively, noted how she became a popular cultural touchstone for Nigerians, influencing hairstyles (a high, tightly pulled-back chignon bun was known as the "Agbani") and touching off an increased appreciation for *lepa* (Yoruba slang for "slim") body shapes that highlighted new definitions of youth, wealth, and health in the country, along with a global appreciation for dark skin. Shortly after clinching the title, she gushed, "I have made history . . . Black Is Beautiful," invoking a global rallying cry to recognize the cultural importance of her win and to counteract a larger history of presenting Black women's bodies as abject.[8]

Feminist scholars have noted the gaps between the idealized beauty standards conveyed in pageants and the "average" bodies of everyday women.[9] Much has been made of how praising Darego's slim, tall body shape accentuated the degree to which her figure remained both out of touch with the bodies of ordinary Nigerians and contrary to the full-figured bodies traditionally prized in some parts of Nigeria.[10] In Southeast Nigeria among the Annang ethnic group, for instance, they have a custom of having fattening rooms where girls and young women are fed starch-heavy and fat-laden meals to encourage weight gain. Participants are kept in seclusion for up to two years until they are ready for marriage. They are tended to by minders and are expected to spend their days eating, drinking, resting, and absorbing lessons about marriage and motherhood. The fattening room is considered a coming-of-age ritual and rite of passage, and increased weight is regarded as a sign of wealth, fertility, and allure, indicating that the woman is well taken care of.[11] Thinness, in contrast, is associated with sickness, neglect, and scarcity.[12] While still practiced today, these practices are largely waning. This decline, alongside the valorization of thinness more generally, has been immediately linked to globalization via Westernization. However, a more expansive perspective on beauty ideals across the world highlights how aesthetic standards are always changing through an interplay of local and global conditions.

Pageant beauty criteria both diverge and dovetail with broader dominant Nigerian beauty ideals, which were described to me as clear skin (spotless, hairless, and smooth); a petite (though not too short) hourglass or pear-shaped body with a flat stomach, wide hips, round posterior, and large bust; lighter skin; and long hair, achieved either through relaxed straight hair, hair weaves, box braids, or cornrows with extensions. Nigerian beauty ideals navigate between a set of configurations that position "global" and "African" beauty norms against each other, leaving space to negotiate between them, and also recognizing their hybrid commingling. Though I set up this dual framework to help make sense of the wide array of beauty ideals that permeate the Nigerian landscape, I do not understand "global" or "African" as pure categories of oppositional difference. Instead, I recognize the diverse media images, beauty industries, and bodily discourses that circulate throughout Nigeria and around the world to capture and make sense of these complex dynamics. Beauty ideals are always situated within specific contexts and are always in flux with regard to class, generation, region, religion, and ethnicity.

In the Nigerian context, the global-African beauty frameworks play out in several ways. The global framework is typically discussed in terms of "international standards" that recognize Western beauty norms such as White skin, blonde hair, blue eyes, and thinness, but also emphasize the ways in which these international standards can be critiqued, reoriented, and appropriated. Moreover, while there is a recognition that "international standards" privilege Whiteness, in the Nigerian context, "international standards" in mainstream media often come through in ways that are not always equivalent with placing Whiteness at the center. While Whiteness may be understood as hegemonic, it is not necessarily aspirational. For example, African American media images and popular culture trends are common reference points in Nigeria and constitute a long history of diasporic engagement on the continent around global Black style.[13]

While many consider South Africa to be at the helm of setting industry standards on the continent in terms of logistics, infrastructure, and policies, many of the Nigerians I interacted with in the fashion, beauty, and modeling industries viewed Nigeria as at the forefront of *aesthetic trends* for the rest of the continent. There is a recognition that global hierarchies may not fully recognize or integrate African beauty and fashion, but in a rapidly changing global context, Nigeria is increasingly viewed as an ideal market demographic to tap into for global brands. The presumed result is that "international standards" long dominated by Western corporations and commodity culture will have to change as a result. For example, I interviewed Xavier, a haute couture fashion designer, former model, and pageant judge, in a large air-conditioned lecture room during an intermission of an association meeting of Nigeria's top fashion designers. Xavier, who proudly boasted about the shows and shoots he had done in Paris, Milan, and New York, cities considered to be established "world fashion capitals," as well as Dubai and Johannesburg, explained how Nigeria was an untapped market for global brands but that these brands would have to shift their strategy if they wanted to be successful in the country. He explained:

> African women have their own statistics. In the fashion world, it creates so many problems [if] you want to sell your clothes here as a designer and you are saying waistline 25 [inches], 32 [inch] hips. What African women are you going to see coming out with hips 32? Where, how, why? At least start from 40 [inch hips]. If you actually want to bring your brand to Africa, not just in Nigeria, there are some things you just have to drop. If it doesn't happen, then I am sorry, no international brand or designer is going to actually do well in Nigeria or in Africa.

When I probed Xavier to explain his reasoning further, he shared that the international fashion industry was changing as a direct result of challenges from markets like Nigeria. He noted:

> Before it was all about drop-dead skinny models, but as of last year they were not picking any skinny model to be on the runway. . . . We need regular people on the runway, a little bit of body. . . . They are embracing the African moment. Everybody is increasing their size for the African market.

Another example of this "African moment" was MBGN's official clothier. The fashion designer's prices range from $150 to $350 for her diffusion (secondary mass-market) line and $350–$1,500 for her signature luxury brand, has showrooms in Lagos and New York, collaborated with *Vogue Italia* (the international fashion world's "bible"), and has dressed A-list celebrities throughout Africa and in the United States such as Lucy Liu, Solange Knowles, and Thandie Newton in her fashions made from West African ankara print and embellished with hand beading, rhinestones, and crystals. Through these examples, participants pointed to African beauty and fashion as reaching a global platform that sustained the continent's viability and competitiveness. This larger global-African context informs how beauty queens' bodies are expected to embody the Nigerian nation.

TESTS AND MODELS OF GENDERED NATIONAL REPRESENTATION

In nearly all contemporary Nigerian national pageants, beauty contestants go by "Miss" and the state they represent. Throughout the pageant activities, contestants wear a sash draped over from one shoulder to the hip with bold block lettering identifying the state they represent. Coincidentally, during the 2009–10 pageant season, when I conducted the bulk of my fieldwork, the MBGN and Queen Nigeria Pageants both crowned "Miss Plateau" as the winner in their respective national pageants. A state located in the Middle Belt region of the country on a disputed dividing line and transition zone between Nigeria's North and South, Plateau is known as the "Home of Peace and Tourism" because of its picturesque sites such as waterfalls, rock formations, and game reserves. With its ethnolinguistic heterogeneity, a large number of ethnic minorities, and a nearly equal mix of Christians and Muslims, who have lived side by side peacefully for decades, Plateau had long been considered a model of national tranquility. However, continued incidents of ethnoreligious violence since September 2001 have shattered that illusion.[14] Plateau, thus, is a fitting symbol for both contests in terms of the rich cultural diversity they want to portray and the complications they seek to obscure and heal. Though "Miss Plateau" won both pageants, the general Nigerian public takes issue with the different ways in which MBGN and Queen Nigeria think about cultural representation, ethnic diversity, and the nation. Their main contention lies with the differing processes that each competition takes for state representation. I diverge from an appeal to scrutinize contestants' backgrounds to ascertain which contest provides a more "authentic" link to the state; rather, in order to unpack the complexities of gendered national representations, I emphasize the primary orientations these contests adopt.

The Queen Nigeria Pageant organized state-level competitions in eighteen of Nigeria's thirty-six states and the federal capital territory of Abuja, the nation's capital. That year, state winners then went on to compete at the national finale in Jos, the capital of Plateau state, which was chosen in part because the previous winner (at the pageant's inaugural contest) was also Miss Plateau. I call Queen Nigeria's version of national representation *tactile* because it presumes a tangible connection to the state the contestants represent based on their cultural knowledge. Each contestant for the title of Queen Nigeria emphasized her connection to a specific state throughout the competition and her grassroots acceptance by the people in her state. They were required to demonstrate to the audience members and the judges that they had a high enough level of expertise that they could convey detailed knowledge about what made their state unique, such as tourist attractions, mineral resources, the state motto, and cultural traditions. This tactile model stressed valuing varied Nigerian customs and unifying the nation's diverse population. By showing how she was in touch with and rooted in the specific state she represented, each contestant highlighted her familiarity with her state of origin, upbringing, or residence.

Reflecting its lack of interest in geographic identity, on the other hand, MBGN did not hold state-level competitions. Instead, contestants competed through auditions in several metropolitan cities, primarily in the South. During the 2010 show, thirty finalists were selected to represent twenty-nine states and Abuja at the national finale, which was held in Lagos. The screening process for the Most Beautiful Girl in Nigeria Pageant filtered hopefuls without regard to their state of origin. MBGN's *tactical* form of cultural representation stressed acquired knowledge, strategy, and open-mindedness about cultural diversity. Adding an element that could play out in a number of ways, MBGN's winner would go on to the Miss World Pageant while the runner-up would go on to the Miss Universe Pageant; this added an additional layer of concern about cultural diversity in the context of global integration.

To spotlight the country's ethnic diversity, both pageants include what they call a "traditional" segment in their shows, which uses a standardized vocabulary to represent specific states. A freeze frame of the traditional segments of both pageants would show contestants wearing similar attire: head wraps (*gele*), coral beads, hand loomed fabric (e.g., *aso oke*), and headpieces adorned with cowrie shells (see Figure 4.3). They hold accessories like handcrafted baskets and scepters made of wood and horse tails. Contestants usually rent, borrow, or assemble this apparel, as most do not have a suitable outfit on hand.

In the Queen Nigeria Pageant, the traditional segment was the contestants' second appearance of the show, after an opening choreographed dance number to the smash hit Afrobeat gospel love song "Kokoroko," which mixed lyrics in English, pidgin English, and Urhobo ("Kokoroko" means "strong" in the language of the Urhobos, an ethnic group from Delta state, in the

FIGURE 4.3. Traditional Costume segment in the Queen Nigeria Pageant (*left*) and the MBGN Pageant (*center*), and Nigeria's National Costume segment at the Miss Universe competition (*right*). *Sources:* Author; Silverbird; Miss Universe Organization. Reprinted with permission.

southern part of the country). For the traditional section, while an instrumental Plateau song played in the background, Mr. Gold, who served as the MC, stood next to each contestant as they strode in one by one from stage left and asked "Can we meet you?" before handing over the microphone to the contestant so she could introduce herself and her state and could describe each part of her "traditional attire" to the audience and judging panel. Descriptions of their traditional wear commonly referenced purity, fertility, wealth, royalty, ethnic pride, and national unity. For example, one contestant, who was dressed in a white cloth wrapper (a garment made from a piece of fabric that is usually worn as a skirt wrapped around the hips and rolled over to secure it) tied and knotted to cover her from her chest to a few inches past her knees, and accessorized with a red-orange coral necklace, a matching coral head piece, and a coral bracelet on each wrist, explained that the outfit signified a maiden participating in a spiritual ceremony, with the white cloth signifying virtue and divinity. Another contestant, who was dressed in a green-and-yellow patterned wrapper with coral beads sewn into it as a form of appliqué, a crown made from coral beads, and four chunky necklaces of varying lengths around her neck on top of a cape made from coral beading that made it look like a lace pattern, described her outfit as representing royalty, wealth, and power.

For MBGN, the traditional segment was the contestants' first appearance on the stage. MBGN's thirty contestants, dressed in their "traditional costumes," made their way down the two long glass stairways that flanked the stage, swaying to the percussive drum beats. First the contestants from the West, then those from the East, next those from the South, and finally those from the North, performed a group dance in succession. Each contestant from her respective regional group glided up to the microphone, introduced herself and the state she was representing, and ended with a motto or greeting in a local dialect from the state, before sauntering away from the microphone.

In both these performances, every state in Nigeria retains discernable ethnic identities that neatly correspond to "traditional" clothing, accessories, music, dances, and gestures. These traditional segments are embodied ceremonial enactments of "ethnicity."[15] I understand these practices as forms of "invented tradition," not because I dispute whether they constitute genuine acts of cultural heritage but rather to acknowledge that these segments are inserted to do the broader symbolic work that signals belonging and legitimacy. These segments work within a set of conventions that are meant to convey to the audience, judges, and organizers that contestants are working with recognizable elements of Nigerian culture. They are meant to showcase pride for Nigeria's rich and diverse cultural heritage; however, the country's over 250 ethnic groups are largely collapsed into uniform parts through the common use of recurrent elements. As Hobsbawm and Ranger note, invented traditions are used to authenticate "continuity with the past" and are staged to maintain national cohesion but may be extracted from a specific context or historical circumstances.[16] In this case, states are falsely presumed to be ethnically homogenous and are reduced to certain identifiable cultural markers without adequate acknowledgment of the complex underlying identities that make up these boundaries.

MBGN also must manage national cultural representations on a global stage. Xavier, who designed some of the national costumes for MBGN during international pageants, settled on a final look by including "ethnic touches" incorporating indigenous fabrics and dramatic accessories such as raffia, wooden buttons, and bright colors. But at the same time, he was careful to choose a design that would be considered "contemporary." MBGN contestants, he reasoned, should have enough "ethnic color" to represent the nation, but not so much that they would stand out as too "ethnic" for the global stage:

It is important so that they will not look out of place, because they are going to the world stage where everybody will be present. They need to look very trendy. They [need to] represent the beauty of the ethnic color, which is significant in such an event where everybody comes in with the best of the best of her country.

He noted that it was important for contestants to not feel embarrassed by a costume that was "too traditional." Some national costumes at international contests have evoked mixed reactions from Nigerian viewers, who questioned their authenticity. For example, on the public message board Nairaland, a post debated the national costumes of African queens at the 2011 Miss Universe. The general consensus among the posters was that Miss Nigeria's outfit, which consisted of a beaded headpiece that covered her face and coral beads wrapped around her torso to form a makeshift armor, was "too edgy," overly focused on "creatively trying to outdo" the other contestants, and "confusing." One user pointed out, "Bini beads are meant to adorn the body not to be worn as an outfit (skirt and blouse)." These conversations pinpoint the additional layer of tradition and embodied performance that MBGN navigated.

As these varied performances of tradition highlight, it is an oversimplification to neatly map the distinctions between MBGN and Queen Nigeria onto a "modern" versus "traditional" set of oppositional differences. The discursive spaces that each contest occupies were always in negotiation and did not exist isolated in a social vacuum. For example, in spite of the different framings around national representation, the pageants attracted some of the same contestants. Contestants were concerned with maximizing their chances of winning and often participated in several types of beauty pageants during multiple cycles to accomplish their aim. They adapted their bodies and discursive strategies to fit the demands of specific pageants.[17] More than a third of the contestants for Queen Nigeria auditioned during the same cycle for MBGN or had auditioned in a past season, though no one participated in both contests during the year I observed them. Most of the other two-thirds said they were open to the possibility of auditioning for a future cycle of MBGN, and some had specific plans to do so. This overlap in contestants highlights the fact that these competing sets of gendered national projects should be understood, not as rigid categories that never intersect, but rather in terms of how the two projects inform each other.

Although evocations of varied state "traditions" are present in both pageants, the two frame the diverse cultures of the nation differently, in ways that fit with their differing national narratives. For example, through debates about direct versus indirect state representation, contrasting prequalifying events, emphasizing distinct sets of skills and divergent ways of managing appearance and dress, the vision of highlighting or obscuring regional differences, and the extent and nature of audience participation, these two contemporary national pageants produce complex ideas about gendered national representation. Though the organizers in particular mold competing visions to orient their discursive claims to Nigerian national identity, both pageants are produced within a broader global-African vortex.

TACTILE NATIONAL BODIES

The finale of the Queen Nigeria Pageant was held in a hotel's event hall. The stage was decorated with swaths of fabric draped from the ceiling and a white banner with the pageant's name printed in green lettering and the Queen Nigeria logo in the center (the same image as on the front of the program). In front of the stage was the judges' table, and perpendicular to that was another table for the designated elders, who would certify the results. Behind the judges' table were rows of black plastic chairs and plastic circular tables with chairs arranged around them for the live audience that would watch the show. The general public could attend the show by buying tickets at the door for ₦1,500 ($10), an affordable amount for most middle-class families and about the same cost as a movie ticket or a meal at a fast food restaurant. During the show, the MC invited audience participation by affirming that "everyone is a judge," and by asking the audience, "Who is your Queen? Has she won your hearts?" At the state-level competitions, he implored the judges to "give us a young girl that is acceptable to the state" and included a smattering of pidgin English and a language local to each state in his act. Audience members often responded with boisterous roars of approval, jeers, or yells of "I want that one!" in a call-and-response rhythm. Contestants on the stage maintained their stance, smiled, and sometimes responded with subtle body movements such as a shoulder shrug, wink, or wave. By stressing the importance of the crowd in selecting the crowned queen, organizers sought to increase the legitimacy of the contestants as state representatives. Once the semifinalists had been chosen, the MC took each one by the hand and paraded them in front of the judges, the special guests, and group of three or four male and female elders who appeared to be in their sixties and seventies. The elders, who were the final group that each contestant passed, certified the results and were thus the final say in selecting the queen. In this way, participants showed their support for the widespread cultural practice of displaying respect for the wisdom of the elderly.

Serving Up a "Touch" of Africa

A key component of the Queen Nigeria Pageant was its cooking competition. Each contestant was allotted a ₦2,000 ($15 U.S.) budget to spend on fresh ingredients for a regional dish that represented her state. Contestants were able to make use of the television network's kitchen to prepare their meals. The judging criteria included speed of preparation, cleanliness, taste, and service (i.e., presentation of the dish and interaction with the judges). The 2014 Queen Nigeria contest upped the ante by requiring contestants to cook outside on a wood stove in an area located on the outskirts of the city (see Figure 4.4). Domesticity was part of the demands of femininity in this contest. Organizers present the cooking competition as an important aspect of the pageant's authenticity.

On the day of the cooking contest, the contestants, the organizers, and I gathered outside of the hotel, preparing to head over to the market to buy the necessary ingredients for the upcoming cooking contest, which was to be held later that afternoon. As one of the organizers, Mr. Edward Richards, handed crisp naira notes to each contestant, he launched into a lecture. "We are going to be watching you closely," he began, and added, "We are going to be paying attention to how you interact with the sellers. How you bargain. How you choose your ingredients. And, when you're cooking, we will be looking at how clean you keep your station. These are things you all should know. I shouldn't even be telling you this." The implication was that the judges' expectations should be obvious: it suggested that a "true" Nigerian queen would know that the flavor and presentation of a meal were only one quality of a woman worthy of praise. Mr. Richards's words echoed the idea that there are culturally resonant practices that the contestants should connect to.

FIGURE 4.4. Queen Nigeria 2014 preparing ingredients for the cooking competition. *Source:* Courtesy of FamFord Enterprises, Nigeria. Reprinted with permission.

The contestants, organizers, and camera crew split up into two large three-row passenger vans, and we drove off to a nearby small off-road open-air market, which was next to a two-story storefront. We tumbled one by one out of the large van and walked over to the market. The contestants wandered through the market inspecting goods and haggled over prices at the different wooden stalls, some covered by faded umbrellas, which were loaded with fresh meat, peppers, tomatoes, onions, and greens stacked onto small tin plates and in burlap sacks, woven baskets, and plastic buckets. Jos, the finale location, is known for its diverse, fresh, and affordable produce since the temperate weather allows for year-round farming. Sellers—mostly women but also a few men—crouched in front of their stands on wooden stools, standing up to attend to costumers; count change; stash the cash away in their aprons, fanny packs, or wrappers; and package the goods in plastic bags for costumers to carry. Some sellers hissed and shouted in pidgin English about the freshness of their goods and their fair prices to attract the contestants' attention to their stalls. In the background was a din of honking cars, the rumbling of motorcycle engines, and the grinding noise of a motorized machine blending corn and tomatoes. All around us, other sellers walked by hawking wares balanced on their heads, transported goods in wheelbarrows, or busily arranged their belongings. The contestants' brightly colored sashes, which were imprinted with the names of their respective states, and the two-man camera crew following close behind them to capture their movements readily identified the contestants to curious onlookers. Some stared; others only glanced and continued their own shopping.

After our shopping trip, we headed back to the television network's canteen. The contestants, who had been divided into three groups so they could use the television station's kitchen in two-hour shifts, prepared a single dish to serve to the preliminary judging panel. In the kitchen, contestants chopped ingredients such as onions and greens; ground and blended tomatoes, peppers, and onions; stirred their pots on the stove; added special ingredients that they had brought from home, such as herbs, spices, and greens, to inject regional touches into their meals; and taste-tested their dishes, before serving them to the preliminary judging panel, which included Lovett (one of the organizers), Mr. Gold, and Mr. Richards. Most of the dishes were fufu-type dishes or stews. Fufu, a staple dish throughout many parts of West Africa, is a starchy porridge-type dish where ingredients, such as dried cassava, semolina, and corn flour, are mixed with hot water into a dough-like consistency to dip into stews made from bitter-leaf, okra soup, and tomatoes.

The contestants served their meals in groups of five, setting their single-serve dish with cutlery as the judges walked up to taste the dishes. Mr. Richards went up to the first dish, a black soup dish served with fufu formed into a round mound. The contestant curtsied, explained her dish as a special delicacy from Edo state made from local greens (which she had brought with her), palm oil, peppers, onions, and seasoning, and offered him a fork and knife to eat the dish. He rejected it, asking for a bowl of water instead so he could wash his hands (many Nigerian foods, which are colloquially known as "swallow," are often eaten with the hands). He preferred to eat the dish with his right hand, explaining that "he was a local man to the core." After washing his hands, he took a small scoop of the fufu, rolled it up into a ball, dipped it into the sauce, and then swallowed it. He then nodded and proceeded to the next station, sampling the rest of the meals in a similar fashion. The rest of the judges (some using cutlery) took one to two bites of each meal without further comments to the contestants. After each shift, the contestants sampled each other's leftovers and invited other members of the crew to taste their food.

When I asked Lovett about the rationale behind including a cooking competition in the beauty pageant, she answered:

> Because we are looking for an African woman. We don't just want your shape or your face or just your intelligence, we want to see you do African things; you have to cook African dishes. . . . African women put their skills to work. . . . We want you to know your culture. We'll appreciate it better. We don't have to be Westernized all through. There is a touch of Africa and there is a touch of Nigeria. It must reflect in your cooking etiquette.

An ideal Nigerian feminine trait was to be "homely," someone who was warm and enjoys keeping a clean and inviting home. When people would use this descriptor as a compliment, I was amused by the opposite American connotations of the word as someone who is unattractive. Lovett's comments contrasted "African women" against the figure of "Westernized women," which acknowledged that practices coded as Western shape the larger expectations surrounding Nigerian femininity, but by recognizing "cooking etiquette" as a set of "skills" linked to African womanhood, the pageant forged an appreciation of Nigerian culture. She expected contestants to bring these skills to the pageant, treating the ability to shop and cook as intrinsic to African women's culture. In fact, contestants received little guidance on what recipes would be appropriate and had gotten no training in basic cooking skills.

Cooking may be the most tactile form of cultural representation within the Queen Nigeria Pageant. The culinary test tapped into a general idea common in Nigerian society, that conventional markers of domesticity such as cooking Nigerian meals, childrearing, and housekeeping are standard elements of femininity. As such, the cooking competition connected contestants to a recognizable domestic element of femininity that would resonate with a broad Nigerian audience. Organizers labeled contestants who could not cook as "spoiled" or "out of touch." As Lovett lamented, "It would amaze you that some are eighteen, twenty, and they have never cooked! [The cooking test] is telling them you don't have to depend on mummy and daddy for everything or a fast food joint." In Nigeria, it is common for middle-class families with disposable income to hire live-in domestic workers to help with cooking, cleaning, and childrearing. Multinational fast food franchises like KFC, which opened in 2009, are more recent imports to the country, with homegrown fast food chains like Mr. Biggs (ironically, one of Queen Nigeria's 2009 sponsors) being more common. These fast food restaurants are viewed as signs of Westernization and middle-class convenience.

By showing off their skill in cooking local cuisines and demonstrating their ability to navigate and purchase staple ingredients at an open-air market, contestants highlighted their cultural competency and also warded off the threat of being seen as spoiled by their parents or overly dependent on Western-derived influences like fast food joints. This also served as an age marker since in this way young women displayed independence from their parents and assumed their own forms of domesticity. Along with being public figures, contestants had to mark themselves as anchored to Nigeria's cultural heritage. Thus, Queen Nigeria presented contestants as the national custodians of Nigerian cultural identity, shielding them against foreign influences.

Challenging International Beauty Standards

Like MBGN, Queen Nigeria's judges evaluated contestants' bodies based on physical appearance according to factors such as height, body size, hair style, skin color and texture, teeth, and smile. The two competitions had a fairly similar range of contestants in terms of skin color and negligible differences in body size. It is typical for pageants around the world to publicize the measurements of contestants by printing them in programs, flashing them on-screen during televised broadcasts, or having contestants announce them at the show. International body norms promote a bust-waist-hip measurement of 36-24-36 inches as ideal. The average self-reported bust-waist-hip measurement in inches was 33.6-28.1-37.8 for Queen Nigeria's 2009 contestants and 33.6-27.4-37.5 for MBGN's 2009 contestants. Both sets of organizers moved away from "traditional" African bodily preferences for voluptuous, heavier-set bodies, but did not neatly fit international standards either. Yet Queen Nigeria's organizers openly challenged "international standards," noting their Western bias and insisting that international standards should be opened up to include a wider variety of appearance ideals.

When I asked Will, Queen Nigeria's choreographer and groomer, what specific beauty traits they looked for, he seemed to express some ambivalence: "In Igboland it is someone who is large that is considered beautiful, because it shows she is well taken care of. But here it doesn't play a role. We are not looking for 'Miss Big and Bold [a real pageant that targets full-figured women].'" Organizers, he said, had to "move with the trend" within the beauty pageant industry. Mr. Gold explained that you could not simply "throw international standards away" but instead had to open up international beauty standards to include African ones, in order to reach a kind of "middle ground," noting, "Even now you have Western girls who can't fit into those standards. They are becoming bigger, with rounder backsides too, so these international standards are changing." Through such remarks, organizers for Queen Nigeria gestured toward a shifting orientation within international standards that must account for, or at least acknowledge, the presence of Nigerian body ideals.

Banning Bikinis

Organizers for Queen Nigeria spent time policing the amount of skin contestants showed in public. They inspected the hemlines and straps of contestants' attire prior to the final show to make sure they were not too revealing, and during excursions to visit public officials and sponsors, contestants were to either wear "native" attire (a colloquial term referring to African-styled clothing such as dresses made of ankara material) or to cover up with a shawl if they were wearing tight-fitting or skimpy "English dress." Ebun, a college student at a private university, took the advice of Noyo, her beauty pageant coach, and arrived at camp in short black shorts, a yellow spaghetti-strapped top, and gold gladiator sandals she had purchased for the event. Later that afternoon, she had put on a pair of black leggings underneath her shorts and had changed into a T-shirt. When I asked her why she had changed, she told me that one of the organizers had pulled her aside and chastised her for her outfit. Noyo's advice, which he gave to all his trainees, that revealing clothing would intimidate other contestants, reflected an understanding of Nigerian beauty pageants in general but ignorance about Queen Nigeria specifically. Queen Nigeria's organizers sought to gain public support from people throughout the country by requiring contestants to dress modestly.

In recalling the on-stage explanations of their traditional outfits, I noted a set of contradictions between the degree to which these costumes were inspected before the show to ensure that they were not too skimpy and potentially offensive to viewers and sponsors, and the sexually suggestive reading of some of these descriptions, which signaled fertility, marriageability, and beauty. A few minutes before the show was about to start, Will led a group prayer backstage for which the contestants held hands and huddled together in a circle around him. He then gave a quick preshow pep talk, instructing contestants that "someone must fall in love with you tonight. Your dowry money must be increasing!" Presenting marriageability as a central aim for the contestants, in which their participation would command an increased dowry (the "bride price" that the groom and his family pay to the bride's family), referenced a cultural practice that varies across Nigeria and other parts of Africa.[18] It also positions the contest as a type of "coming of age" ceremony,[19] in which heteronormative and feminine ideals converge, mirroring some specific rituals in Nigeria that announce marriageability by having young women parade in public.[20]

Organizers specifically branded Queen Nigeria as a no-bikini show. They commonly referred to bikinis as underwear (bra and panties), calling them un-African and representative of a major roadblock in the effort of pageants to gain greater acceptance throughout the country. Organizers told me that they hoped to attract young women who, due to religious concerns about modesty, might not normally enter a beauty competition. The concerns over modesty cut across religious lines in the sense that pageant affiliates consistently raised it as a concern for both devout Christians and Muslims and highlighted cultural values that united Nigerians irrespective of their faith. However, there was typically a set of assumptions in which pageant participants considered Muslims, and Northern Muslims especially, to be the most hesitant about taking part in pageants. For example, when Lovett described Queen Nigeria's vision of including all the states in the finale (at the time, only eighteen out of the thirty-six states and the federal capital territory were represented), she explained that to fulfill their vision, they might have to recruit contestants who currently lived in other parts of Nigeria but could trace their lineage to specific states in the North. This in part stems from the degree to which perceptions of, and practices surrounding, Islam rely heavily on public piety and pious subjectivities that centralize women's bodies.[21]

Most pageant participants viewed Muslims as automatically opposed to pageants since they associated their religion with being pious, modest, and conservative in ways that coded women's bodies as always covered, hidden, and not on display. Many understood the positioning of women's bodies in Islam as entirely contradictory with the aims of pageantry, which stages women's bodies for a broad public to project communal ideals. Moreover, they reasoned, while modesty is important to Christianity, in Islam it is considered by some to be a mandatory component of the religion. I was often told that Muslims would *never* participate in any type of beauty pageant. Though Christian contestants dominated Nigerian pageants, there were assumptions of a fervently vocal segment of Christians who were also harshly critical of beauty competitions. There was a recognition that among those that shared the Christian faith, there was enough ideological wiggle room to allow some contestants to rationalize their participation, as Faith did to her pastor father. However, Christians were seen as also potentially critical of the industry, especially over its inclusion of bikinis.

Pageant organizers aimed to assuage anxieties from conservative parents and guarded against wary politicians, who did not always want to openly be associated with pageants, and cautious corporate sponsors, who feared blowback from a critical general public about bodily display in pageantry. Raul, an organizer of a state-level pageant for Queen Nigeria, explained:

> Especially in Africa, we believe that nudity is wrong, women should not be exposing their body; they [Queen Nigeria] didn't want to celebrate nudity and especially as a national brand. It's family TV, where the young, the old, and children would be able to watch. . . . We want to celebrate our culture, without celebrating bikini.

Raul insisted that as a national brand seeking to attract a broad audience, Queen Nigeria could not be seen as supporting "nudity." In contrast, Will observed that an international audience would not have to navigate these issues:

> Not all mothers can allow their daughters to go on in a bikini. And if you watch pageants here, you will see that those bikini segments, they don't air it. The norms and values here are different. There are some things that we don't appreciate. It might be abusive to viewers. If it's international TV, it's something that is not new. It's not a big deal.

Raul and Will's comments indicate that they saw the pageant's audience as national, rather than international. Will's point that Nigerian television does not air bikini portions of pageants is not entirely accurate, as evidenced by MBGN's own bikini segment, which is aired on their network. Will's statements, however, do speak to general media controversies concerning sexuality. While sex scenes are common in Nigerian media, the actors are typically not nude. Movies, music videos, and music lyrics with sexually explicit content risk censorship and fines by the regulatory agencies.[22] During the primetime television hours of 7–10 P.M., broadcast television networks must abide by what's called the "family belt" period, during which foreign content, overt sexual behavior, and offensive language is banned. Moreover, "naked" and "nude" are not equivalent terms, since the meanings attached to nudity also include ideas about "indecent" dressing, such as skimpy clothes.[23] By banning bikinis and remaining attuned to regional, religious, and cultural concerns over bodily display, Queen Nigeria sought to present itself as a legitimate arbiter of Nigerian culture. It advanced an inclusive stance that recognized locally based differences as a means to unify the country and establish a successful African-centered national brand.

Regional Spotlighting

Over the course of the state-level competitions and during the preshow rehearsals for Queen Nigeria's national finale, contestants routinely answered questions about the best assets that their states had to offer, including tourist sites, natural resources, and the names of political leaders. Queen Nigeria's judges and organizers expected contestants to display an easy familiarity with a comprehensive body of knowledge about their state. In answering detailed questions about the symbolism of their traditional outfits, the ethnolinguistic makeup of their state, and how their platforms directly affect people in their state, Queen Nigeria contestants presented themselves as if they had an automatic, habitual, and almost innate connection to the state they represented. Participants believed that being rooted in a specific community granted them more genuine access to the grass roots, and allowed them to have a more authentic voice on the national scene.

Each contestant in the Queen Nigeria pageant had to demonstrate a cultural tie to the particular state she represented. The state-tiered organizational scheme was used in part to emphasize a "genuine" connection to the state at the national events. Organizers demonstrated that contestants were plugged into the Nigerian Television Authority stations in their state through their participation in the competition. The first ladies of the contestants' states or a representative often crowned them at the state-level competitions and sometimes provided winners with scholarship funds and logistical support for their charity work through the state governments. These measures served to legitimize the contestants bearing the states' names as rightful representatives. Mr. Gold referenced the importance of geographic identity as their "selling point":

> Participants at our national events are Queens who come from various states of the federation with the active participation of people and the government in those states, [who] could identify that a girl is truly from that state. They would want to come because they were part of the process which produced her.

Mr. Gold emphasized that choosing queens at the state level prior to a national finale, with government representatives verifying each contestant's claimed tie to a particular state, enhanced contestants' connections to the culture of the states they represent. Also, by highlighting the need to "sensitize communities" and solicit "active participation" as part of the pageant's goals, Queen Nigeria established the understanding that the beauty queens remained in touch with everyday Nigerians at home.

The traditional costume segment expressed both state identity and national identity. At the state-level competitions, some contestants wore traditional clothes that were meant to symbolize the nation as a whole, for example, by wearing green and white, the national colors of Nigeria. Most wore an outfit associated with a specific ethnic group that was prevalent in their state. Some mixed state costuming with national symbols. These eclectic mixes helped to buttress Queen Nigeria's maxim of unity in diversity. Contestants described their attire as part of their commitment to their country and community. Prior to the show, organizers asked pointed questions about how they had selected their costumes by barking out questions such as, "Who wears this?" "When do they wear this?" "Why do they wear this?" Such detailed questions required a proper justification for the contestants' sartorial choices and sought to authenticate the participants' cultural knowledge. One contestant, Deola Ogunyemi, spoke about the importance of integrating traditional attire into pageants and made a direct comparison between Queen Nigeria and MBGN:

> You get to know who you are and what you represent and the state you represent and the home town you come from. That attire is your tradition and you have to fix yourself into it to be Queen Nigeria. . . . You have to know the origin of the attire that you are wearing. In Queen Nigeria pageant, you don't have to start going anywhere. You represent where you've come from.

The Queen Nigeria contestants emphasized that they had an easy time representing their states because talking to community and family members told them everything they needed to know. Deola pointed out that, in contrast, an MBGN contestant might have to travel to another state to learn enough about the culture to properly represent it.

When I asked Lovett to explain the difference between Queen Nigeria and other beauty pageants in Nigeria, she emphasized contestants' "authentic" representation, which was anchored in their cultural knowledge of a particular state:

> It's different in the sense that actual state queens are created and when we say actual state queens, [I mean] you have the right to contest [compete] if you have full knowledge of the state. . . . We have to make sure you understand their values 'cause it's all about Nigeria. It's a kind of cultural integration program like the NYSC [National Youth Service Corps], bringing people from this state sending them to that state. . . . You have to know what you are doing. Even if you are sleeping, we can wake you up to tell us something [about your state]. You have to know the nitty-gritty of a state.

Lovett's insistence that a contestant should be familiar with the "nitty-gritty" of the state she represents and should be ready to communicate this knowledge at any time of the day or night highlights the cultural fluency and agility that organizers expected from the contestants. The invoking of the NYSC, a mandatory year-long national program that stations college-educated youth in service programs all over the country, suggests the Queen Nigeria Pageant wishes to promote national unity above all. The NYSC purposely posts participants to parts of the country outside of their states of origin with the aim that they will learn about ethnic and cultural backgrounds different from their own. Lovett's points also conveyed that contestants were supposed to share and learn from each other. Queen Nigeria's vision of national unity sought to bring together the country's diverse parts in order to strengthen the country as a whole. Moreover, she emphasized that this cultural fluency was not necessarily tied to ethnic heritage (e.g., as an indigene) but could be attained through residence and the desire to make a contribution to local communities at the state level.

Organizers of the Queen Nigeria contest often struggled with the question of how to translate a cultural import of Western origin into the Nigerian context. They inserted Nigerian cultural references throughout the casual wear, traditional wear, and evening gown segments. During the finale, Mr. Gold continually stressed the need to "start appreciating our own." The choice of a Plateau regional song for the dance number recognized the state government's

FIGURE 4.5. Queen Nigeria contestants performing their opening dance number dressed in adire. *Source:* Photo by author.

role as an official sponsor. The contestants wore green and pale yellow tie-dyed [*adire*] material sewn into scoop-neck tank shirts and capri-length pants (see Figure 4.5). This type of regional spotlighting was appropriate for Queen Nigeria because it served to promote the federation model of the nation, in which the national union and the self-governing states are considered to be mutually reinforcing rather than incompatible.

The Queen Nigeria officials sought to incorporate the North, even as they understood that it would be difficult. Lovett explained that Northerners were especially resistant to pageants because of cultural sensitivity over bodily display, but a possible workaround would be recruiting contestants who could trace their origins to states in the North but lived elsewhere in the country. She clarified the difficulty in getting contestants from the North:

They are religiously conscious people. Their religion is their culture. They don't believe in pageants. Like I said, they feel they are not supposed to expose any part of their body . . . [and] they weren't convinced that [Queen Nigeria] was going to be different. When they hear the [word] pageant, they think it's something exposing. They can disown their daughters for contesting.

Lovett stressed that Queen Nigeria was a different kind of pageant, which sought to accommodate those who normally would not enter a contest because of cultural concerns.

Aisha Haruna, a Muslim who had attended college in Southeast Asia, was one such contestant. Will asked her to lead a prayer to officially kick off the camp program, stating that he started each day of camp with a prayer to help the contestants focus and give thanks to God. Aisha declined, simply stating that she was Muslim. A moment of awkward silence briefly hung in the air. The other contestants and Will were visibly surprised by Aisha's declaration that she was Muslim. Will did not encourage her to lead the prayer anyway and instead solemnly nodded his head. A few of the other contestants appeared puzzled and taken aback by her response, as judged by their raised eyebrows and quizzical expressions.

Some of the contestants were surprised because of the common perception that Muslims do not typically participate in pageants. They had preconceived ideas about how Muslims, and especially Northern Muslims, look and act. For example, the previous evening before camp officially kicked off, some of the contestants and I were walking over to a restaurant to grab dinner. I overheard a few of them talking about how this was their first time in the North (for some contestants this was the furthest North they had ever been, though Plateau is not really considered to be part of Northern Nigeria by some). They had been warned to avoid wearing trousers and that they were likely to encounter many women who were "covered head to toe." Aisha's flamboyant personality, hair weaves, and trendy outfits did not fit the mold of their perceptions. Her curt reply implied that she could not conduct the prayer because of the assumption that the remaining contestants were Christians and that she would not pray in the manner that they would recognize. Another contestant offered a prayer for the contestants and organizers "in

Jesus's name" and began leading the others in Christian praise songs and Christmas carols in anticipation of the holiday, which was just days away. I should point out that Queen Nigeria is ostensibly open to anyone regardless of their religious background. While the pageant has remained open to including religious diversity by stating the need to target contestants from varied ethnoreligious backgrounds, by failing to encourage multifaith prayer experiences, the pageant's affiliates positioned Christianity as the default and Islam as out of place.

TACTICAL NATIONAL BODIES

At the entrance of the MBGN finale, attendees stepped onto the red carpet, posing for photographers in front of the multiple step and repeat vinyl backdrops, which featured the names of the companies under the Silverbird imprint and MBGN's corporate sponsors. Celebrities dressed in long evening gowns, cocktail dresses, and tailored suits were stopped by entertainment reporters, microphones in hand, asking them what they were wearing and what they were looking forward to at the show, and for updates on any current projects. Inside, the recently renovated banquet hall had a newly engineered sound system and stage, as well as state-of-the-art lighting equipment. The seating arrangements were divided into three sections. The VVIP table sections were located in the center at the front of the room, directly behind the judge's table, the VIP tables were on the sides of the room and behind the VVIP section, and rows of chairs were set up behind the tables for regular admission. The VIP tables were decorated with black tablecloths and had red and gold upholstered chairs surrounding them. Soda bottles from one of the corporate sponsors of the event, small chop appetizers, and flutes, which bottle service servers milling around the room carrying gold sparklers attached to Moët bottles filled with champagne upon request, covered the tables.

MBGN tickets cost far more than Queen Nigeria tickets. Attendees had to purchase them up front and paid between ₦5,000 ($33) and ₦50,000 ($300) apiece, depending on the VIP status. MBGN organizers expressed their desire to put on a dynamic show for the live audience, the national television fans, and international viewers at subsequent competitions outside of Nigeria. Whereas Queen Nigeria made a show of involving the local audience in the decisions at the state level, fans could participate in MBGN by voting via text message for their favorite contestants. The contestants who won the viewers' vote would automatically get a spot among the top fifteen semifinalists. The organizers, however, said that they viewed this mostly as publicity hype to get the audience invested in the show. The decision making was placed in the hands of a carefully selected group of judges whose credentials in the business, entertainment, and political worlds could bolster the goals of the pageant. That year the judging panel, half of whom were expatriates, included business executives, former beauty queens, the owner of a performing arts organization, and a high-level civil servant who worked for the state government (who ended up dropping out at the last minute).

Modeling the Self-Confident Nation

The skills the contestants must display for the modeling segment of the Most Beautiful Girl in Nigeria pageant reflected the organizers' vision of an international audience. During the show, one contestant would be crowned the "Face of Select Pro," serving as an endorsement ambassador for one of the sponsors of the event, Select Pro Cosmetics, a makeup and styling line. At the finale, contestants posed and strutted in shiny black minidresses made from trash bags, with a techno beat soundtrack (see Figure 4.6). The host's banter praised their style, attitude, and presence. This eight-minute onstage segment took hours of behind-the-scenes work. Gina, the African American producer flown in each year to drill the contestants on poise, etiquette, catwalking, and posture, spent most of the rehearsal periods teaching the choreography needed for the modeling sequence as a Lady Gaga track pulsed in the background. By using imported experts from the United States and South Africa, in addition to elements of global culture, MBGN's organizers intended to secure cosmopolitan prestige. During an interview, Gina emphasized the focus on modeling in many international pageants. She said she had to train contestants not only in the mechanics of walking, posing, and grooming but also in gaining self-confidence and professionalism, qualities needed to be successful in the field. When I asked her to describe her ideal candidate, Gina responded forcefully: "Someone really competitive. It's a game they play, and it's about learning to play that game and playing it well."

FIGURE 4.6. A contestant at the MBGN Model Competition. *Source:* Akintunde Akinleye/Reuters Pictures.

Learning to "play the game" of self-confidence was a theme woven into MBGN's ten-day camp. The first night, the panel of organizers and groomers sat in a row of chairs facing the thirty contestants. Following introductions and the national director's opening remarks, Gina stood up. "I only have one question: which one of you is my queen?" she said. Five hands shot up immediately. A few more followed, tentatively halfway up in the air. Gina commented,

> A lot of you seem unsure. We have to work on that. Part of this process is about having confidence. You have to be sure that all of you can say you can be a queen. I'm going to work on instilling that confidence. If you don't want to win, you might as well go home now. I want you all reaching for that crown!

She ended her pep talk with, "Again I want to ask, who's my queen?" This time everyone's hands shot up. Through such tactics, Gina continually instructed contestants in the rules of the game.

The skills MBGN contestants were supposed to acquire—especially those promoting self-confidence, professionalism, and competitiveness—were meant to be used off as well as on the stage. But unlike Queen Nigeria, they did not include cooking. One lunchtime discussion revolved around the perception that African contestants operate at a disadvantage in international contests like Miss World or Miss Universe because they lack self-confidence.

Eliza Meyer, a South African production specialist, pointed out, "African girls are so soft. They are trained to be quiet and obedient."

"Oh, but you know those Latin girls! Watch out. They are so aggressive!" Emeka, a reporter for Silverbird Television, interjected.

"They have to be trained to be firm. They can be a lady on the catwalk, but firm off of it," Eliza concluded.

Emeka and Eliza's exchange comparing Nigerian women to Latin American women—who are statistically likely to win international beauty competitions—highlights the specific transnational poles of feminized gendered ideals that contestants were expected to navigate. Eliza's point of view that they could train contestants to be "firm" was typical of MBGN organizers. They directly engaged in "grooming" contestants, using experts like Gina to seek a competitive edge for MBGN in the international competitions that would follow. They envisioned assertiveness (e.g., firmness) and self-confidence as signals of cosmopolitanism.

Strategizing Within International Standards

Like the contestants in Queen Nigeria, MBGN's contestants used their bodies to signal the gendered form of nationalism expected from their respective contests. Unlike Queen Nigeria's organizers, however, the MBGN organizers did not question international beauty standards. Gina openly described her role as pushing standards toward thinner and taller contestants, in line with international criteria, and opined that it had led to the 2001 crowning of Miss Nigeria as Miss World, a triumph that she took credit for. Similarly, the organizers warned the judges before auditions with instructions such as, "We don't want any big-leg girls. If you have any of those local guys pick the contestants, they will just be looking for girlfriends. We don't want that, so watch out for that." These comments suggest a distinction between local standards of desirability and the quest for a candidate who would fit internationally defined notions of attractiveness.

MBGN in fact sought women conforming to two different sets of standards, both internationally set and correlating with Miss World and

Miss Universe. Organizers noted that Miss World is considered to be more popular in places like Asia, Africa, and Europe since it is a British-owned pageant, while the American-based pageant, Miss Universe, with its "confidentially beautiful" motto, is more popular in North and South America. They described Miss Universe contestants as "model-types"—tall, slim, and dark. They pointed to the influence of the modeling industry on the pageant, which the mogul turned American president Donald Trump once owned. According to organizers, dark skin was an asset for African contestants in Miss Universe as it evokes glamour and makes them stand out as commercially viable. In contrast, organizers said that they looked for a "girl-next-door" type to send to the Miss World Pageant, which is a British pageant organized and privately owned by the Morley family. To appeal to Miss World's "beauty with a purpose" tagline and emphasis on raising money through charity functions, organizers and judges focused on picking a fresh-faced, innocent-looking, wholesome candidate with mass appeal.[24] These candidates tended to be more shapely, shorter, and lighter-skinned than candidates for Miss Universe. Mr. Tim described the difference in the following way:

> Well for Miss World, it is a family-owned organization. They are looking for a likeable personality in a woman—someone they would consider a daughter. A nice person, sweet and lovable person who can achieve goals. For Miss Universe, I see them looking for an exotic model who can model for Gucci and the rest, you know, a high-flying person.

As these comments reflect, even the tall, skinny bodies that are integrated into international standards are in need of racialized difference through their skin tone. The choices the judges at MBGN make highlight their tactical approach: they judge according to a perceived strategy.

Beyond highlighting the social dimensions of skin color by both marketing light skin as a marker of global "mass appeal" and capitalizing on dark skin as a form of desired "exotic beauty," MBGN manages beauty ideals through a global cultural economy, demonstrating flexibility in striving for international legitimacy. These ideals are strategized within international standards to simultaneously signal belonging and to stand out. While preferences for lighter-skinned candidates for Miss World fit within the commonly accepted paradigm of outside global influences that perpetuate Western-dominated ideals of beauty, a few contestants disagreed with this interpretation. Lota, for example, who herself is light skinned, claimed that during her experience competing at Miss World, there was an expectation that contestants from African countries should all have dark skin, and she felt she was at a disadvantage. She discussed how, among the other African countries present, most also were light skinned, which left observers confused about their origins. The discussion of race and beauty through an international lens brings to light complex interactions between domestic intentions and global expectations.

Pageant participants such as Mr. Abe viewed Africa as the next frontier for beauty. He explained:

> If you are looking at [international] pageants today, Americans never win . . . . I will tell you why: because Americans are so programmed from birth, they are so mechanical that there is no natural beauty in an American woman today. Now the world is looking for natural beauty and guess what the future is? Africa . . . African beauty is becoming exciting. All of a sudden, we are becoming the future and we could win every year, but we've got to stay focused.

Like several others, Mr. Abe claimed that women in Western countries like the United States were plastic-looking, unnaturally thin, and plain. In contrast, African beauty was raw, natural, and striking. Beauty contestants viewed women from countries in the Global South such as Venezuela as their main rivals, not women from the United States or England. Even in the Miss World Pageant, they felt that darker skin gave Nigerian beauty contestants an edge over White women—if not necessarily over Latinas.

Bikini Barbie Turns

Whereas Queen Nigeria drew a firm line against including bikinis in its show and actively policed bodily displays, MBGN included a bikini segment (see Figure 4.7) and contestants often wore short, tight cocktail dresses to attend dinner parties, meet-and-greets, and press functions. Early in auditions, the women had to introduce themselves to the screeners while wearing bikinis and five-inch heels, making "Barbie turns" (slow, 360-degree spins)

FIGURE 4.7. Contestants strike a pose in the MBGN 2008 bikini segment. *Source:* Sunday Alamba/AP Photos.

so that screeners could inspect their bodies. Calvin, the White South African producer, explained to me:

> We have to have them in bikinis to look for scars. Some of them have such bad scars from accidents, or really bad belly buttons, or those big tribal markings and we have to see all of that. We need to eliminate anyone with really bad scars or else they could get disqualified at Miss World or Miss Universe.

Uneven skin texture, poorly proportioned bodies, cellulite, stretch marks, protruding navels, and scars all justified elimination. The screeners openly discussed and debated these elements. Markings on the body, either in the form of "tribal markings" or scars, served to indicate specific ethnic traits or membership in a community with low socioeconomic status, and were thus seen as inconsistent with the cosmopolitan femininity meant to signal Nigeria's international prestige.

Rejecting scars was in part a means of distancing the pageant from the scarification that represents an old Nigerian tradition and is associated with outdated cultural beliefs of uneducated people from rural areas. Many ethnic groups in Nigeria have long made different patterned incision cuts, piercing the skin with sharp instruments to form a scar on various body parts (including the face) for a wide variety of purposes including medicinal healing, spiritual protection, ethnic identity, and beauty, but it is a practice that is typically associated with the Yoruba ethnic group. This cultural practice, which used to be more or less obligatory two generations ago, has faced mounting calls to be outlawed by the government and has declined in practice since the late 1990s. However, its association with backwardness remains.

Bad scars were also linked to class status and national modernity. Calvin signaled this awareness when he leaned in to point out a faint pink line that extended across his neck. He said, "This scar is from a car accident that split my neck open. But you can barely see it. If the surgery were done here [in Nigeria, rather than in South Africa], the scar would be all jagged. There is no way they could have done it here." Some bodily alteration, however, was completely acceptable and even desirable for a few contestants. Blessing Osagie, a former beauty queen, described how Nigeria's lack of access to plastic surgery potentially put contestants at a disadvantage at international pageants, noting:

> [Miss] Puerto Rico actually got free plastic surgery as one of her prizes. When you win it, you get anything on your face or body. They don't hide it over there. For the first time in my life, I saw silicone boobs, I never knew there were injections for pushing out your booty, there were nose jobs everywhere, tummy tucks everywhere.

Blessing's comments suggest that an unblemished body reflects modernity; by betraying a lack of access to good surgery or the resources to travel abroad for medical care, prominent scars would suggest that Nigerians were backward.

Calvin's remarks that bikinis were necessary suggest why MBGN organizers included them, even though they recognized that they alienated some Nigerians, who were uncomfortable with such levels of bodily exposure. "What is a beauty pageant without a swimsuit section?" they asked. Some said defensively, "When you go to the beach what do you wear? A bathing suit." My own observations visiting Nigerian public beaches at least a dozen times in the past decade reveal that beachgoers rarely wear bikinis, though this is changing gradually. Women wear T-shirts, shorts, jeans, tank tops, and cover-ups. Bikinis are more common at private beaches and exclusive swimming pools. Through rationalizations such as that offered by Calvin, MBGN signaled the importance of the international audience over a national one.

National Balancing

Contestants for the Most Beautiful Girl in Nigeria were assigned to represent states with no regard for their place of residence or knowledge of the particular region. Organizers positioned the contestants' obligation to learn about areas of the country that they might never have visited as a way of valuing Nigeria's diversity. Should a contestant go on to an international beauty contest, she would bring the knowledge she had learned about a state in Nigeria with her. Thus, contestants established themselves as national cosmopolitans by transcending provincial understandings of cultural representation.

MBGN organizers justified the audition system as a means of securing participation of the most qualified contestants.[25] Reflecting the location of the auditions, most of the contestants were from the South. At the end of the Lagos audition, after all the finalists were selected, Octavia, the pageant coordinator, gathered the finalists around her and asked some of them where they were from. She then began the process of assigning them to states. One of the contestants requested to represent Rivers state, which was her home, but Octavia dismissively replied that it did not matter. When the same contestant insisted that she did not know anything about the state to which she had been assigned, Octavia instructed, "Just browse [online] and do some research on the basics. It doesn't really matter, just do your best." It seemed to me that expressions of distaste often followed assignment to states in the North. When Lagos was assigned to one contestant, others told her that she would have to work hard because people expect a lot from Lagos. Octavia soothed some of the sulking contestants, urging them to smile, and insisted that the states they represented had no bearing on their ultimate chances of winning the pageant.

When I asked one contestant, Kamdi, to express her own thoughts about the state assignment process, she explained nonchalantly, shrugging her shoulders, that it was just a form of "balloting" (drawing straws), and that no one received any special treatment. She said she was just "lucky" Octavia had assigned her to a prominent state. I asked why she was pleased, and she replied:

> I just thought it was good. You know I felt that some states could bring you to the limelight without you struggling to do that, places like Lagos, Abuja, Rivers, and [Cross River]. If you find yourself representing those states, people will want to see who is representing and then if you are good enough, fine [pretty], and if you represent that place well enough, it will be easier for you to shine. I just felt good about the state that was chosen and for me it was a good sign.

Kamdi felt that judges would scrutinize contestants assigned to states with major cities, and that her assignment conferred an advantage because of that. In short, contestants viewed the state assignment process through a strategic, rather than a cultural lens, unlike Queen Nigeria contestants. Kamdi admitted that she would have preferred to represent her own native state, because she "pretty much knows all about it," but she said that she appreciated MBGN's system. Belying Octavia's statement that a cursory Internet search would do, she said:

> Having us tagged by the states of this country is important because it's a national pageant. I'm not from there but I had to wear the costume, I had to research on that thing. You know it teaches us something and gets you to appreciate it in a very interesting way. You don't just want to come out looking like a normal Muslim lady; you will want to add flavor to it to make it beautiful. It makes you appreciate another state and with that I think it helps you see the beauty of Nigerian culture.

MBGN awarded prizes for the best traditional costume, and contestants also saw the selection of traditional attire as a creative process in which they stood out as well as represented their states. Other contestants agreed, sharing similar sentiments like that of Oluchi Mbanefo, who described the process as more "open-ended than it is imposing. It doesn't make you sit in the bus of your hometown. It makes you get exposed to other traditions. It adds to your library of things you know." Blessing noted that "if you are a good Nigerian, you should be able to represent any state. I don't think that should be a big deal." These contestants observed that MBGN's selection process, which did not emphasize local recruitment, was forcing them to move beyond their insularity and loosen their provincial attachments. They described themselves as eager to learn about unfamiliar cultures. This allowed them to buttress their claims to be cosmopolitan not just outside the country, but within the country as well. They insisted that the randomized method was logical because you often had multiple contestants from the same state and all states had to be represented in a national pageant since it would be considered biased otherwise.

Contestants sometimes hurriedly learned basic facts about their states during rehearsals while getting quick language lessons to incorporate into their greetings or practicing movements that would best showcase their assigned region. As they were preparing for the opening dance sequence, a couple of contestants asked to use my Internet-enabled smartphone to help them look up the slogans of their states and the ethnic groups that lived there. On the first day of MBGN rehearsals, one of the contestants seemed to forget the state that she was representing; she failed to respond to it. "Get used to being called by your state," Octavia admonished. "Everyone, look down at your sash. This is your new name. We do not know your names; we only know you by the state you're representing." Women at Queen Nigeria never seemed to forget their state, which is unsurprising given that they were each assigned to the state where they had been crowned. The organizers of the Queen Nigeria Pageant probably would describe this self-education process, just days before the show, as a signal of MBGN's inauthenticity.

While the MBGN contestants said that the random assignment of contestants to states was reasonable, the practice was a source of continuing controversy among the public. Apart from the random and inauthentic-seeming aspect of the assignment, the practice broke with specific tradition. Nigerians traditionally determine ethnic group affiliation through patrilocal lineage. Thus, the practice flouted traditional perceptions of intersections between ethnic identification and state or regional divisions. One audience member reported that during the MBGN show some audience members yelled, "How can an Igbo girl represent Kogi state! It's not right!" This skepticism did not stem primarily from stereotyped distinctions based on physical appearance, but rather from ideas about cultural familiarity and heritage. Right before the start of the final debriefing meeting for the contest, the national director, Mr. Tim, queried, "So how many Igbos did we have this year?" Octavia responded, "I think at least three-quarters of them were Igbo." Scanning the roster of contestant names to confirm Octavia's estimate, he exclaimed, "Almost all Igbos!" "That's the problem, it's mostly Igbos," Mr. Tim reasoned. Because the contestants are usually dominated by Igbos, they have represented states where Igbos are not indigenes of those areas.

In Nigeria, indigenes are understood as those who can trace their heritage back to ethnic groups who originally inhabited and settled in any given community. Those from other ethnic groups are seen as non-indigenes or settlers. Indigene/settler divisions are hotly contested because they are tied to conflicts over resources like land access, career opportunities, and political rights. For example, constitutional mandates stipulate that university slots, civil service jobs, and army enlisting are tied to state quotas where only indigenes qualify. In describing this "federal character" model of Nigeria's political system, political scientist Mahmood Mamdani shows that this arrangement results in rigidly matching specific ethnic groups with certain states. He advocates for a focus on "common residence over common descent—indigeneity—as the basis of rights."[26] A 2009 NOI-Gallup Poll reported that 67 percent of Nigerians supported the idea that settlers and indigenes should have the same political benefits, providing some evidence about shifting opinions about the significance of indigeneity.[27]

Queen Nigeria disrupted traditional notions of state membership by including birth, residence, *and* grassroots recognition as being equally acceptable forms of proving state allegiance and cultural representation as paternal ethnic heritage (i.e., indigeneity). However, critics view MBGN's flouting of tradition as more blatant and obvious, as so few of the contestants would qualify for state allegiance even based on more flexible conventions like those from Queen Nigeria. Queen Nigeria's redefinition of regional and state membership as transcending ethnic ties aligns with shifting understandings of cultural and political belonging, whereas MBGN's does not. This debate nonetheless triggers a tension between federalism and indigeneity that is key to the conflicts between ethnicity, nation, and identity within the country.

MBGN's organizers were well aware of the criticism that contestants were not ethnically diverse enough to represent all the states. But they resigned themselves by lamenting that would-be contestants from the North rarely bothered to audition so it was difficult to find representatives from Northern states to participate in the pageant. I also commonly heard the belief that people from the North were the most beautiful, but that they would not "come out to take part." Reflecting on the disproportionate number of Igbo contestants, Mr. Tim lamented, "Northerners just don't come out [to enter the contest] . . . even though they are the most beautiful." He then turned to me and said, "You know people from the North are the most beautiful, right?" When I asked him to explain why, he explained that women from the North have arresting features with excellent bone structure, a tall stature, and a bright complexion. I often heard the explanation that the "most beautiful don't come out to audition" because of specific assumptions about class and ethnicity. While I was working in Silverbird's main offices, one of the clients who rented office space in their building remarked, "They have to be very careful! Silverbird is looking for trouble if they think they can continue this process of just assigning girls to any state. One of those northern states just might sue them." When I asked him what he thought might be a suitable solution to their predicament, he replied that they needed to just go to that area and recruit people.

I realized the extent of MBGN's complicated relationship with the North one evening when I was helping the chaperones sort through a bag of sashes that had just been delivered from the seamstress. I helped Ada and Jenifer, the chaperones, go through the sashes one by one before they distributed them. In addition to setting aside sashes with misspellings to go back to the seamstress, Ada tossed aside the four sashes for Sokoto, Kebbi, Kano, and Kaduna. "Those are sharia states," she explained, saying that MBGN had never assigned contestants to them. The seamstress had gotten the order mixed up.

When I asked Mr. Tim the rationale for not including all the states, he sighed heavily and replied, "I would love to. [But] I am wary of religious issues. Some states don't favor pageants. Because of that I shy away from states that are anti-pageant, because they have sharia law. Imagine if a girl won the pageant and she was from one of those sharia states. How would you handle the homecoming, for example?" He later admitted that he was thinking about doing away with the policy and having all thirty-six states plus the federal capital territory represented in the pageant. He explained his likely change of heart, noting, "I think it's unfair. Not everyone in that state might feel that same way. It's a national show. It's not just the states that I like [laughs]. Although we might have dabbled into them [sharia states] in the past without knowing it, we try to avoid it. But, it's beyond sharia. Now, it's about the nation. Next year I will probably do all thirty-six." The following year the pageant did increase the number of contestants from thirty to thirty-four, leaving out three Northern states, but including Jigawa, Kaduna, Kano, and Katsina states. By 2015, all states were represented. Mr. Tim's fear of large-scale reprisals from the Northern sharia states have yet to materialize. This is likely because by hosting the contest in the South, MBGN flies under the radar. While their assignment process is still viewed as controversial, this geographic containment means that the motivations for staging organized backlash do not register.

While Queen Nigeria selected a regional Plateau song for the traditional number which included all contestants in homage to the host state, MBGN worked hard to ensure that the dance number was regionally diverse. Ngozi Elendu, the assistant choreographer, instructed the contestants to separate into groups, clustering states into specific regions. She taught some traditional dance movements to each group separately, asked them to put their own spin on them, and worked with them on the final product. In the course of preparing for the contestants' introductions, Ngozi told the contestants: "Look, this is carnival. This is traditional. This is Africa! Bring that joy from the carnival into your introduction. Don't try to be cool." She struck a stereotypical beauty pageant pose—right hand on her hip, tossing her hair with her other hand, and cocking her head to the side. "You can do that in the evening [gown] section." The traditional segment was a time for them to let their hair down, to be loud and boisterous. These were clichéd expectations of a type of physical embodiment meant to portray "authentic" cultural imagery to the audience. Each girl introduced herself by state, naming the state motto, usually followed with a greeting in one of the state's native tongues.

The regions were the South, East, West, and North. The North was the largest group, with eleven contestants. This group of eleven contestants representing the North appeared to be an undifferentiated group, suggesting that the North has a monolithic, unified culture, in contrast to the South, whose representatives were separated into culturally distinct subregions. This representation of the North, like the exclusion of states that have sharia law, highlights a discomfort with the region that was evident during the dance number.

Later on, in MBGN pageant rehearsals with a traditional dance troupe and live drummers, someone pointed out that they were only incorporating one ethnic group (Yoruba) into their dances and that the regional dances did not match up to the regional parts of the contestants' introductions. When I asked Emeka why they were concerned about it, she replied, "It's a national pageant, [so] you need to be PC [politically correct]," alluding to the idea that MBGN had to achieve regional representativeness in a balanced manner. Ngozi, the choreographer noted, "[Originally] they end up with a Yoruba number, so that can't work, [as] you are indirectly saying Yorubas rule Nigeria. You [need to] represent everybody and you end up on a general note and I tried to make them understand that and they just couldn't see it."

Mike Thompson, an American-based producer, and Chinedu Ukpabi, the head choreographer from the dance troupe, were positioned near the racks of traditional costumes and were debating some changes. Mike insisted the choreography should represent the region individually and conclude with a unifying dance at the end of the number that would combine movements from all the regions of Nigeria. Chinedu spluttered, "There are over 200 cultures in this country, you can't represent them all! You can't do a unifying dance with Edo which is a more graceful dance mixed with a Fisherman's dance. I don't know how people will feel from those regions, because it's not elaborate enough." Mike responded, "So, there is no kind of unifying dance? Well, just end with whatever region we're in." Chinedu paused, apparently racking his brain. Mike said, "Look. I just care about the production value, so pick which costumes will add to the production and look best on stage and on TV." He then pointed to a couple of costumes and walked off.

Ngozi told me that her solution would have been to choreograph a contemporary Nigerian dance piece at the end, which would enable audience members to have both a backward (signaling tradition) and a forward (signaling the future) outlook on Nigerian cultural performance. While Queen Nigeria had paid homage to Plateau without showing any concern for the possibility that it would not be nationally representative, MBGN's organizers made no mention of paying homage to Lagos, the host site. Lagos is a

cosmopolitan city that brings together diverse ethnic groups, due to migration from other cities, surrounding countries, and expatriates from places
such as China, Lebanon, and India. However, Lagos's association with the
Yoruba ethnic group persists, since they are indigenous to the area. This
made it impossible for a Lagos-themed number to be seen as nationally representative.

CONCLUSION

This chapter has described configurations of practices that construct different representations of femininity, and by extension, separate visions of national identity. By focusing on distinct sets of skills, debates over appearance
and dress, and differing ways of representing cultural diversity, MBGN and
Queen Nigeria constructed distinct versions of gendered nationhood. Each
version incorporated its own take on ethnoreligious and regional distinctions as a way to mark femininity and its relationship to the nation. Each
contest reflected different and distinguishing levels of belonging to the global
community, to the nation, and to the local community, as negotiated and
managed by the participants. Queen Nigeria constructed a *tactile* model of
gendered nationalism, which emphasizes *testing* cultural competency, for
example, through a cooking contest. This cultural competency test served
as a means of connecting contestants to a broad Nigerian community and
showing appreciation for Nigerian culture, with the ultimate aim of unifying the nation. In contrast, the Most Beautiful Girl in Nigeria Pageant
featured a modeling competition that emphasized *cultivating* skills, such
as self-confidence, viewed as integral to success at the international phases
of the pageant. This *tactical* model stressed Nigeria's compatibility with an
international community, with the effect of globalizing the nation. Through
the cultural production of idealized femininities, the two different pageants
consolidated varied contours of the nation—as inclusive of cultural and ethnic diversity geared to different local audiences *and* part of a global community for a transnational audience—in tandem through the multilayered
process of nationalism.

5 | THE BUSINESS OF BEAUTY

ENTREPRENEURIAL RESPECTABILITY

After being cooped up in the NTA Jos television station for over five hours, waiting for a scheduled interviewee who was a no-show, I stepped outside to enjoy the cool, fresh air. Outside, I met Jonas Wabaranta, one of Queen Nigeria's support staff, who was wrapping up a phone call. Jonas, a college graduate in his late twenties, was dressed in pressed khakis, a gray button-up shirt, a black belt with a gold Gucci buckle, and brown leather shoes. He worked as a pageant promoter and often trawled university campuses scouting for possible beauty contestants. Learning of my interest in beauty pageants, Jonas declared, "Nowadays beauty pageants are being entered by girls with integrity. Christians who fear God and university students. This work is my ministry. I build contestants up!" Jonas told me he had just finished a call with a beauty contestant who was feeling a little down as she prepared for another upcoming pageant. Their quick phone chat was meant to pump up her confidence before the start of her pageant. In seeing his work as a form of ministry, Jonas, a devout Christian, viewed his participation as a dignified vocation that developed the potential of young, morally upright Nigerian women. Though his use of the term "ministry" was meant to signal religious connotations, his word choice also reminded me of another factor that enters into Nigerian pageantry—the role of the state and public officials who manage government agencies (referred to as ministries in Nigeria). Nigerian pageant industries often court their support for financial backing, logistical support, and legitimacy.

As we headed back inside to grab a seat and a snack in the television network's canteen, Jonas handed his phone to me so I could read a text sent by Peter, an organizer of an Abuja-based pageant. The text, which was littered with exclamation points, announced that the impending pageant would feature special musical guests Jay Z, Chris Brown, and Mary J. Blige in the contest's musical line-up. "Last year there was a bill with pictures of the top celebrities in Nigeria and the names of senators in Abuja, and at the end of the day there was nothing there. They also promised a car to the winner, but there was no car given," Jonas said. Describing these pageants as fraudulent "copycats" run by shady charlatans who dupe hopeful contestants and expectant corporate sponsors, Jonas explained to me that these types of contests corroborate pervasive assumptions that Nigerian beauty contests are filled with dubious business ethics—with broken promises and quid pro quo propositions. By seeking distance from the seedy underbelly of the pageant industry and highlighting their reliable business practices, contests like Queen Nigeria and MBGN sought to build their reputations as credible brands.

My conversation with Jonas evoked flashbacks to an incident that had happened several weeks prior. When I caught up with Doyin, one of Noyo's trainees, a few days after her pageant, she revealed that she had to leave that contest early because masked robbers had infiltrated the hotel they were staying at for camp and robbed her and other contestants at knifepoint. Doyin, who was still visibly shaken up and very angry, claimed it was an obvious insider job and a setup, placing the blame squarely on the shoulders of the pageant owner. A gossip column later ran a story about the robbery, lambasting the owner as a scam artist. Contestants must carefully navigate the deluge of beauty pageants that continuously crop up in the Nigerian landscape and attempt to lure them in with tempting prizes such as millions of naira, a brand-new car, all-expenses-paid trips, job contracts, endorsement deals, magazine features, and international exposure. Nigerian beauty pageants in particular have a reputation for fleecing unsuspecting contestants by forcing them to pay exorbitant camp fees, sell tickets in order to secure their spots, and pay additional money to claim prizes in exchange for the prestige of being a beauty queen. Among industry insiders, fans, and critics alike, there are constant rumors that contests are rigged through political scheming, that contestants must sleep with someone influential to win, and that the crown is available for purchase to the highest bidder. On the flip side, pageant owners who do not take care of their contestants properly develop reputations as businessmen who should not be trusted.

Beauty pageants are not unique in their association with dodgy business schemes but are rather part of a larger public perception of Nigeria's difficult business environment.[1] Because of their associations with young, impressionable women, however, many people considered untrustworthy pageants to be even more egregious. Beauty pageant stakeholders worked to push against the trope that Nigeria is a bad place in which to do business due to rampant corruption, poor regulation, and unvarnished greed. Through a strategy I call *entrepreneurial respectability*, which involved remaining attentive to amplifying repute while acknowledging profitmaking motives, varied stakeholders viewed their participation in the industry as a viable venue to redefine Nigeria's business environment and, by extension, improve the nation's image and generate additional economic capital. This logic hinged in part on discourses and practices of masculinity that positioned pageants as legitimate pathways for entrepreneurship, promoting integrity and diligence in a risky but lucrative business environment. Pageant contestants form symbiotic relationships with various groups like groomers, owners, and sponsors, which results in differential material and symbolic benefits for these groups. Symbolically, these groups cultivate status, build their brands, and boost their reputations through their connections to beauty queens. Materially, they seek a return on their investments. Through what is seen as a feedback loop, improved symbolic gains generate further material revenue. However, these aims are shaped by the structural realities of the tensions between state and market, forces that both facilitate and constrain their aims. Though entrepreneurial respectability uses the refrain of women's empowerment to distance men from any of its benefits, this strategy is ultimately underwritten by men both financially and symbolically.

THE POLITICAL ECONOMY OF BEAUTY PAGEANTS

Money and status connect major stakeholders within the Nigerian beauty pageant industry. Relationships between these groups are a microcosm of Nigeria's emerging nationalism and reflect and contribute to Nigeria's broader political economy. Sociologists Kimberly Hoang and Ashley Mears connect body work to various forms of social and economic capital in ways that highlight intricate relationships between status, money, and morality.[2] Hoang argues that the intimate labor of sex workers in Vietnam facilitates the complex flows of capital for varied groups of male clients who are differentially placed in the global hierarchy. Mears, in turn, coined the term *girl capital* to refer to the ways in which elite businessmen appropriate the bodily labor of attractive women to serve their own ends. Transactional intimate relationships depend in part on conventional gender norms that place men in the category of providers who compensate women through relations of exchange.[3]

In Nigerian competitions, beauty queens depend on owners, sponsors, and groomers to build their aesthetic capital, but these groups also benefit from the contestants' labor materially and symbolically. The political influence of the state as well as the economic clout of a transnational business class are additional actors that shape Nigeria's pageant economy. For example, owners use these contests to develop relationships with politicians and with executives of multinational corporations headed by expatriate immigrants from countries such as Greece, India, and Lebanon, whose businesses cover big-ticket items such as hotel lodging, event venues, cars, and travel through barter agreements. Though these competitions are centered around women's empowerment, through which young women are able to get ahead in ways that would otherwise be impossible, the industry is underwritten by men and masculinity. Beauty queens' relationships with varied stakeholders are crafted as mutually beneficial, but differential symbolic and material benefits ultimately accrue to elite men at the levers of state power and financial capital.

THE GROOMERS

Noyo relished his job as one of the most well-regarded pageant coaches in the country. He started his career by "packaging" (promoting) university pageants while he was a college student. When I first met him, grooming was mostly a side job for him. He did not have his own office space or full-time staff. His bread-and-butter position was working with a modeling and events management company, where he regularly encountered potential clients. He charged ₦150,000 ($1000) for a standard two-week, all-day training package, and typically had two to five clients a month, though it was not unusual for him to go a few months without a single client.

One of Noyo's claims to fame as a pageant coach was that he taught cat-walking in heels. When we went shoe shopping, Noyo asked the sales clerk to bring him a pair of size 41 or 42 shoes (US size 11), claiming that they were for his sister. She brought him a pair of shoes and he put them on his feet, saying that since he and his sister were the same size, he could use his own feet as a guide. Noyo then stood up and began catwalking with the shoes on. He strutted with his hands on his hips and did a quick spin. The sales clerk's mouth was agape in shock and then she started giggling. The shoes Noyo was buying were meant for him, not his sister. The sales clerk's shock rendered his own body peculiar and odd within the shop's space, due to normative ideas about masculinity and embodiment.[4] Noyo was not bothered by the sales clerk's outburst, but instead wore this skill as a badge. He was a self-professed divo (a male diva), by which he meant someone who exuded confidence, style, and originality.

Noyo was a fountain of information about the Nigerian beauty pageant in-dustry, especially its more prominent ex–beauty queens who became regulars on the socialite circuit. He viewed his trainees as his protégés who, through his coaching lessons, would become the next generation of famed queens. He often complained, however, that they failed to show him enough appreciation and would quickly forget about him once they became famous. One analogy he used to describe his concerns compared these beauty queens to "angels in a devil's dress." I took this to mean that beauty queens were easily allured by the temptations of the industry, while leaving him behind without hesitation.

Noyo not only provided lessons on style and protocol, but also taught those under his tutelage important life skills that would help them in the industry in which they were eager to succeed. For example, during one les-son on "office protocol," he paced back and forth in front of his trainees and instructed them:

With a smile on your face, always be aware of any possible suspicious circumstance by asking questions of the people around you, confirming an address before going anywhere to avoid dangerous areas, and taking permission from security guards on where you park your car. Always observe door signs to confirm that people are who they say they are, and request mission statements of any organizations, especially before agreeing to any interviews.

This lesson in particular was meant to ensure that contestants kept their eyes wide open to avoid the hazardous pitfalls within the industry.

Noyo had bigger aspirations. One day, while sitting in his workplace's reception area, Noyo showed me some mocked-up logo designs for a proposal that he was putting together. He dreamed of opening his own full-fledged grooming business and modeling school. He said that he and his business partner were planning to apply for a bank loan to cover their expenses, and he talked about charging large groups of aspiring models and contestants ₦60,000 ($400) for a three-month course that would entitle them to a certificate at the end. Noyo noted that this would add a much-needed element of professionalism to modeling and pageantry in Nigeria. He hoped to advocate for making the course mandatory for all models and beauty contestants. He shared the difficulty in securing sponsorship and leveraging enough capital to get his business off the ground, lamenting that in Nigeria, "money travels in circles," so if you were not plugged into the right social circles, it was nearly impossible to secure enough sponsorship. He grumbled, "They either say they will get back to you and never do, or they say they don't sponsor fashion, yet they spend money on nonsense things." One of those "nonsense things" that Noyo identified was what he saw as the government's misplaced priorities. He ticked off the ways in which the government provided logistical and financial support for male sports teams, but dismissed beauty pageants, modeling, and entertainment as irrelevant. In the backseat of a cab, as we were headed to visit a fashion designer, Noyo commented, "If I could ban football [soccer] and get rid of the Minister of Sports, I would. I'd have a Minister of Entertainment instead."

Sports and beauty pageants are parallel institutions in that both draw crowds, have corporate sponsors, and involve domestic and international

national representations through their participants' bodies. Sports are associated with physical strength, aggression, and competitiveness. Women's sports tend to attract fewer sponsors, less adulation, and fewer financial opportunities. Beauty pageants are also highly competitive arenas, but are linked to physical appearance, a kind disposition, and criteria that emphasize attractiveness, speaking ability, and humanitarianism. In Nigeria, male beauty competitions are fewer in number and have reduced budgets and smaller prize packages. During my fieldwork, I observed the 2010 Mr. Nigeria pageant, whose winner went on to compete in Mr. World, an international competition. While MBGN was held at the banquet hall of a five-star hotel, Mr. Nigeria was held at a club where the audience was almost entirely women (the audience at female beauty pageants are typically a near-even mix of men and women). Mr. Nigeria's preliminary activities included a swimming competition, arm wrestling matches, and horseback riding, tasks meant to signal athletic prowess to counteract the stigmatizing impact of participating in an event coded as feminine. Both sports and beauty diplomacy engage with similar public dynamics, but these gendered differences mean that they play out in distinct ways. Like beauty diplomacy, sports diplomacy uses star power, events, and its relationship with states, international agencies, the private sector, and NGOs through non-profit charity work to paint a country in a favorable light.[5] Both forms of diplomacy are shaped by and are used as tools to influence foreign policy, philanthropic efforts, and national politics. Noyo's criticism showed that the government failed to realize that both sports and beauty pageants used different means to achieve the same ends. Noyo described tactics that he believed would further give the industry legitimacy. While he recognized the industry as fast-growing and expressed a desire to tap into that growth, he identified the lack of proper structures, the mistreatment of contestants, and a need to fully celebrate the importance of beauty pageants and show business as a whole, as important to the country.

While Noyo was enthusiastic about furthering his career as a pageant coach by opening his own business that would celebrate his skills, Will, who was in his early thirties and worked as Queen Nigeria's choreographer and groomer, was more tentative. Will had gotten his start in the industry as a runway model, working with one of the top modeling coaches in the country.

He was a self-taught choreographer who learned dance moves by watching music videos. He expressed a desire to "go to the next level" by owning and producing his own pageant and entertainment company since he felt he was getting too "big" to still just be teaching contestants choreography and how to walk, calling it "shameful." Comparing his teaching style to Noyo's, Will said he believed he could teach effectively by observing the contestants and correcting them as needed.

Part of Will's embarrassment rested on perceptions that his job allowed others to question his masculinity. However, as we chatted in his hotel room after rehearsals had wrapped up for the evening, he told me that, on the contrary, he had to be an even stronger man in order to do this job, using as an example the fact that he had to constantly control his own sexual urges and rebuff the advances from beautiful contestants. He referred to an example that I had witnessed earlier in the day. A contestant, leaning up against the van waiting for another contestant to finish up at the bank before we took off for a courtesy visit to the local radio station, flirted with Will by asking if he was married and then stating that she was looking for a husband. Will gave a noncommittal response, but in a whisper he asked her more about her dating life. The contestant then shifted the conversation to ask more about the pageant's judging process, inquiring if Will knew who the judges would be. Transitioning her speech pattern to pidgin English, she questioned Will, "Wetin judge dis ting na?" Will responded that he had no knowledge of the process, and the conversation abruptly ended. Referring to the banter I had observed between Will and the contestant, he explained that this was just one of many examples of how he had to be steadfast in the face of seductive contestants.

Like Noyo, Will complained that contestants were "greedy" and did not properly thank him after all the work he had done to teach them how to properly walk, stand, sit, and dance. During training camp, a few days before the finale, we were chatting in his hotel room and the subject turned to his expectations of what would happen after the final show. He launched into a diatribe about beauty queens. "They can't even send me a simple SMS [text message] afterwards. After all, I'm not the one making money from the crown, but they can't even send a few naira my way," Will grumbled. These grievances were meant to signal that contestants reaped financial rewards, yet rarely acknowledged how groomers like Will helped them build their popularity. As his complaints illustrate, while groomers add value to beauty contestants by teaching them much-needed skills, beauty contestants are able to capitalize from their bodies in ways that body laborers like Will and Noyo cannot.

A few weeks after the pageant, I caught up with Will at a sports bar where, in between sips of beer, he reiterated how, while he provided the tools for beauty queens to be successful, contestants needed to realize that they would have to put in extra effort to fulfill their roles as public figures, instead of expecting pageant organizers to do all the work:

> Being a queen, everybody expects the whole world from you. . . . As a queen, you need to work very hard and if you don't work for it, you should not expect us to do it for you. As a queen, you cannot sleep in the luxury of your bed and expect us to pay you money. Who will work for that money? People know *your* face. You were the ones crowned, not me.

Will's statement pinpointed the potential beauty queens had to attract further capital, which he later specified was possible through public relations and branding campaigns, but he also warned that it was not an automatic process. It required a strong team of organizers, but more importantly to Will, there had to be more buy-in from contestants who would put in the work to propel their own careers. As Will and Noyo alluded in our conversations, beauty queens are able to capitalize on their bodies, the same bodies that these groomers helped to perfect. While Will and Noyo differed in whether they wanted to continue to work as groomers, they both shared a desire to be owners in their own right, since they felt that having their own full-service businesses in the industry would help them reap greater financial rewards.

THE OWNERS

Pageant owners worked to project an image of their contests as safe, trustworthy, and legitimate pathways for contestants to pursue their future careers. In doing so, they were able to make a case for corporate sponsorship, national support, and global recognition. They worked to strengthen their relationship with the state in order to pursue more lucrative financial opportunities through government sponsorship and assistance. However, the relationship to the state remained tenuous. Owners recognized the importance of securing a connection to the state in order to increase their access to capital, but also understood the state to be corrupt, inept, and possibly working against their interests.

The state-owned Nigerian Television Authority's (NTA's) TV Enterprises, the broadcast network's business arm, which cosponsored Queen Nigeria, launched in the same year as Queen Nigeria. TV Enterprises was formed to establish collaborative and strategic partnerships with private entrepreneurs and companies in order to add profit to NTA. NTA faced rising competition from private broadcasting networks and meager government budget allocations. The organization devised innovative initiatives to remedy this problem. Queen Nigeria was one such solution. Partnering with Mr. Gold's private marketing firm, they struck an agreement that his company would keep all the proceeds from the local state pageants and NTA / TV Enterprises would retain profits from the national grand finale.

NTA's corporate edge remained in having the largest television network in Africa, with stations covering all the Nigerian states. Though it is an established brand, many considered it an outdated media outlet struggling to keep pace with competitors. Insiders noted that NTA used Queen Nigeria to attract a younger audience and to directly compete with Silverbird. As Will explained to me during our conversation in the sports bar, starting Queen Nigeria was part of a larger process of NTA rebuilding its brand:

> [Queen Nigeria] makes NTA have a name and then it can compete with MBGN, because NTA is not happy that Silverbird came and overshadowed them. The Most Beautiful Girl in Nigeria should be handled by NTA as the largest network. If you are showcasing or presenting a girl to represent Nigeria and the medium through which Nigeria should be known [and] NTA is not there, it means there is something wrong. That was why NTA said let's do something of our own. . . . Now NTA showed people their level of thinking is not old anymore. It is like a new revolution in activities in NTA, so that is why I think they ventured into pageants. They're into shows and entertainment too now.

To further complicate Will's point, and highlighting the competitive streak between NTA and Silverbird, Ben Murray-Bruce, the former chairman of

Silverbird, was also the former director general of NTA, having started Silverbird TV shortly after the end of his tenure at NTA. NTA officials viewed their collaboration with Queen Nigeria as a way of injecting youthful vigor into their network and also one-upping Silverbird.

MBGN is primarily run by middle-aged male executives who cast themselves as providing the economic means to help contestants fulfill their career goals and financial needs. MBGN budgets ₦18 million ($120,000) to produce the annual show, which they offset through sales of entrance forms, sponsorship deals, and vendor discounts. MBGN winners sign a year-long contract with Silverbird that entitles the company to between 50 and 70 percent of their proceeds from any appearances or promotional campaigns, depending on if the booking is in or outside the country (international appearance fees generate a lower cut of the proceeds). They offered three sponsorship packages: a platinum level, at ₦50 million ($333,333); gold for ₦40 million ($266,666); and bronze at ₦30 million ($200,000), with the "value-added proposition" (a marketing term that was included in all sponsorship pitches, which is meant to describe how clients or partners will benefit) of local and international publicity through MBGN. Although it strains credulity, MBGN owners claimed they lost money organizing the pageant but were compelled to organize it annually in order to fulfill a national duty to have representatives at international competitions and benevolently help contestants fulfill their aspirations.

The industry as a whole is run by male owners, though women tend to hold the position of the pageant coordinator or executive director, who manages the day-to-day operations of the pageant. Female-owned beauty pageants are an exception, and nearly all are run by former beauty queens or women who have worked for other major pageants as organizers. Christina Aimanosi, Queen Nigeria's makeup artist, expressed disapproval of the gender imbalance of pageant owners and asserted that the industry would be dramatically different if more women were in charge:

> If you look into these contests, there is usually a man. I think women should handle such beauty pageants because it is also a sensitive thing as you are dealing with women, [introducing issues of] privacy and sexuality. . . . Women should handle it because you can't trust your daughter

in the hands of just one man. Things can go wrong but having a woman makes it safer so to say. You know that a lady will handle her fellow lady respectfully.

Male pageant owners reversed the logic of Christina's statement by pointing to contestants' confidence in them as proof that they were trustworthy businessmen primarily interested in contestants' success.

MBGN owners repeatedly stressed that the pageant ran at a net loss. Mr. Omo disputed this view and urged me not to be naïve:

> If they don't make money, will they keep doing it? Don't let anybody fool you, my sister; pageantry is full of money. I give it to them, they understand what making money is all about. The people who have done pageants in the past are dishonest, they make money, they don't deliver and at the end sponsors don't go back to them. That is why pageants come and go in Nigeria.

Labeling these dishonest pageant owners "half-baked cashers" who are just after easy money, he admitted that though MBGN had some shortcomings, the owners had business acumen that attracted contestants and sponsors alike. He noted that their media savvy and ownership of television and radio outlets meant that they were able to control the pageant's publicity.

Even as they downplayed their financial returns, it was clear to me that working with beauty pageants was an investment strategy for owners, since they used them to brand their marketing and entertainment companies and to gain access to political and economic elites. MBGN is a signature event for Silverbird, and executives often capitalized on beauty queens as household names by taking them on business outings and galas since they commanded attention. Inviting contestants to special courtesy visits with state dignitaries, to meet-and-greets at social gatherings and industry parties, and to business meetings, helped pageant owners seem more approachable and facilitated their desired relationships with others. Beauty queens attracted attention and intrigue from prospective partners. It was common to find contestants hanging out at the corporate headquarters, chatting and associating with the executives in between meetings. Gina, MBGN's groomer, described how inviting beauty queens to events helped build up Silverbird. In particular, she discussed the presence of having the top five winners attend various events:

> It makes Silverbird look more powerful, and with the kind of queens we produce, we've gone to many events that the people will be like wow! Are they all with Silverbird? And we replied that yes they are, they are all Silverbird queens.

Having beauty queens at social and corporate events helped raise the presence of pageant owners by emphasizing the work they did to bolster the success of beauty contestants, but there was a synergetic relationship between these two groups. Associating with beauty contestants provided the owners of these contests some measure of credibility as well.

Through the success of MBGN, Silverbird has built its brand around the image of being cutting-edge and in tune with international trends. Silverbird's beauty pageants serve as its frontline marketing campaign. An executive explained the role the contest plays in the overall company as follows: "MBGN brings us out there. Silverbird is not a dull brand, it's a bright brand. People want to know where she is. Be associated with her. And know what she's up to. She helps our brand and adds a lot of value to the company." Part of Silverbird's brand depended on the longevity of the pageant due to MBGN's consistent track record. For example, Octavia, a pageant coordinator, emphasized how MBGN's dependability helped sustain Silverbird as a durable brand:

> Some people will ask you how many years [have you been in business] and you tell them for twenty-three years they will be like how? Probably because most pageants after a year or two you will not hear anything about them anymore, like Miss Nigeria they don't exist anymore. It is really not easy to sustain it.

Octavia points to the difficulty in sustaining business in Nigeria, which contributes to the irregular intervals of other pageants like Miss Nigeria. Fred Ebele, a Silverbird crew member, described the company as having earned a big name in media and entertainment due in large part to MBGN: "I feel that is why a lot of people have that faith and trust in us. With MBGN being part of Silverbird, [people] are always looking forward to what we will offer.

There is always this excitement when people talk about us." Because MBGN was a yearly event that drew captivated fans who were interested in keeping up to date on the latest beauty queen, there was a constant reenergizing and sense of intrigue about Silverbird.

When I asked what made MBGN distinct from other pageants, Ope Alabi, a vendor who had designed MBGN's program several times over the years, replied, "People appreciate and respect it more. It has lasted years and that is very rare in Nigeria. Others just do something for like five years and they pack up whereas this is MBGN's twenty-third edition." MBGN's consistent track record was contrasted with those of other contests, which were described as erratic and quick to abandon their efforts. As Ope and his team holed up in a hotel room, hunched over Apple laptops and pulling an all-nighter to complete the brochure by their deadline, Ope explained to me, in between making edits on his computer, that MBGN was "classy" because the organization was reliable. Ope had gone back and forth with Mr. Tim before settling on a final price to help produce the brochure, offering a substantial discount as a mea culpa for some errors his company had made in the previous year's brochure, and to ensure that they would continue to keep MBGN as a customer. Ope did not seem very bothered by having to write off some of the expenses that came with discounting his typical fee. He noted:

> MBGN [doesn't] promise you a price and [then] fail, they promise this is a price and you get it immediately. They have good deliverance. They keep to their words. And for the girls they pay them immediately, which allows the girls to invest. Most of those who participate in the pageant are paid before the end of the pageant. This makes the pageant the best.

By building their reputations as trustworthy in the pageant world, the organizers boosted their repute as businessmen. The logic went that if young women, who were especially vulnerable, could put their trust in them, then others should as well. Through this logic, organizers showed their concerns, not only to promote their own pageant, but also to boost business culture in Nigeria overall. Through business practices such as paying their vendors on time, providing contestants with a steady income through prize money they could use to "invest" in their future, and upholding their promises, owners guaranteed their standing as honorable businessmen.

Pageant owners also pointed to the steady income stream and job opportunities that they offered through their contests. They not only were providing a means of upward mobility for contestants, but also by hiring and giving opportunities to a crew of people who helped produce the show, doing everything from manning cameras, to designing sashes, to printing brochures, they viewed themselves as propelling Nigeria's economy forward. These practices may not seem very important, but business norms in Nigeria are not always easy to navigate. In fact, it is not uncommon for government jobs, which are coveted as stable career paths, to have salary in arrears. In 2015, the Nigerian Labour Congress, a trade union organization, disclosed that 23 out of the 36 states owed public workers months of salaries, including nurses, schoolteachers, and other civil servants.[6]

Organizers encouraged contestants to view their participation in beauty pageants as a form of entrepreneurship which prepared them for the responsibilities of the real world. Octavia noted that contestants were not just chasing after a crown but rather it was about using the crown to "reach higher goals." They considered multiple pathways as successful transitions after participating in pageants including educational pursuits, working in the entertainment world, starting a business, founding an NGO, or getting married and starting a family. Organizers recast their involvement in beauty pageants through the lens of respectable entrepreneurship, in which their contributions in building the industry helped contestants pursue careers in a wide-range of fields. Mr. Tim, connected their main aim to "women's empowerment":

> What it does for young ladies is that it creates a platform for them to choose a career of their choice and propels them into any field they want. It's [also] symbolic. When you have a beauty queen like an MBGN girl, you will like young girls to emulate them, to say let me help develop my community in some form or the other and let me lead in an industry where women are not known to lead. I think it encourages young girls to emulate this character. Hopefully even if you are not The Most Beautiful Girl, it makes you realize that your dreams can be realized if you work hard at it, and it gives women an equal opportunity as men. We promote entrepreneurship. Our contestants have become international models and have gone onto the

House of Representatives. This is just another form of business that parents should accept.

Mr. Tim pointed out how MBGN provided contestants access to male-dominated careers, which should help level the playing field between men and women in the Nigerian economy. By using an entrepreneurial lens, they also sought to legitimize the industry as a possible pathway for success.

Organizers recognized that there were negative stereotypes about beauty pageant contestants, which they actively worked to counteract. These stereotypes presented contestants as sexually promiscuous and poorly educated, an image that pageant organizers directly combated by elevating beauty queens as wholesome, morally upright, and economically mobile citizens. Organizers felt the beauty pageant industry had made major inroads in presenting a positive image of contestants that centered on their positions as role models and cultural ambassadors with budding political and economic clout. Organizers often claimed that parents now bring their daughters to audition for the pageant as evidence that people view beauty pageants as family-friendly and a viable pathway for success. I saw very few parents at auditions. The clear majority of those whom I saw audition came either alone, with friends, or with handlers. However, I understood this constant refrain as a rhetorical strategy that was meant to show that beauty competitions had gained enough brand recognition that parents escorted their children as mark of approval. Still, organizers constantly complained that parents needed to view participating in pageants as something to be encouraged and respected.

Early in the morning, as we were preparing for the Lagos tryouts, the hotel manager checked in with Mr. Tim about whether guests of the applicants would be able to watch the audition process. Mr. Tim shook his head and replied, "It's just the uncles that I'm worried about. We have to keep out the uncles." By then, a few months into my internship, I had figured out that "uncle" was a code word for older male sponsors. By noting this preference for not having older men as spectators during the auditioning process, Mr. Tim aimed to publicly distance MBGN from the association between contestants and relying on older men to finance their participation. Mr. Tim's distancing, however, served to support a larger stance of entrepreneurial respectability that worked to present a wholesome image and professionalize the industry.

This reliance on personal sponsors was viewed as potentially sullying the reputations of beauty contestants.

PERSONAL SPONSORS

In the middle of my lunch with Iris and her business partner, they detailed their understanding of how personal sponsorships work in Nigeria. Personal sponsors are typically older men who help out some contestants financially so they can afford the associated costs of participating. Iris explained to me that there were two types of ways sponsors help out contestants: directly, by offering cash so they can buy needed items such as shoes, gowns, and hair extensions, or indirectly, by lobbying pageant owners to have contestants win either through personal connections or money. Iris, who participated in her first pageant at age fifteen, had competed in over ten pageants in ten years. When she started college, she would use the money her parents intended her to use to cover school fees to travel five hours to Lagos every few months from her college town so that she could compete in pageants and audition for modeling gigs. She described the shuttling back and forth as going from having a regular life at school to living in the fast lane in Lagos as a wannabe celebrity, meeting new people and posing for pictures at events. One day Iris met a White man at the mall who, after drinks, invited her over to his house. After hearing of her pageant aspirations, he gave her some money and offered to call up the pageant owner to make sure she would win the pageant since he knew him personally. While she was in camp, she continued to text him, "posting" him (leading him on) so that he would not renege on his promise. Iris did not end up winning but did finish in the top ten. Though she was unhappy, she was satisfied with walking away with that consolation prize because not placing at all would have been an embarrassment to her. She gave credit to the man she had met for making the first cut as she had gotten wind that she had upset one of the judges at the preliminary rounds of the pageant. She was convinced that this man had pulled the strings to make her stay in the pageant. She then told me she probably did not place any higher than top ten because other "big men" had likely paid for their own favored contestants to win.

After she told me this story, I assumed that she viewed this man as her sponsor. Shaking her head to refute my interpretation she told me, "He wasn't my sponsor. He was just doing me a favor. I didn't give him anything. I just flirted with him." Iris then explained to me that to have a sponsor was a mutually beneficial relationship. Contestants help out a sponsor as much as a sponsor helps them. Since she had not given him anything in return and never spoke with him again, she had just been leading him on; it was not a sponsor-type relationship, but rather a onetime courtesy. While I was less certain that the man had only offered to assist as a good deed rather than as an expectation of something further later on, our conversation did clarify some things for me. I asked Iris to tell me what she thought the sponsors get in return to help clarify some pieces of the puzzle that were slowly fitting together. Though I had directed the question to her, Iris's business partner, Junior, who had largely been silent up until then, answered the question as if it should have been plainly obvious to me. "Bragging rights," he stated in a monotone as he took a final bite of food. Iris nodded.

This conversation with Iris and Junior made me recall a past conversation with Frankie. As we sat in a lounge bar with an R&B song playing in the background, the topic turned to sponsors. He dismissed the idea that contestants participate in pageants to support their pet projects, claiming that these charity projects were jokes and a cover-up for contestants' real motives of finding a rich man to marry. He then began talking about Michael, an infamous bachelor businessman who was known for his flashy rotation of luxury sports cars and penchant for dating beauty queens, whom he spoiled with lavish gifts. Stating that he did not get the appeal, he said sponsors like Michael had a "fetish" for only dating beauty queens. Frankie then said that these beauty queens were equivalent to Michael's rare sports car, a status symbol that those around him could fawn over. As soon as their reign was over, he had his sights set on the next batch of reigning queens. Frankie's description positioned sponsors like Michael as having an insatiable urge to be gratified by social recognition and asserted that beauty queens helped satisfy those needs.

Chibuzor, a branding expert for one of MBGN's corporate sponsors, said that personal sponsors were synonyms for "an Aristo," which he explained was a wealthy, older man who can take care of contestants. He similarly described it as mutually beneficial:

> These guys don't just spend on one girl. There are so many girls to choose from. They spend so much money because they have too much money.

What does it cost to give ₦500,000 ($3,333) to a girl in a competition?
These guys are used to making billions of naira on a yearly basis.

Though these sponsorships were just a drop in the bucket for well-off sponsors, these sponsors traded on the aesthetic capital of contestants to boost their own social capital as well-connected men who had a bevy of attractive women to select from. Though these relationships were described as mutually beneficial since contestants profited financially and sponsors gained symbolically, there was some measure of inequality in terms of how respectability played out. Openly admitting to having a sponsor was a negative mark for contestants, while being a sponsor boosted the sponsors' "bragging rights," even as contestants and sponsors navigated the same social circles.

While I was not able to officially corroborate the degree to which indirect sponsorship happens, I heard this from enough people that it would not surprise me if there was some measure of truth in these statements. For example, I met Victoria through Will, who was starting up a new pageant for a businessman based in the United States. She described how, though there were some contests that were "free and fair," most winners were "handpicked" by boosters who pay ₦15–₦20 million to "bid for the crown" as indirect sponsors for contestants. Since this was the first year for the pageant she was organizing, she claimed that they would have a much lower price. She explained that this underground bidding process included influential politicians at the highest levels of government, wealthy entrepreneurs, and executives in sectors such as finance and oil and gas. I took Victoria's descriptions in as situating the beauty pageant ecosystem as central to the off-the-books process that connected members of Nigeria's elite to each other.

THE CORPORATE SPONSORS

Both sets of organizers maintained that pageants not only helped build their own brands, but also promoted other companies due to their associations with the pageants through sponsorship agreements. They leveraged their connections to major media companies, offering free advertising in exchange for services and monetary sponsorship. In a meeting with a potential sponsor, Lola, an MBGN coordinator, explained barter arrangements and cosponsorship packages during a meeting with Seye Tiwalope, a hair salon owner who was interested in being a sponsor. We were in Silverbird's main office, sitting at the glass-topped conference table, while Lola grabbed nearby items on the table to illustrate her points. "A barter arrangement is, let's say I have this newspaper," gesturing toward a newspaper on the table,

> And you have this phone. You want my phone and I want your newspaper. We trade and everyone is happy. A sponsorship is when you have this phone and this newspaper is our event. You provide free services and we give you PR at our event. Whenever we promote MBGN we mention you as an official sponsor. We can mention this on the website, on the radio, on TV, and in our cinemas.

In detailing the varied options that were based on Silverbird's self-devised valuation of their media brand, Lola communicated that this arrangement was an equitable financial agreement that would be mutually beneficial. After Lola provided details about the arrangement, Seye's face visibly relaxed and she nodded, saying, "Yes that sounds good. That's what I want." Lola then assured her, "I will just put it all in writing for your approval. MBGN is such a superbrand that you will get a lot of exposure, it's just hard to break in." Lola had originally agreed to meet with Seye because of her family connections to one of the wealthiest businessmen in Nigeria. But once she learned that Seye was open to offering her services for free, she was ready to move ahead with the deal.

In exchange for free or discounted services, all official sponsors of the pageant earned naming rights and promotional consideration during radio announcements and television spots ten times daily for three weeks prior to the event, acknowledgment on all print and digital communications, an advertising spot during the televised show, a full-page ad in the event brochure, and venue branding. MBGN valued this total package at ₦30,000,000 ($200,000) and stipulated that this sponsorship arrangement was a deal for official sponsors who provided their services. Through this agreement, sponsors gained ambassadors for national brands who brought their products and services to a more high-end clientele as well as an international audience.

Several up-and-coming vendors, such as photographers, graphic designers, and stylists, often agreed to work for pageants pro bono or with heavily discounted rates in exchange for promotional advertising and exposure.

Beauty queens provided many local Nigerian brands and designers with a body to publicly promote their products. These brands got symbolic returns on their investments through the hope that promoting their brand on a public stage would help them acquire everyday consumers to purchase their labels and services. A number of aesthetic services used the attention directed at beauty queens to help promote their brands to both domestic and international markets and attract new clientele. They formed a complementary service industry through which they mutually supported one another. Just as for the sponsors, body laborers, from makeup specialists to fashion gurus, gained national brand ambassadors who brought their products and services to a more high-end clientele as well as to an international audience. Bodily laborers often granted them free or discounted beauty treatments and goods, with the expectation that they would plug their brands at events and in the media. Contestants were given free access to hairstylists and makeup artists who were official sponsors of the beauty competition. Being known as an official consultant or service provider to the latest "it girl" on the beauty pageant scene increased their business and their credibility.

For example, Seye, the owner of a full-service hair salon and spa, talked about how she had approached MBGN to become a sponsor because she felt that her business was in a good place to move to the next level. All contestants underwent a hair consultation for the finale, and Seye brought in her team of twelve male and female hair stylists to put in nine-hour days for two days before the show, tirelessly hand sewing human hair onto contestants' scalps, where it was attached to their own corn-rowed hair. The "fixed" hair was then arranged into chic hairstyles that could easily transition between the show's many costume changes. The hair was meant to blend seamlessly with the contestants' own hairline so that it would appear as natural as possible. While contestants had to pay for their own hair bundles ($300–$800 depending on the length and quality), Seye wrote off the cost of the hairstylists' labor, reduction in hours at her own salon, transportation expenses, and additional hired assistants who helped with shampooing and organizing the hair extensions, as a worthwhile business expense. She paid her hairstylists a monthly wage of $150–$200 a month but regularly charged customers $30 per weave. In Nigeria, labor is typically cheap, while customers pay a premium for consumer goods and services, meaning that owners like Seye, who was not trained as a hairstylist herself, ultimately accumulate profits. Seye also brought in manicurists ($5–$15) and eyelash specialists ($5), which contestants had to pay for out of pocket. The winner and the first and second runners-up were given free hair and styling services for the year from this sponsoring hair salon. They often visited Seye's chic hair salon, which was decorated in swaths of red and black, to receive complimentary hair services, manicures, facials, and waxing. After their official sponsorship ended, Seye racked up industry awards, held a grand reopening with the beauty queen as a special guest, and, after a month-long discount promotional period, raised her rates by 20 percent. Seye was pleased with the media attention that her sponsorship brought, which included a review that stated, "This hair salon will surely make a Miss World out of you."

Through the glitz associated with the pageant, corporate sponsors sought to elevate their own brands, which they viewed as a fair return on their investment. I chatted with Mrs. Ellen, the wife of one the Silverbird executives and owner of the official makeup and skin-care line for MBGN and a formal-events clothing boutique, in her backroom office, in between time spent attending to her staff and taking phone calls. The makeup line products ranged in price from $5 to $15 and the skin-care products ranged from $15 to $30. She discussed her desire to work with beauty queens since they could serve as a blank canvas to help promote her recently launched makeup and skin-care line. Mrs. Ellen explained to me what she was looking for in a brand ambassador, "I was looking for an innocent face. I want a face that will easily be transformed through makeup . . . and that can easily be attributed to real beauty." After stopping our interview briefly to attend to one of her staff members, Mrs. Ellen returned to discuss what she hoped the new face of her brand would be able to accomplish, including attending seminars in Nigeria and abroad:

> Our selection is not just for the Black skin. It is for women of all skin
> types, and if she goes out [of the country], I want her to take that out with
> her. She should be able to represent the country very well to the extent
> that when they see her, they should be able to ask her what do you use
> on your face? I want the queen to be able to pull the crowd irrespective
> of where she goes. . . . I want them to be active and bring back glory to

the country. We're not just looking for the face of a product, but the face of a nation.

Through this statement, she asserted the connections between aesthetic transformations and nation branding. By expressing these hopes, Mrs. Ellen communicated that she effectively wanted Nigerian beauty queens to be considered "mainstream" internationally, such that their makeup looks would not only be praised but would entice interest in the nation as a whole. She also stressed that while hers was a Nigerian-based company, it sought to appeal to women with a variety of skin tones and selections that anyone around the world could use in order to establish itself as a global brand. Through the Nigerian beauty queens' global visibility, Mrs. Ellen sought to grow and develop her company as an internationally renowned brand that would also translate into a stamp of approval for the future direction of Nigeria as a nation.

These different service industries use the public exposure and newfound celebrity status of beauty queens to grow their own brands through endorsement campaigns, advertising, and requesting contestants at their events. Mrs. Ellen's formal-events clothing boutique provided ball gowns to the queens. She connected providing contestants with gowns that cost between $200 and $650, and which were sometimes worn at international pageants, to a specific material gain in increasing interest in her business by "rolling in the money" from other customers, commenting, "[People] say whoa, best evening gown and [the dress] is from [us]. That helps us because we have that knack in picking those winning gowns. [The beauty queen] uses her face to roll in the money." Then she laughed. As Mrs. Ellen saw it, gaining prestige also brought very real material benefits for her business.

Beauty queens gave the companies media mileage. These different service industries used the public exposure and newfound celebrity status of beauty queens to grow their own brands through endorsement campaigns, advertising, press junkets, and requesting contestants at their events. While many of these returns are symbolic, there is the promise of indirect material revenue through reaching new clients that would further enrich their businesses. It is important that the owners of these brands (as compared to those who served solely as laborers) profited the most, both symbolically and materially. Moreover, gaining positive attention for these beauty services was seen as directly related to raising the national prestige of the country.

SECURING SPONSORSHIP

Beauty queens were a main draw in being able to get sponsorship, but they paradoxically also served as a roadblock to getting a wider array of sponsorship opportunities because of the controversies that surround pageants in Nigeria and the presumption that beauty contests do not attract a wide enough marketing demographic. Pageant organizers revealed that one of the biggest hurdles they faced in their jobs was securing adequate sponsorship for the event. Their goal of generating revenue was often thwarted by skepticism, neglect, and sometimes even outright hostility from potential sponsors. Other industries, especially football (soccer), were often brought up as a silent rival to beauty pageants since they drew considerable financial support from the government and corporate sponsors. In contrast, beauty pageant organizers wrote countless proposals in the hopes of attracting funding from the state, local companies, and multinational corporations, yet received only a small fraction of the level of support generated by football. Lamenting the lack of financial backing, particularly from the federal government, Emeka noted:

> The beauty pageant industry here deserves more attention because of the role they play in developing countries. In other places they treat their queens like second first ladies. But the Nigerian government is not really as interested here. The government is not really taking advantage of this platform, they don't see the value. They just pay lip service to us.

Emeka observed that the state does not fully capitalize on the value-added potential of the industry and thus missed out on a viable economic initiative. Nonetheless, pageant owners and organizers worked to court state support for these businesses.

One of the major hurdles organizers sought to overcome was the fact that some corporations viewed beauty pageant sponsorship as too limiting because of its association with women. When I asked why they encountered difficulty in securing more sponsorship, Frankie explained:

> Because it is just about ladies and people don't want to limit themselves to brands just for women. Most brands are for everybody. If you start limiting your brands to only women, then, you'll lose sales. Like having a women's drink, you'll surely lose sales from men also, so it is very hard.

Frankie noted that while they were able to easily get beauty-related sponsors on board, they were unable to attract enough sponsors with deeper pockets—the larger multinational corporations and state governors that they coveted—because pageants were viewed as too limiting. Chibuzor seemed to confirm Frankie's point of view with regard to how certain brands are gendered in specific ways. The manager for a cloyingly sweet soft drink that served as one of the sponsors for MBGN gave me a quick lesson on gender and marketing from his perspective. He noted that some brands, such as his own and Fanta, are coded as feminine because they are light-colored, sweet, nonalcoholic drinks, while Gulder, a beer, is coded as male because it is dark, bitter, and alcoholic. It struck me that part of his assumption about gendered branding incorporated normative embodied assumptions about women and men.

Nigeria's political economy entangles the state and the market with national and global forces. Both MBGN and Queen Nigeria contended with barriers in attracting sponsorship though both pursued multinational corporations and the state as ideal boosters. Organizers and pageant owners navigate the tension between subscribing to the demands of the state and the strains of private capital. Each contest maintains an uneasy relationship with the state, in which it faces various pressures to serve specific political aims. Oil and its surrounding politics provide a key example of these contradictions. Although oil is nationalized in Nigeria, it still remains a part of the international marketplace due to its tie to multinational companies and its export to countries around the world. Ownership of oil is controlled by the federal government according to national decrees. Political officials govern the access to state revenues, which they distribute to themselves and their constituents to secure their loyalty. In a form of politics that political scientists dub *prebendalism*, government officials use their access to state resources to secure loyalty with their constituents, who are often divided by ethnicity, religion, and regional interests.[7] This patron-client relationship allows for the use of political offices for personal gain and is one of the key reasons why the state is highly susceptible to corruption.[8] In other words, state control over capital becomes a source of political power and commingles the public with the private. The attempts to deregulate the oil industry by decreasing state subsidies and moving toward privatization of the market further highlight this tension between state and capital. The state not only consolidates class power, but also male domination. Political theorist Achille Mbembe describes postcolonial state power as a "phallocratic system" to understand the overlapping categories of masculine authority, political leadership, and embodied symbolism that centers unhindered male pleasure and the sexual control over women's bodies to mollify "anxious virility."[9] Nigeria's national beauty pageants navigate within this context, aligning themselves with these interests to advance their organization's goals. By aiming to develop close relationships with state officials, pageant owners strengthen masculinity across the private sector and state power. Moreover, since economic capital is concentrated in the hands of the state, gaining access to the state is typically viewed as the fastest means of securing upward mobility and stability. Nigerian politicians are some of the highest paid legislators in the world, earning $540,000 a year once the base salary and generous allowances are accounted for.[10] Because of state control over oil, government officials have financial power that private players like beauty pageant owners try to tap into.

I spent most of my time as an MBGN intern reaching out to sponsors, drafting proposals and presentations, writing letters to government officials, and putting together sponsorship packages. On my first day on the job, Lola asked me to brainstorm a list of ideal companies to focus on for sponsorship. The final list included Moët, Blackberry, Rolex, and Range Rover, among other luxury brands. One day we ran into Vijay Patil, an Indian expatriate who worked for Silverbird, at the nearby pharmacy. He asked about our progress and then proceeded to give us a pep talk with specific tactics to increase our chances. "Look, when you deal with multinational companies [through their Nigerian satellite offices], go directly to the head or as far up as you can go because they don't trust anyone below them. When you deal with the local Nigerian businesses, go for the middle, because they will be able to convince their bosses." Vijay's strategy was meant to target the specifics of the Nigerian business environment; while multinationals that are almost entirely headed by expatriates expecting more formal dealings, Nigerian corporations would be more comfortable with using connections to help broker a deal. By being sensitive to the "Nigerian factor," which differentially influences multinational and local companies, Vijay believed that we could optimize our prospects.

For MBGN, with its attention to international competitions, private multinational corporations seemed like a natural fit. MBGN viewed multinational corporations as the key target for sponsorship because to them they were the only companies with sufficient resources to afford the full benefits of the partnership. The organizers felt that multinationals were a logical match with their brand message, even as they found it difficult to convince a large number of multinationals to buy it. Mr. Tim noted:

> Multinationals need to realize the benefits of using these young delegates as ambassadors for their products. It's hard for them. You have to sell the fact that they can sell your product. And it's a lifestyle. Why shouldn't Coke Light realize that they can be used to symbolize this new diet drink that they have? Because our contestants are young and fit and Coca-Cola Light is just perfect for such girls.

They insisted that while in other places in the world, clothing, jewelry, and beauty companies flocked to pageants to promote their products, in Nigeria, local companies were not cash-rich and disregarded the importance of advertising. As a result, multinational corporations were preferable. Public billboards that dot the urban landscape, commercials that regularly air on television, and newspaper advertisements marketing local and regional products and services belied Mr. Tim's point. I interpreted the disjuncture in part through the differential success Nigerian pageants have had at the international level as compared to other countries with record-breaking pageant wins. The Nigerian pageant industry has not fully emerged internationally. Perhaps the industry had not yet fully proved its financial mettle to potential multinational corporations.

Mr. Tim explained that one of the key hurdles they faced with appealing to multinational corporations (MNCs) as sponsors was that these brands were overly cautious and did not want to offend segments of the country that found pageants to be unsuitable. He clarified that these companies had to be mindful of a "national perspective" rather than focus only on big cities like Lagos, where most residents would not bat an eye about a pageant. He further explained:

> A lot of the multinational brands in Nigeria shy away from getting involved in pageants for one or two reasons. The primary one is that the

multinationals which sell their brands across the nation are religiously sensitive. What I mean by that is that they will not want to upset the Muslim community in the North. If they are promoting Lux soap in the North where women are seen to be covered up, to be more conservative. . . . We still have the problem when we get to the North because of the religious reasons. The people from the North don't let their girls to take part in any competition. The only experience they have is their pulpit, that's it. They shy away from publicity like that.

His view seemed somewhat plausible to me, though I think my earlier explanation about perceptions of the lack of financial returns appears more likely. Mr. Tim's logic may seem counterintuitive. We might expect multinational corporations to be less aware of local politics. However, multinationals must often work with local intermediaries who help with distribution, consumer marketing, and navigating the regulatory environment. Moreover, multinational corporations have a ready association with international capital, making them easy targets for anti-globalization efforts that decry how local culture is being encroached upon. These factors may make potential MNCs prudent about their investment in the Nigerian beauty industry. Mr. Tim's comments frame religious concerns about modesty and body display in pageantry as an economic concern since multinationals seek the broadest appeal for their products. As a result, they would be disinclined to sponsor beauty pageants because of opposition from some segments of the Nigerian population.

Both pageants developed an ambivalent relationship with the state, switching between a level of mistrust and sought-after patronage. At MBGN, I spent hours writing invitation letters and finessing sponsorship presentations for state dignitaries, requesting financial backing and their attendance as special guests of honor for the show. In the weeks before the pageant, I was asked to write and revise these letters, making sure I researched the proper titles for the government officials. The organizers hand-delivered the typed letters to personal assistants and couriers, hoping that politicians' attendance at their event would facilitate further political access. They also included the pictures and titles of relevant governors and heads of the state ministries in their programs. In turn, government officials often penned letters promoting the tourism and investor potential of their states, which were included in the event brochure.

MBGN executives, however, would often deny a reliance on the state for assistance, noting a shift in Nigeria's economic landscape toward embracing private enterprise. Mr. Abe noted:

> Historically, government accounts for all jobs, all patronage and all income in Africa, especially Nigeria. Now the private sector in entertainment, with no support from the government, is becoming successful with pageants on their own. They are the ones that should get all the national honors. They are the greatest Nigerians ever!

Mr. Abe was onto something. The Structural Adjustment Program introduced into Nigeria's economy in 1986 resulted in the downsizing of Nigeria's public sector. Over the course of two years, civil jobs were cut by 40 percent. However, many of these jobs have been replaced by people working in the informal sector such as vending and running small businesses.[11] Mr. Abe talked about private companies like Silverbird as transforming the economic landscape of the country by generating income, wealth, and success independent of the government. He later insisted that government officials were useless "illiterate village guys," stating, "They can discuss village politics [but] they are not going to talk to me about pageants and shows." In his next breath, however, he insisted that the government should play an active role in supporting the entertainment industry by passing a law that required all banks to reserve 1 percent of their loans for the pageant industry. Mr. Abe's comments pinpoint the tenuous position of the state in Nigerian public consciousness—he acknowledged that the state has long been viewed as the main source of provisions for its citizens due to its control of the country's political economy and patronage relationships, but then noted the state's incompetence as an institution comprised of leaders who could not be trusted to run the state efficiently.

MBGN has made a few inroads with getting governor sponsorship, a deal which means that state governments cover the expenses for the pageant. For example, in 2013 the Bayelsa state tourism development agency, which was barely a year old, was the main sponsor of MBGN. In a public statement, the agency lauded Silverbird's executives as entertainment impresarios and competent professionals and name-dropped special guests and dignitaries who would be present at the show including Agbani Darego. Promising a

night of "glitz, glamour, and razzmatazz," the agency explained that the
pageant would provide them an opportunity to "display the rich, vibrant,
and colourful cultural heritage of our people," including hospitality, cuisine,
and tourism. They hired trained tour guides especially for the event, and
heralded events like MBGN as attracting both goodwill and making the state
"a tourist destination of choice in Africa" for international event managers.
They also discussed the promise of beauty queens "flying the Bayelsa state
flag" at international contests. The statement further declared:

> For the two weeks that the contestants and event crew will be in town,
> the hospitality industry will be agog as hoteliers and entertainment spot
> owners will be smiling to the bank daily because of the boom in the in-
> dustry. Transporters will also enjoy brisk business all through the period.
> MBGN pageant provides an ideal platform to project the rich and vibrant
> cultural heritage of the state. It provides a veritable vehicle for promot-
> ing our tourism, hospitality and entertainment industries. Events such
> as the MBGN beauty pageant and other entertainment shows creates an
> ideal platform to address the misconceptions outsiders have about the
> state because of the antecedents of our youths in the resource control
> agitation of the past. The Ijaw nation was the arrow head of that strug-
> gle. The government may use the occasion of the event to showcase the
> laudable transformation that is presently going on in the state courtesy
> of the Restoration Agenda of Governor H. S. Dickson.[12]

The state agency viewed the pageant as a moneymaking enterprise, but also
as a way to showcase social change in the country. Bayelsa state is located
in the Niger Delta region in South Nigeria. This region has the most oil
deposits in the country. Because of environmental degradation and high
rates of poverty despite this oil richness, youths have turned to militancy by
destroying oil production, kidnapping, and piracy to vocalize their concerns
about global exploitation since foreign oil companies and the Nigerian
state benefit financially from oil while citizens of ethnic groups who live
in the region, like the Ijaw, do not. The tourism agency viewed their hosting
of the pageant as a way to change the image of the state as dangerous. The
agency's press release, which was posted on a public blog, garnered two anonymous comments. One commenter wrote, "Don't bayelsa state n d bruce's

[the Murray-Bruce family] have something better to do for d state than all dis nonsense?" while another commenter noted, "A good one and welcome development for the upliftment of tourism and security in the state." These comments typify the range of responses of the general public to this tactic.

Queen Nigeria pursued governors as the ideal primary sponsors for their events, and in the 2009 cycle, Plateau state served as an official sponsor. Getting official state sponsorship that year was an uphill battle, however, since, as organizers explained to me, the then-governor was concerned that as a devout Christian, he would be seen as a hypocrite for supporting an industry focused on women's bodily display. By emphasizing Queen Nigeria's no-bikini stance, the college credentials of candidates (the previous winner from 2008, also from Plateau, was a pre-med student), and contestants' charity work, organizers were able to convince the government to offer state support. The 2009 pageant brochure included photographs of the governor, the deputy governor, and the commissioner of information, offering visual proof of the contest's state-sanctioned activities (see Figure 5.1). Throughout the pageant season, there was also much fanfare around the pageant's close relationship to first ladies, since the first lady or her representative was supposed to crown the beauty queens at both the state- and national-level pageants. Some first ladies were more supportive than others. The most supportive ones provided state-level winners with scholarship money, pageant-coaching packages, and a clothing allowance. Amina Mama dubs the public influence of the wives of heads of state in Africa the "First Lady Syndrome," since they wield a great deal of authority. Mama questions whether the concentration of financial and political power in the hands of a small group of elite women is a promising sign of equality or further signals authoritarianism in gender politics.[13] In Queen Nigeria, contestants are viewed as "mini first ladies," in the hopes of elevating their social status and highlighting their importance to the public.

For Queen Nigeria, this close alliance with the state meant that contestants and spectators viewed Queen Nigeria as susceptible to partisanship. At the grand finale of Queen Nigeria, when the winner was announced, the hall erupted in cheers and screams. Miss Plateau, the contestant from Queen Nigeria's host city, had emerged the winner. I slipped backstage, going through the side door to observe the reactions of some of the contestants and their minders. "PDP!" [the name of a political party] one of the girl's handlers

FIGURE 5.1. The inside pages of the Queen Nigeria program with photos of political officials. *Source:* NTA/TVE. Reprinted with permission.

yelled. I also heard other people shouting "PDP!" in the hallway and outside in the audience. One man had a chair raised above his head and looked like he was about to throw it. The PDP (the People's Democratic Party), which was Nigeria's ruling political party at the time, had produced both of Nigeria's presidents since its return to democratic rule in 1999, and was referred to in this case as shorthand for political power run amok. The shouts and yells of "PDP!" that filled the event hall's space were accusations that the organizers had rigged the contest so that the host state would win (mirroring allegations that the elections, in which PDP emerged the winner, were fraudulent).[14]

The audience's jeers and yells vocalized their disapproval, but the judging decision stood. I was instructed to collect the small, laminated placards that the contestants had pinned to the outside of their clothes to identify their state. As I collected the placards, the contestants' reactions ranged from visible anger, with some contestants storming out and crying, to nonchalance. I hugged one of the contestants, who whispered in my ear, "Now you've seen how a pageant can be influenced," spun on her heels, and walked away. On the short car ride back to the hotel, some of the contestants sullenly grumbled that the show was a "family affair," which allowed Miss Plateau, a contestant from the host state, to emerge the winner.

When I met up with Ebun a few weeks after the national finale at a fast food restaurant, she was accompanied by her new manager, who was developing a new plan for her to build her office as the state winner. Ebun was furious about how the finals had played out and placed the blame squarely on the organizers, saying they were more concerned with making money from the state government than having an impartial process. She explained:

> Your "yes" should be your "yes" and your "no" should be your "no." Not because you want to collect money or peanuts from your government, then you turn to. . . . Like the Yoruba saying goes "because you want to eat meat, then you will now be calling a cow *brother cow*." It is not supposed to be like that. It was so obvious. The result was there and they stroked [checked] like three names. And you know it was regional stuff, one person from the West, one from the South, East. Then Plateau won.

She pointed out that the winner and the runners-up each represented the major geopolitical regions of the country, serving to placate concerns about favoritism in the pageant. The day after the pageant, Ebun and other contestants had been invited to the governor's official residence for a courtesy visit. A representative of the governor had given each contestant ₦50,000 ($333), an amount that Ebun ridiculed as too small. She explained to me that the organizers had likely made much more than that from the state, and that they would not have even been able to set foot into the governor's house if not for using the contestants as a cover to thank the state for its support. She felt she had wasted her time going to the contest and compared Queen Nigeria to MBGN, "Even if you do not win the pageant you get offers that will compensate. From there you get the opportunity to do billboards, movies. Even if you do not win you get to connect. MBGN is still the best." The various layers in securing sponsorship for these contests showcase some of the constraints that pageants navigated. Accepting state support meant running the risk of the pageant being viewed as a political pawn. Moreover, the difficulty of penetrating multinational corporations lies in the fear of alienating local sentiments.

PASSING THE BUCK

Various stakeholders who formed relationships with Nigerian beauty queens understood them as mutually beneficial, but some contestants did not share this sentiment, feeling that under this system, they did not get the full benefit of their work and others actually hindered them from reaching their full potential. Immediately after the Queen Nigeria finale, we rode back in the van to the hotel. We had just passed a security checkpoint, which was in place because the city was under a 10 P.M.–6 A.M. curfew due to political unrest and ethnic clashes. The pageant had wrapped up thirty minutes late. After explaining to the police why were out so late, we were finally waved through. After passing the checkpoint, one of the contestants loudly sucked her teeth, using pidgin English to bitterly protest the contest's outcome: "*Na wa o!* [Wow!] This silly pageant! After all effort we put for dis here contest! Abeg, they better come give us our money o! We no go leave dis city without our money o!" Others also expressed their irritation and agreed with her assessment. Another contestant piped up, "They can't even compare themselves to MBGN. If you see the gift bags they get filled with jeans, T-shirts, even Sleek makeup!"

When I visited Yinka at her dorm after she had resumed college a couple of months after the finale, she bluntly pointed out that MBGN was a more worthwhile endeavor. She was especially fixated on the car Queen Nigeria had given the winner, a base-model hatchback Kia Picanto (worth about $12,000). Pointing out that MBGN winners got mid-range makes like Subarus and Toyotas, she taunted the new queen, giggling, "All other beauty queens are rich, big girls [slang for "rich girls"], who live a good life but you just got a Picanto, so what?" She then described MBGN as a pageant in which "everything's worth it, the prize, the money, the exposure, the event. Even if you don't win you are exposed. In my own pageant we didn't get anything." Like Ebun, Yinka did not see the money given to her from the government as anything special. When I visited Aisha after the pageant, she seemed to concur with Yinka's views about the Kia. When I asked her about it, she told me that it was parked in the back of her compound without gas and she refused to drive it. Aisha, who had been pursuing a modeling career, came from a well-connected, upper-middle-class family. She explained that she only had done the pageant for "fun," a common refrain I had heard from others, but she was one of the few whose statement seemed earnest. As she explained to me, she did not need the money from the pageant like the other contestants did, so the fact that the financial rewards were not as high as others had expected did not bother her.

While Queen Nigeria contestants painted a rosy picture of MBGN, one that viewed even those who didn't win as living in the lap of luxury, many MBGN contestants would beg to differ with this assumption. One example is Delilah Nwozuzu. Delilah was raised in Lagos, the last born of six children. Her father died when she was eight years old, a loss that plunged the family into economic crisis. As Delilah explained it, her father's death "took the wealth with him." A spiritual person with an independent streak, Delilah described herself as "very principled. I have a code. . . . I don't want anybody coming to take away any glory." She did not want anyone else to veer her off the morally righteous path she had set for herself. She had resolved to be successful while keeping a moral compass. This self-determination, a result of her father's early departure from her life, drew her to register for MBGN. Two years earlier, when she had just graduated from secondary school, her neighbor recruited her for another pageant. The queen had been dethroned at the last minute and the pageant's organizers were looking for a replacement since they had committed to sending a representative to an international pageant in the small West African country of Gambia. The neighbor was able to convince Delilah's overprotective mother to let her be installed as the new queen without having to compete. That experience "broke the barrier" for her mother, who became very supportive of her taking part in MBGN and her budding modeling career, even accompanying her daughter gown shopping as she prepared for camp. Delilah did not work with any stylists, advisers, or coaches before the show, but she had done some modeling, through which she had met a designer who loaned her outfits for camp and the show. As a result of her participation, she won an endorsement deal. Delilah was invested in doing behind-the-scenes work for the brand and not just being the face of a product. Though she was eager to work as a brand ambassador, she felt limited in what she was able to accomplish and felt she had few "next-world opportunities," narrating to me the series of challenges she faced, namely in not having "mobility," meaning a car to get around Lagos. Having a car was seen as critical for beauty queens due to the combination of their status and logistics.

Like many other contestants, she complained that the pageant was only interested in the winner and winning Miss World, and as a result did not fully invest in the contestants as a group. Other contestants I interviewed shared similar complaints, saying that the main focus was only on the show itself, building hype around the finale, before allowing the excitement to taper down and then starting the process all over again the following year. After eight months of rising frustration from hitting several brick walls, and feeling drained, Delilah signed with one of the top modeling agencies in Nigeria and launched her career as a professional model. She had the opportunity to travel to Los Angeles to do some modeling work, and upon her return to Nigeria, she began commanding the booking fees of an "international model" due to her experience abroad. She gave very little credit to MBGN for her accomplishments and instead griped that its organizers needed to do more to provide all contestants with the financial resources to match the new heightened expectations they navigated.

The contestants expected the owners and organizers to help fund their new lifestyles, but the organizers deviated from this opinion, absolving themselves of that responsibility. They felt they provided contestants with sufficient media exposure, entry into elite social circles, and enough training for them to personally invest in securing their own futures. But the contestants found an unlikely ally in Mr. Omo, who stated, "My sister, Nigerian girls are hungry, for as low as ₦2.5 million ($16,666), they can deny their mother in public, that is the truth and that is why pageantry is still thriving. [MBGN] has done their best, they've produced finalists, but there is still room for improvement." Mr. Omo explained that MBGN had been able to maintain momentum because of the pageant's attachment to a media juggernaut—including television and radio stations that generated publicity for their company and the queen. However, he identified several shortcomings, namely, the need to spend more money on beauty queens and to do more publicity. Claiming that MBGN's organizers had begun to rest on their laurels and viewed the contest as a part-time hobby instead of a full-time passion, he explained that the contest should "go back to the drawing board." He believed the pageant had become a "means to an end and no longer an end to a means," meaning he believed Silverbird now only viewed the pageant as a marketing strategy to help its other business ventures. As a journalist, Mr. Omo had a vested interest in MBGN's commitment to publicity. He complained, "How many stories have you read about the current queen? She can walk around the mall today and no one would know her. Show her picture to a thousand people, maybe fifty would know her. She has not been publicized properly." Mr. Omo had written a piece about the newest queen but said he did it as a favor since she had asked him directly. Taking one last impatient look at his watch, he wrapped up our interview by stating that, as far as he was concerned, the climax of Nigerian pageantry was in producing the first Miss World, and given the way he saw things going, he thought that was not likely to happen again for a long time.

CONCLUSION

Multiple stakeholders use pageants to get ahead by generating revenue and boosting their reputation. Though the relationships between beauty queens and these stakeholders are presented as mutually beneficial by helping contestants thrive in a structural environment in which they regularly encounter barriers, the financial and symbolic benefits largely accrue to pageant owners, sponsors, and the state, groups at the helm of Nigeria's political economy. While beauty pageants around the world are used to enhance national reputations, Nigeria's especially poor international image, juxtaposed against the high hopes for a promising future, heighten the stakes. Despite the hopes surrounding the possibility of an upward economic trajectory for Nigeria, a number of problems persist in guaranteeing a secure business environment due to dodgy business schemes, bureaucratic institutions, and murky legal policies. Associating with young women who are positioned as responsible role models through their charm, beauty, and intellect, re-casts pageants as a form of respectable entrepreneurship that benefits young women and brands the nation in a positive light. Although the owners presented beauty contests as open sites for determined young women ready to make their mark on the nation, contestants often felt that the symbolic and material benefit from their participation went to others. This complex process intermingles money, status, and power in Nigeria's political economy.

6 | AS MISS WORLD TURNS

BLACK SWAN

In risk management circles, the term *black swan* is a metaphor used to under-stand unforeseen outlier events.[1] This seems a fitting analogy to understand Agbani Darego's November 2001 win. Darego was a long shot. Oddsmakers had put her chances at winning at 66–1.[2] Her history-making feat as the first Black African to win Miss World is still talked about as the apex of the industry to this day. Silverbird employees scouted Darego at a zonal contest for MNET's Face of Africa contest, a modeling search that aimed to launch the international careers of African models. Darego did not make the cut for the search, but Silverbird employees urged her to compete for MBGN.

The Silverbird executives were eager to clinch an international title. They brought Gina onboard to help reorient the pageant and inject what she called "international flavor" into the show. Gina instituted a strategy of aiming for tall, thin, modelesque contestants. At one point, MBGN used precise body proportions, measuring everything from neck circumference to hip to toe lengths. At six feet tall and with long limbs, high cheekbones, and deep-set brown eyes, Darego fit the bill. Silverbird hired a dedicated team of experts, including top Nigerian hairstylists, fashion designers, and etiquette coaches, who trained Darego on posture, poise, how to work a room, and how to eat with different place settings for three months straight. Darego, who was described to me as shy, blossomed under this tutelage. The intense coaching paid off—Darego was a top ten semifinalist at the 2001 Miss Universe contest held in Puerto Rico. Naomi Campbell, an international supermodel and cohost of the 2001 Miss Universe Beauty Pageant, invited Darego to participate in "Frock-N-Rock," a benefit fashion show in Barcelona Spain, which further honed Darego's skills. Six months after making the top ten in the Miss Universe Pageant, Darego won Miss World.

The Silverbird team stressed the amount of time and money invested into ensuring Darego was well prepared for the pageant. Early on a Saturday morning, Mr. Abe leaned forward in his black leather office chair and explained to me that his vision came to fruition not because of sheer luck, but because he had thoroughly analyzed international pageantry. Making a comparison to the Nigerian football (soccer) teams, which, he claimed, did not reach their full potential on international playing fields because they "never have smart players and smart coaches at the same time," he said that Darego's win was due to a combination of her intelligence and Silverbird's ingenuity.

Mr. Abe and others stressed Silverbird's hard work. However, I also heard rumors from others that Darego's win was linked to a broader strategy to justify hosting Miss World in 2002. Those inclined to believe such conspiracies described an orchestrated business ploy put into motion when Julia Morley, Miss World's owner and the reigning Miss World at the time, made a three-day visit to Nigeria in May 2000 to support the charity work of first lady Stella Obasanjo, who was a close friend of the Murray-Bruce family. In published news reports from 2000, an unnamed source claimed, "The coming of Miss World [the visit from the 1999 Miss World beauty queen] is to test the ground towards Nigeria's dream of hosting the pageant someday. . . . I tell you with the relationship that is going on between Silverbird and the Presidency, nothing will stop Nigeria from bidding for the Miss World pageant someday."[3] Those I spoke with who subscribed to this theory portrayed hosting the pageant as a way to secure business deals tied to Nigeria's oil industry, promote the sale of more beauty products in Nigeria, and gain political connections to the Obasanjo regime. These pageant affiliates viewed this as a business arrangement that implicated both Silverbird and Miss World. Those who speculated that this rumor was accurate pointed to the fact that in 2001,

Miss World introduced a new twist to public voting through a component called "You Decide," in which viewers could phone in or cast a vote online for their favorite contestant during either the pretaped preview events or the live broadcast, during which an onstage top ten scoreboard tabulated votes in real time. Viewer scores were combined with the judges' marks.[4] In 2001, the government fully deregulated the telecommunications industry, which meant that Nigerians gained unprecedented access to mobile phones. Moreover, these speculators explained, Nigerians, who were already well known for well-publicized Internet schemes, doubtless crammed into cybercafés and easily gamed the system, bypassing the public voting formula, which weighted scores according to the country of origin. Those who bought into this plot offered as additional proof Darego's reaction to her win: she did not burst into tears when her name was announced, which is a typical response for pageant winners, but instead smiled broadly, implying, according to cynics, that she already knew the outcome. While I took these rumors with a grain of salt, it did strike me as likely that hosting the pageant was part of a long-term business move to further entrench the country into global capitalism and link private corporations to state politics.

Sociologist Leslie Sklair uses the term *transnational capitalist class* to describe how corporate owners, politicians, and consumer-driven elites control the reins of the global political economy. Through the concept of global nationalism, he argues that this group aims to boost national interests by identifying a lucrative position for the country within a globally integrated political economy.[5] I expand this concept to consider the broader transnational forces that build and respond to nation-building projects through domestic and international political actors who align, not only with a profit-driven transnational capitalist class, but also with religious civic society, such as advocates of Political Islam, who push for a realignment of state and society through moral principles,[6] and with the global equity regimes, which push for compliance to universal mutually agreed-upon principles enacted through conventions, treaties, and legal instruments.[7] These social actors not only do their work through an economic logic, they also insert politics and culture into constructions of global nationalism. Varied groups discursively use women's bodies to project specific national narratives with wide-ranging material consequences. Women's bodies are frequently a locus of tension over potential solidarity and strife in that issues such as women's dress, reproduction, and sexuality, generate global moral panics, a generalized fear about potential social breakdown. These debates about women's bodies serve as important national symbols and as instruments of control during international crises and shifting geopolitics that signal consolidation and fragmentation.[8] This event brought cosmopolitan and cultural definitions of the Nigerian nation to the fore on a global stage. I use the term *global-nationalism* to depict how nations are not only symbolically constructed internally, but also in dialogue with external perceptions of the country. That is, responses to and input from external definitions also contribute to nation building. National trajectories are jointly defined within and outside of countries.

Using the tensions engendered by the buoyed confidence of Darego's victory alongside the dashed hopes of hosting the pageant just one year later, I develop the concept of *gendered embodied protection* to show how women's bodies played critical roles in defending globally inflected visions of the Nigerian nation. This tactic is a discursive political strategy that centers the vulnerability of women and their tangible bodies to justify intervention for varied cultural, political, and economic ends. This tactic is a tool to advance moral claims on women's bodies, determined by competing views on globalization and Nigerian national identity. Different groups centered certain embodied figures as needing protecting—attractive foreign delegates, nude women, and women punished with stoning—to project national images on the world stage. Discursive politics are often embodied through mobilizing different facets of women's bodies (in this case physical, spiritual, and civic) to draw out contested visions of the nation-state and destabilize international politics. Local and international boycotters and supporters of the Miss World hosting used this critical world event to define nationhood, modernity, and global belonging.

A PERFECT STORM

Eric Morley, a British entertainment businessman, founded the Miss World Pageant in 1951, conceiving of it as a onetime publicity stunt to coincide with the Festival of Britain, a government-organized national exhibition to encourage the arts, technology, and industrial design held during the post–World War II recovery period. The pageant steadily grew into an annual sensation, attracting delegates from around the world. Morley died in 2000 and his widow, Julia Morley, took over the enterprise. Miss World is the longest-running international beauty contest in the world today and is currently franchised in over one hundred countries.

In 2002, the Miss World Beauty Pageant website boasted: "Miss World 2002 will be the most lavish and spectacular production that we've ever undertaken. It's second only to the Olympics for international participation."[9] Since 2000, Miss World has claimed participation from over one hundred contestants from around the world and an estimated audience of 2 billion viewers from close to two hundred countries, making the Miss World Pageant one of the most widely watched events in the world. Its viewership rivals those of mega–sporting events like the Olympics and the World Cup, which attracted about 3.3 billion and an estimated 2 billion viewers on average, respectively between 2002 and 2016.[10] Following Darego's triumph, Silverbird leaped at the chance to enter a hosting bid for Miss World the following year, viewing it as a prime opportunity to proclaim Nigeria's rising status. In February 2002, a delegation from the Miss World Organization toured possible venues in Nigeria and four other countries that had entered bids. In June, Silverbird secured hosting rights to host the pageant in Abuja, Nigeria's capital. At a press conference, First Lady Obasanjo announced plans for a partnership between her office's Child Care Trust charity project and the government ministries of Culture and Tourism and of Aviation. She pledged that the federal government would provide logistical support for the event but expend no public funds.

As organizers prepared to hold the planned event, a variety of protests ensued. Originally slated to be held in November, organizers shifted the date by a week to accommodate complaints by some Nigerian Muslims, who were angered that the date interfered with the final week of Ramadan, the Muslim holy month of fasting and spiritual reflection. Problems escalated after Isioma Daniel, a Christian, British-trained Nigerian journalist, opined in a newspaper article titled "The World at their Feet" that the Prophet Muhammad would have likely approved of the contest and chosen one of the Miss World contestants as his wife. Daniel's article, which ran in *ThisDay*, a Lagos-based newspaper with a national circulation, exacerbated preexisting

tensions between Christians and Muslims. The editor-in-chief was detained
for three days by state security agents. The deputy governor of Zamfara state,
Mahmud Aliyu Shinkafi, issued a *fatwa* (a religious edict; it was later revoked)
calling for the death of Isioma Daniel for blasphemy.[11] Daniel resigned and
fled to Benin, eventually finding asylum in Norway. The paper issued a re-
traction two days later and repeated it the following day, faulting a technical
glitch during the editing process that prevented deletion of the passage.
The newspaper later issued a formal front page "apology to all Muslims"
and denounced the article as "utterly provocative."[12]

The damage was done, however. Protests, which turned violent, erupted
in Kaduna, a Northern Nigerian state capital with a mixed Muslim and
Christian population, over the inflammatory article.[13] Rioters burned down
the local offices of *ThisDay* because it had published the offending article.
Hundreds were killed, thousands more were injured, and buildings were
destroyed. The rioters vandalized mosques, churches, shops, and hotels. They
marched through the streets chanting, "Down with beauty!" and "Miss World
is sin!"[14] Security agents imposed a curfew, patrolled the streets, and stopped
and searched motorists to enforce calm in the city. Following Jummat services
(Friday congregational prayers), protests also took place in Abuja, Nigeria's
capital and the intended venue for the beauty contest. The police reportedly
made twenty-seven arrests.[15]

Yet another conflict developed over the selection of Nigeria as the
Miss World event site, in the first place. International human rights organizations
called for a boycott of the event, in light of the mistreatment of women under
the newly codified sharia law (Islamic legal doctrine) in some Northern Nigerian states. In particular, the case of Amina Lawal had risen to international
prominence in March 2002. Lawal was a thirty-year-old Muslim woman
from a small village in Katsina state in Northern Nigeria. Nine months after
her divorce was finalized, she gave birth to a baby girl. Lawal claimed that
her daughter's father had promised to marry her but later rescinded his marriage proposal. Nonetheless, the state sentenced her to be stoned to death for
alleged extramarital sexual relations, just two months before Nigeria secured
hosting rights, but stayed the execution for two years so that Lawal could
wean and care for her daughter. On September 27, Amnesty International
presented a petition with 1.3 million signatures gathered online to Nigerian

officials at the London High Commission in protest of Amina Lawal's sentence. Lawal's case was eventually overturned in 2003 by a five-judge panel in the Katsina court of appeal, but the case became embroiled in the Miss World events due to the timing.[16] In solidarity with Lawal's plight, several contestants including Miss Norway, Miss Panama, and Miss Denmark withdrew or threatened to boycott the competition to rally behind Lawal.[17]

This reaction unfolded and reached a crescendo over the twelve days the delegates spent in Nigeria. In Abuja they had met with state officials and worshipped at the Aso Rock Villa Chapel. They also traveled to Cross Rivers state, which is located in the southeastern coast of the country, where they attended events and toured preselected tourist sites, including the Obudu Cattle Ranch (now known as the Obudu Mountain Resort), Mary Slessor's house (Slessor was a famous Scottish missionary stationed in Nigeria during the 1800s), and a cultural regatta in the form of a procession. Late on a Saturday night and two weeks before the scheduled pageant, however, the organizers made the final decision to switch venues to London for the "sake of the nation." The eighty-eight contestants, the organizers, and their entourage boarded buses headed to the airport to leave the country on a specially chartered aircraft.[18]

The final crowning of the pageant occurred at Alexandra Palace in London. The winner, Miss Turkey, was the first winner from a predominately Muslim country since the pageant was won by Egypt in 1954. Some commentators speculated that this was yet another political move on the part of Miss World's judges, who selected her to promote a moderate version of Islam. Footage shot at preshow events were shown during the airing, and the organizers insisted that the show was still "Nigerian at heart." They also claimed that the finalists, including the newly crowned Miss World, were inclined to return to Nigeria. Like the carefully edited "fun tape" footage captured at popular Nigerian tourist attractions, organizers hoped to show controlled images of Nigeria that highlighted the very best of Nigerian culture, hospitality, and luxury. Sean Kanan, the announcer and American soap star read a statement on stage, stating "Our hearts go out to the families who have suffered, and we hope that Nigeria recovers swiftly and will finally be recognized for the beauty it possesses." A moment of silence was held in tribute to Amina Lawal at the contestants' request. The event was clearly an international public relations nightmare for the country. The initial optimism surrounding the bid as an effective tool for positively showcasing the country to the world shifted to understanding the events as a deeply humiliating event that revealed a wide-scale failure. The mayor of London rebuked the contest for bringing tragedy and strife to Nigeria. Accusations of "swimsuits dripping with blood" were plastered throughout the British newspapers, and no British television station agreed to broadcast the pageant, though it was televised in other countries. The newly crowned Miss World, Azra Akin, never returned to Nigeria for a visit.

The Miss World crisis unraveled due to a confluence of complex factors. While accounts by pundits, scholars, and the public typically explain the protests as an inevitable outcome of Nigeria's communal conflicts, this chapter presents a different view.[19] That view is that the conflicts surrounding the 2002 Miss World Pageant should not be understood as merely a product of religious convictions and misunderstandings. I propose alternative framings that, while drawing in part on religious tropes, highlight a broader set of political issues that involve divergent understandings of the Nigerian nation-state both within and outside of Nigeria. The geopolitical dimensions of these protests, as well as the plans that prompted them and the adjustment that followed, were symbols of contested understandings of globalization and an unsteady vehicle for nationalism that were projected onto a world stage.

The 2002 Miss World beauty competition served as a platform on which to crystallize and declare the larger agendas of various groups. These heterogeneous groups speak to the broader political interests that directly engage with the Nigerian nation-state and the global community including Nigerian entrepreneurs, Nigerian religious groups, and international human rights organizations, each of which had a stake in how this event was framed. Local and international supporters and boycotters debated the trajectory of the Nigerian nation through rhetorical framings that drew on ideas about national identity and global belonging.

Miss World brought with it the global spotlight. It mattered that this event was an international one rather than a local or national pageant. After all, pageants have existed in Nigeria since the 1950s, and while there have been moments of controversy throughout their history, they have continued without any large-scale protests against them. However, the global scope of the Miss World Pageant brought accompanying debates about globalization to the fore. The political crisis that accompanied the 2002 Miss World Pageant was as an example of a *critical world event,* which I define as an event that transnationally situated institutional actors can leverage politically to demand attention and focus their agendas. Anthropologist Veena Das points to "critical events" as watershed historical moments that often incite violence. Through a case study of contemporary India, Das argues that critical events make visible specific historical rifts, pointing to larger issues of ethnic conflict, state power, global processes, and gender that figure into the crossroads of nations.[20] I extend Das's concept to show how critical world events throw the idea of a unified nation-state into question, allowing multiple projections of the nation to emerge in response to these events. Critical world events garner broad international scrutiny, are broadcast throughout the world, involve many countries, and depend on multiple interest groups. Institutional actors view them as both an opportunity and a threat because they speak to underlying social conditions and political struggle.

Institutional actors highlight the global political dimensions of cultural events as sites of both potential solidarity and friction. Groups capitalize on critical world events as political openings to move their agendas forward within contested discursive frames. Activists, private corporations, journalists, state officials, and spectators can use critical world events to reshape broader social processes in symbolic ways. The events during the Miss World Pageant constitute a contested site of public debate that brought together a variety of political actors, which together shaped national narratives about Nigeria. Critical world events highlight and make visible competing perspectives of the nation-state and globalization. These events in particular revealed existing anxieties and anticipations about Nigeria and its place in the world in which embodied gendered claims of protection played a prominent role in substantiating larger political claims. Critical world events serve as fraught political platforms for focusing and announcing social concerns on a public global stage, thus providing local, national, and international collective actors a way of moving their agendas forward to publicize their views, project broader conflicts, and spur social action.

The Miss World crisis happened at a critical historical moment, which was rife with conflicts over sharia law, Nigeria's newly reinstated democracy, and the impending 2003 elections. In 1999, following decades of military rule, the country returned to democracy. While sharia has long existed as a form of customary law governing practices like marriage and inheritance in some Northern Nigerian states, starting in 1999 sharia law was formally enacted as the basis of the *legal criminal* code in twelve Northern states.[21] Broadly, sharia refers to the religious commandments and code of conduct based on the Quran (Muslim holy book) and sunnah (traditions of the Prophet). Islamic jurisprudence varies based on different legal schools, which have diverse interpretations, legal rulings, and analytical reasonings. In Nigeria, implementation of sharia had populist support since it was framed as a means of redressing moral decline, political corruption, and economic insecurity through redistributive economic reforms and political accountability. Sharia has served as a flashpoint in the country, and people on the ground have noted the contradictions and conflicts surrounding its implementation.[22]

In 2002, President Obasanjo, a candidate from the South, was in his final year of office and up for reelection in 2003, the first time in fifteen years that a civilian government had organized democratic elections in the country. His major rival was Muhammadu Buhari, a Muslim Northerner. The broader jostling for regional control was important as Buhari drew his base of support from the North. The North wanted a turn at the seat of presidential power, wanting to see one of its own in office for the upcoming election cycle. Obasanjo was seeking to appeal to the North. Nigerian supporters construed the protests as a political strategy to distract Obasanjo who would not provide a forceful response so as to not alienate the North. The reelection bid spurred an understanding of the Miss World crisis as politically motivated. As Mr. Abe explained:

> When they started attacking the girls, they were attacking President Obasanjo. Obasanjo was seeking re-election, they were attacking him, they were discrediting him because the North wanted to produce the next presidential candidate. . . . You know in Nigeria everybody takes advantage of your weak spot and everybody goes after you.

By identifying the protests as a way for the North to benefit from regional divisions and as an attack on then-President Obasanjo's "weak spot," Mr. Abe deflected the blame onto internal politics.[23] President Obasanjo spoke about the Lawal case but refused to directly intervene in the judicial process or grant her an immediate pardon. In a radio and television address to mark the forty-second anniversary of Nigeria's independence, he remained equivocal, saying, "We cannot imagine or envision a Nigerian being stoned to death. It has never happened. And may it never happen."[24] In interviews, Nigerian supporters of the pageant argued that a desire to appeal to the North prevented Obasanjo and other politicians from issuing more forceful denouncements of the Amina Lawal case. Many members of the Silverbird Production team met with high-ranking officials to seek formal confirmation that the government would commute Lawal's sentence and quell the riots, but to no avail. When I asked them about it, they described a series of events that became a mishandled diplomatic affair.

It was also significant that the attempted hosting of Miss World in Nigeria happened in the relatively recently inaugurated capital city of Abuja. Abuja is a planned city, the first of its kind in Africa and the seat of administrative political power in the country. In 1991, the capital officially moved from Lagos, the previous colonial capital in Nigeria's Southwest region, to Abuja, a city in the midpoint of the country. The objective of choosing Abuja to re-site the capital was, in part, to mitigate regional and religious splits since city planners and government officials viewed the new location as a neutral center.

Since it officially became the capital in 1991, Abuja has grown from a quiet civil service town to a fast-growing metropolitan city. The city is divided into several districts and cadastral zones, with clusters of satellite settlements along the outskirts of the city. The city's tree-lined streets are surrounded by hills, Savannah grassland, highlands, and tropical rain forests. Features such as open green spaces, shrub vegetation, and two massive granite formations—Aso Rock and Zuma Rock—are prominent geographical features in the city, blending a tranquil backdrop against bustling city life. Abuja's cityscape contrasts with Lagos, which in the 2000s was known for crumbling infrastructure neglected by the federal government's relocation, heavily congested highways, and potholed roads. The Lagos metropolitan area is densely populated. There, an area 2.5 times smaller than Abuja holds a population that is 3.5 times higher.

In hindsight, nearly everyone I spoke with suggested that hosting the event outside Abuja, most likely in Lagos, might have protected it from some of the uproar.[25] The site selection for Miss World called into question the issue of state funding for the event as well as regional divisions between the North and the South. Debate about whether parts of this area belong to the North or the South is constant, and people who opposed the pageant frequently described Abuja as Northern and thus an inappropriate site for the contest due to the region's conservative atmosphere. In contrast, Nigerian supporters of the pageant viewed Abuja as a neutral center and the clear choice for the site of the Miss World Pageant, and they referenced its cosmopolitanism and robust infrastructure. Organizers felt that Lagos's overcrowding, gridlocked streets, and poorly maintained infrastructure would make preparations logistically difficult and might embarrass the country. While organizers' concerns about hosting the pageant in Lagos were likely well-founded, it seems possible the pageant would not have simultaneously touched off issues of Obasanjo's pending reelection campaign, diplomatic affairs, the state's backing of the pageant, and Nigeria's return to democracy in 1999 if not for the selection of Abuja as the host location.

GENDERED EMBODIED PROTECTION

The multiple responses to the Miss World Pageant encompassed a wide range of institutional actors, including private entrepreneurs, religious groups within Nigeria, and international activists who interfaced with global publics and the Nigerian state and had a diverse array of concerns. While these three groups were not entirely monolithic in their responses, commentary at the time and since reflects distinctive competing frames within which the 2002 pageant was understood. These three different groups all drew on common claims of protecting women's bodies to lobby for or against the pageant yet relied on distinct discursive strategies that reflected varied ideologies about women's place and interpretations about the responsibilities of the nation-state and the consequences of globalization. Nigerian entrepreneurs focused on security and the political economy, Nigerian Muslim opposition groups emphasized piety and culture, and international human rights organizations and their allies stressed advocacy and the law.

Security, Economic Capability, and Physical Protection

The Nigerian organizers and their supporters were thrilled to use Darego's win to bankroll their financial motives. They emphasized how her physical beauty and acumen proved to others around the world that Nigeria was a capable country on the brink of an economic breakthrough. Through personal relationships with state officials from Cross Rivers state, Rivers state, and the federal government, the organizers secured financial sponsorship and logistical support to host the event. I interviewed eight supporters who backed the pageant. They were largely high-powered Nigerian entrepreneurs affiliated with the Silverbird Group who stood to benefit financially from the contest. This team advanced a security discourse centered on the physical safety of attractive foreign pageant contestants. Security signaled financial fitness, military ability, state strength, and compatibility with international standards. Mobilizing state resources, they used ramped-up security as a way of linking local initiatives with established international expectations of order, wealth, and competition, directly seeking to resist the framing of Nigeria as a poor, violent, conflict-ridden nation. Contestants' physical bodies came to stand in for representative nations since they were viewed as international delegates that organizers of the pageant were charged with protecting through their access to state-sponsored strength. Nigerian supporters prized the physical safety of foreign beauty pageant delegates. Their ability to provide this protection was directly linked to broader interpretations of the nation-state as an economic force that centered on Nigeria as a central node of globalization and fostered international belonging.

Nigerian organizers justified their spending on the event as worth it at the time because of the long-term investment. They anticipated a large financial return in the form of increased foreign expenditure in the country since a successful event would showcase Nigeria as an economically prosperous and safe country with untapped wealth. They also rationalized accepting state support for the pageant, counteracting critics who expressed hesitation over the Nigerian state using federal money to support a private event in the face of national problems such as poverty and poor governance. In contrast, the pageant organizers emphasized the economic responsibility of the Nigerian state to provide logistical support through state-backed security. Countering critics, they actually viewed the contest as addressing national concerns by boosting the country's reputation, which would attract financial investment and allay fears about political corruption and economic instability in the country. The security narrative was a means of evaluating the country's financial strength.

Mr. Omo's words elucidated the connections between Darego's win and the 2002 hosting as an economic initiative:

It was a hallmark. We needed to prove to the world that if we are capable of producing a Miss World then the idea was to showcase Nigeria positively to the world. We needed to showcase some of our tourism facilities. The government capitalized on that for them to increase the GDP of the citizenry. The government wanted to use that as an opportunity to invite investors that despite all the farce, all the noise that we are terrorists and all that, we wanted to show them that there was something still good about Nigeria. We lost that because of a few stupid Nigerians, backward people that are not ready to get civilization into their veins.

Talking about Cross Rivers state, one of the sponsors of Miss World, as a one-of-a-kind destination with gushing waterfalls, top-notch resorts, and sanctuaries for endangered monkeys, Mr. Omo explained that managing to hold the Miss World Pageant there would have helped Nigeria increase foreign investment, boost GDP, and become a magnet for ecotourism, one of the sectors the then-governor, Donald Duke (who had a reputation as a young, forward-thinking, and gregarious leader), sought to further harness. Nigerian supporters framed Miss World not as lining their own pockets, but as augmenting the bottom line for the country as a whole. Growing increasingly impatient with my questions and glancing repeatedly down at his watch, Mr. Omo angrily decried "religious fanaticism" and placed the blame on "hypocrite infidels," who protested and rioted against Miss World as preventing these economic dividends from coming to fruition. Speaking of these "fundamentalists," he started, "You know they usually cover themselves from head to toe. The Miss World [Pageant] goes beyond covering your head. You need to show some of the anatomy that makes you a woman."

As our conversation wound down, however, he concluded that it was the international press that ultimately "killed" their hopes of staging Miss World. Like many others, he portrayed Nigeria as peaceful and downplayed the violence that had occurred. Instead, he indignantly blamed the foreign media for sensationalizing the turn of events:

There is no violence in this country. It was just a handful of people who were there making noise, trying to set up fires on the street, opposite the hotel. That was what CNN and the American motherfuckers saw and started showing to the world because we had produced one Miss World, so they figured that, if given that opportunity, we might produce a second Miss World. It was a gang-up against the Black man. That was racial discrimination.

He characterized the international media as envious and racist, and Darego's physical beauty as threatening to Western domination. He complained bitterly that foreigners wanted to "pull us down. They thought nothing good comes out of Africa," presuming that Darego's win was "just a flash in the pan." He then described Miss World as losing its glamour and said that Agbani's win had brought originality and excitement back to the international competition. He focused specifically on Agbani's answer during the question-and-answer round, in which American talk show host Jerry Springer, the evening's MC, asked, "In this man's world, what do you think you can change that a man cannot?" Darego's response emphasized charity by assisting the needy and her love of humanity. Mr. Omo underscored Agbani's perfection and exclaimed, "Beauty goes beyond being a White person! Beauty has to do with intelligence and Agbani showed to the world what intelligence is all about. Agbani proved to the world that a Black woman can also be very intelligent but the White people didn't like that. No White woman could have done that." Mr. Abe had similar misgivings about the international media, sharing that one of the moves that solidified their decision to shift the pageant to London was that the *Sun*, a British tabloid, was threatening to charter a plane to "rescue the girls" and splash it all over their headlines. For Mr. Abe, the risk of humiliation was too great to call their bluff.

Nigerian organizers stressed that foreign pageant contestants were to be treated as cultural ambassadors from their respective countries. Nigeria's ability to adequately protect these delegates became an important symbol of the country's desire to improve its international reputation and increase their global standing. The Nigerian supporters emphasized the twenty-four-hour surveillance of contestants, through appointed chaperones, a heavy security detail at the five-star Nicon Hilton Hotel in Abuja, and access to armored vehicles, intelligence operatives, motorcades, and chartered private jets, as proof of their ability to provide adequate protection for all contestants. Several uniformed

FIGURE 6.1. A security force member stands by Miss World contestants. *Source:* Boris Heger/AP Photos.

security guards with guns holstered on their hips followed contestants everywhere (see Figure 6.1). Pageant supporters did not view these security measures as portraying Nigeria as dangerous, but rather as a signal of wealth, power, and tactical maneuvers. I interviewed Mr. Kalu, who was one of the strategic organizers of Miss World. After offering me a glass of water, Mr. Kalu's secretary showed me into his office, where he sat behind his large mahogany desk with his arms folded. Mr. Kalu recalled the planning stages which included intense meetings with the state security services (or SSS; this is the country's domestic intelligence service, which is similar to the U.S. FBI), the police, immigration officials, and the national intelligence agency (which oversees foreign intelligence and counterintelligence operations, akin to the U.S. CIA). In our interview, he repeatedly stressed the financial loses that nearly led to Silverbird's financial collapse. He claimed that he lost 375,000 pounds alone in a matter of hours because the air cargo plane that was scheduled to bring the stage and other equipment had to be turned around at the last minute and they chartered additional planes to move everyone to London. He continued to emphasize the protection they offered contestants from bodily harm, even in the midst of the turmoil of switching venues, stating, "When the girls were moving, NICON [Hotel] shut down. We had one hundred female mobile police officers guiding us. We had SSS. We had soldiers. We had five girls to each chaperone. You couldn't even move close to them."

Mr. Kalu then went on to observe that the international media was overly concerned with the Amina Lawal case and reporting stories of Nigeria focused on "stoning women," which he found to be a mischaracterization of the country. He continued:

> We had a press conference and all the press wanted to know about was, what do you feel about this Amina that was [supposed to be] stoned to death? What do you feel about armed robbery? And other related questions. They were not even asking about the pageant, what they were after was Nigeria's problems. They don't see anything good in Nigeria. They say Nigeria is not safe. How many people were killed in the city of Chicago within twenty-four hours?

In response to these negative questions, he devised a strategy of asking reporters where they were from and then researching their countries to say something equally atrocious. He used other countries as yardsticks and framed Nigeria's problems as similar to, if not less severe than, those faced by any other country.

Many other Nigerian organizers also made direct comparisons to other countries to emphasize that their need to physically protect the contestants was a general concern facing events of this magnitude, and not a specific problem in Nigeria. They stressed their competence in protecting beauty contestants through state-backed security agents and attempted to minimize the potential risk faced by contestants by limiting the public's access to and contact with them. Catching her in between meetings, I met Mrs. Abigail Nansel in a conference room at Silverbird's beachfront television station. A trained lawyer-turned-journalist who directed public relations for the event, liaising between the Ministry for Foreign Affairs and the diplomatic missions of the contestants' countries, she assured me:

> We were working closely with security agents and at no time did they tell us the girls were in danger. The girls had the protection they needed. . . .

The federal government ensured that they were all protected. The girls
were ensconced at the Hilton. Because of how pageants are and how
society works, it generally would have been difficult for anyone to have
access to the girls, even if they were in London or the U.S. The girls were not
fair game. These girls were not objects of affection. They were here for
a purpose.

Like others, she repeatedly downplayed the potential danger the contestants
faced, emphasizing their continuous communication with security agents
whose professionalism and effectiveness should be trusted. By bringing up
other places like London and the United States, she framed safety actions as
also required in other sites around the world and described outsiders' general
difficulty in having direct contact with contestants. These international contestants were viewed as untouchable women who could showcase Nigeria's
ability to successfully host other elites. Lamenting that the media had caused
everything to "go up in smoke," Mrs. Nansel continued that the rationale
behind hosting the pageant was to "sell Nigeria to the world" and redirect
Nigeria's image as a country undergoing rapid economic development:

> Everybody [sees] Nigeria as a poor nation. If you don't know Nigeria and
> you have not visited the country and you see how she is being reported
> internationally, you will think, the country is backwards. One of the
> things I wanted to do was to tell them that Nigeria is undergoing develop-
> ment, it is an important country, it is a good place and if she [the country]
> breaks up today [splintered into separate countries between the North
> and the South, for example], there will be issues in Africa. . . . Nigerians
> are enlightened people; they travel all over the world. I am sure; there is
> no part of the world that there is no Nigerian.

Hosting Miss World was meant to highlight the country's fledgling economic
status, high potential for development, and position as cosmopolitan citizens.

Hosting rights alone cost 5 million pounds (nearly $8 million), and in-
formants disclosed that the Nigerian organizers never fully paid off the fees.
Beyond attracting investment and tourism, reported estimates predicted that
Nigeria would make about $180 million in television rights alone. With the
relocation of the pageant, government officials placed the overall revenue
loss at over ₦10 billion ($100 million in 2002), with insurance money only

covering ₦2 billion.²⁶ Security served as a proxy for an image of a stable Nigerian financial system. The security framing, demonstrated in part through the physical protection of beauty queens, was also meant to highlight Nigeria's economic stability. Nigerian organizers justified their hosting of the event as a means to promote financial investment in and tourism to Nigeria. Ensuring meticulous security provisions was meant to combat negative perceptions of Nigeria as a risky place. The protection of these elite international beauty delegates served as a proxy for projecting an image of not only physical safety but also a broader trust in Nigeria's financial system. Through access to state-sponsored logistical assistance and the billions of naira invested in the event, Nigerian organizers sought to establish Nigeria's regional importance and that the country was deeply integrated into the international political economy.

The Nigerian supporters' emphasis on security arose as a response to an existing global narrative about insecurity in Nigeria. They voiced concerns that global media and international human rights organizations were determined to portray Nigeria negatively, creating a major stumbling block to their aspirations. Supporters of the pageant viewed the international media as suppressing positive stories of the African continent and opposing Nigeria's hosting rights. Mr. Abe was one who held this view. We sat in his office, which was decorated with framed black-and-white photos showing him with celebrities including the Reverend Jesse Jackson, Muhammad Ali, and Harry Belafonte. He described how the foreign press was determined to diminish Nigeria's status, either to sell newspapers through sensationalized stories or to attract charity donations by presenting Nigeria as downtrodden. Mr. Abe said:

> The media in the West started attacking Nigeria because they felt that Amina Lawal was going to be stoned to death. They said people were going to cut the arms and the legs of the girls [contestants]. All those folks like Bianca Jagger²⁷ [a well-known human rights advocate,] who specialized in pretending to protect the dignity of the human race, they found Nigeria a sitting duck. . . . I didn't find out how these guys make money before. They spread this information, frighten the West, then the West gives them money and they go out to say they want to save Africans. They do it for financial reasons. I found out a lot of stuff about

these so-called [people] who say they want to protect and save Africans,
it's a game.

Mr. Abe's logic echoed the critique of postcolonial feminist scholars such as
Lila Abu-Lughod, Gayatri Spivak, and Chandra Mohanty, who have pointed
out that Western discourses use a savior rhetoric as a way of justifying impe-
rialist intervention and to create ideological distinctions between the Global
North and the Global South.[28] Mr. Abe's reasoning was that the West, which
was anxious about Nigeria's emerging position in the international political economy, sought to hamper the country's development. He positioned
himself as a "global player," who was not satisfied with being the best in just
Nigeria or even Africa, but rather sought to conquer the world. He explained,
"Once you want to just be the best in Africa then you accept yourself as a
second-class citizen of the world. I'm just as good as any other guy out there
in the world!" Using himself as a prime example as someone who measured
up to global standards, Mr. Abe pushed for a shift toward acknowledging that
Nigerians were also central to the global order. This questioning opened up a
view of globalization that destabilized a static hierarchy between "advanced"
and "developing" countries, and instead embraced a perspective that allowed
for a more even playing field in the international political economy.

Though Mr. Abe attributed a great deal of culpability to the international press, he also viewed the federal government, and in particular the
foreign minister, as not doing enough on the frontlines to defend the country,
which he said was "under attack" from foreign dignitaries and the press. He
stated, "When you have eighty young girls from eighty countries in your
custody and you do not defend them, it makes us look bad. The government
of Nigeria was just as guilty in what went wrong as the militants who made
it very difficult for us to organize the show." Another organizer commented
after Nigeria's hosting unraveled, "We lost a great opportunity to showcase
Nigeria to the world. And people will say, if you can't look after 18-year-old
girls, who can you look after? It's dangerous. . . . It's one that will hurt us for
a long time to come. We've got to understand the consequences of what has
happened. This will be with us for a long time." The "Miss World crisis," as it
has come to be called, has been etched into Nigerian collective memory as
an example of ethnoreligious conflict. It further imprinted a negative image
of Nigeria, which has had a long-lasting impact, mobilized in part through

(in)security. The country continues to recover from this. For example, Boko Haram, the insurgent Islamic fundamentalist group in Northeast Nigeria, has been central to contemporary concerns about Nigeria's insecurity. In an eighteen-minute video posted in 2012 claiming responsibility for the bombing of *ThisDay* offices in Abuja, Boko Haram explained that it was in retaliation against the 2002 Miss World article, resurrecting concerns about the inability to mobilize state security measures.[29] Effectively mobilizing security would have been a boon for Nigeria. Instead, inadequately marshaling this security discourse raised alarms and dented Nigeria's national image.

Nigerian supporters emphasized protecting the *physical* bodies of contestants through discourses of policing, surveillance, and military access. This was meant to signal the *economic* prowess of the nation-state and highlight Nigeria's readiness to be fully inserted in the global political economy. The focus on security became a means of not only confirming the stability of the Nigerian state, but also of serving to legitimize its global aspirations. By focusing on the similarities between Nigeria and other countries, Nigerian supporters sought to emphasize local integration of global expectations. Through gendered discourses of protection, supporters directly linked the ability to effectively handle the custody of eighty-eight delegates from around the world to Nigeria's broader national project of becoming an essential member of the international political economy. Through a focus on security, Nigerian backers of the event sought to resist framings of Nigeria as volatile. Nigerian supporters downplayed the threat faced by potential attackers to protect an image of Nigeria as a safe place for investment and tourism. They instead accentuated their sheltered protection of elite women via their access to the militarized arm of the state and to economic resources.

Nudity, Piety, and Spiritual Protection

Nigerian opponents to the Miss World Pageant included different Nigerian groups such as civil rights and labor organizations that opposed the federal support of the pageant on the grounds it showed misplaced priorities given the larger social problems in the country. Some Christian religious groups also opposed the pageant for moral reasons. However, Nigerian Muslim opposition groups garnered the greatest media attention. I interviewed seven leaders of civic religious organizations who were vocal in their disapproval, labeling the pageant an indecent spectacle. Nigerian Muslim opposition was not without internal variation. Some were solely against the originally scheduled time during Ramadan, others were against the intended host venue in Abuja, and still others opposed the pageant in its entirety. Regardless of these varied stances, the overarching discursive strategy focused on piety to explain their opposition to the pageant. Opposition groups expressed a need to spiritually protect all women, though were specifically focused on Nigerian women, highlighting the corrupting influence of nudity and Westernization. They placed Nigeria on a higher ethical standing than other countries in the West. Nigerian opponents sought to enforce the state as a neutral moral arbiter that was responsible for maintaining the cultural authenticity of the Nigerian nation in the face of rapid globalization. The framework of protection stressed the *spiritual* bodies of all women as mandated by Islam. They expressed unease about female contestants and the polluting effect of their presence on other women in the country, which endangered African culture.

I met Mr. Yunus Bashir, a semiretired senior law partner in his seventies, at his law office. A council member for one of the leading Islamic civic organizations, Mr. Bashir had spoken extensively with reporters during the turmoil surrounding the Miss World Pageant. I asked him to explain his stance to me. and in a gravelly voice he responded:

> I am against the whole idea of this beauty thing, any beauty pageant because of the way it is done. I do not believe that women should expose themselves. There is nothing wrong in watching someone who is a beautiful person. It doesn't mean that the beautiful person should be nude. If you are properly clad, it is alright, but that nudity is not right. So, I am opposed to beauty pageants the way they are conducting it; the criteria which they introduce.

Using Muslim women's participation in sports as a counterpoint, Mr. Bashir noted that there were some sports where athletes wear trousers or shorts, which are inappropriate clothing options because they show too much skin or the contours of women's bodies. His words resonated with other interviews I had conducted in which respondents accused Miss World of exposing scantily clad bodies, which they equated with nudity and the contaminating of cultural values. For example, Alhaji Khalil Akanni, a legal scholar and community activist, declared, "As far as Muslims or Islam is concerned, a woman is a sacred being that needs to be given proper protection and dignified. We don't consider women to be objects or commodities for sale or a contest for sexual products." Phrases describing women as "sacred beings" and "dignified" peppered all of my conversations with interlocutors and were meant to defend their need for women's protection through an emphasis on piety. Similarly, Mr. Bashir noted, "We think it's immoral for young girls to expose their nudity just because you want to do a beauty pageant." Incidentally, their sentiments echoed much of the conventional Western feminist backlash against beauty pageants throughout the world for their commodification of women's bodies, yet relied on assumptions about piety and morality rather than women's rights to self-determination to justify their opposition.[30]

When I pointed out to Mr. Bashir that there have been pageants in Nigeria since 1957 and that the formats of some Nigerian contests were not altogether different from international ones, he brushed me off, pointing out that this was not new information to him:

> I have told you. There are a number of young ladies that have become Miss Nigeria. We also have Miss World, Agado or what's her name now. You know everybody hailed her. I think that was rather tactless. This was not imposed on us by outsiders but Nigerians. It shows the tendency of some enlightened people to be contemptuous.

When he brought up Darego's win, I asked him if he thought it was good for Nigeria's image. He retorted, "To us, it was not important. It is not as important as Nigeria hosting the World Cup in football." Like some of the other opponents I spoke with, Mr. Bashir viewed sports as a practical venue for promoting a positive image of the country. But unlike Nigerian supporters, he was dismissive of the cultural relevancy of the events surrounding Miss World and characterized the pageant as disgraceful. Describing himself as a Muslim first and an African second, Mr. Bashir bemoaned his belief that the world was quickly "going upside down" and sought to resist what he defined as externally imposed criteria that were out of step with African standards: "The international community feels that what is tolerated and accepted in their own climate, that we must do the same here and I think that is going too far." He pointed out that his perspective was in part about "protecting our religion, our beliefs and our own way of life." He continued to emphasize the importance of freedom of expression but insisted that outside forces were not ready to respect Muslim autonomy. Mr. Bashir said, "They are not ready to observe that rule, they felt that you must accommodate. They think that we are not modern enough. I think that is a wrong impression on their part." Mr. Bashir did not view piety and modernity as incompatible logics. Our discussion then turned to sharia law. An expert on the topic, he was a staunch supporter of its implementation. When I asked him about the Lawal case and how it had influenced the events surrounding Miss World, he scowled, saying, "No. They were totally different. Maybe they were occurring about the same time and the international media in order to portray Nigeria badly put them together, but they were not related."

I interviewed Justice Faruq Abayomi, a judge, in his home in one of the ritzier neighborhoods in Lagos. His maid served me tea with condensed milk and sugar cubes in the living room as he emerged from his room upstairs in a long white kaftan from what looked like a mid-morning nap. Like Mr. Bashir, Justice Abayomi viewed the Lawal case as unimportant to how the events during the Miss World Pageant unfolded. I sensed that, like Nigerian support-ers of Miss World who decried how the international media used the Lawal case to further hamper Nigeria's image, Nigerian opponents were suspicious of international motives for linking the case to their own disavowal of the pageant. He shared his displeasure with Nigeria's hosting of Miss World, but framed his thoughts as not only about religious interpretations of strict Islamic doctrine. He felt that "core" or socially conservative Christians would hold a similar view as him based on shared cultural background—it was a Nigerian consciousness and sensibility that held at bay, at least momentarily, the ethnic, religious, and linguistic differences in Nigeria. Nigerian oppo-nents frequently contrasted "African culture" with Western influences. In a statement typical of those who shared his views, Justice Abayomi explained:

> Look, in traditional African society, women don't go catwalking on the stage because they want to look beautiful or whatever. It's not done, it's not part of our culture, it's not even [about] religion. It's not part of our upbring-ing. So, it's an aberration to us. Miss World has come from the Western influence. The influences we have in this country are: traditional African society, Islamic, Christian, and the Western influence. It is un-Islamic, it's not traditional, it's not Christian. It can only be a Western thing.

He concluded that the contest was a Western element, oppositional to African culture that unites Nigerians regardless of religion. In enumerating the various cultural influences in Nigeria, he mirrored others who interpreted Miss World as an encroachment on Nigerian cultural values and an adoption of Western culture, rather than a means of securing Nigeria's place in the global political economy on its own terms, as envisioned by Nigerian supporters. As a closing point, he then went on to lambaste the criteria used to crown "the so-called Miss World" as also un-African since thin women typically win, which he said was further evidence of his point about Westernization.

Shifting directions, he started on a tirade about the transplantation of Western culture due to nefarious marketing strategies that only served Western interests and the concomitant abandonment of Nigerian values. He explained this as being attached to colonial baggage that justified the bad influences imported from the West. Referencing a recent CNN broadcast on excessive drinking and antisocial behavior, Justice Abayomi stated that even those in the West viewed their culture as depraved. He compared Nigerians to the Chinese and the Indians, countries he viewed as embracing their culture, which, according to him, paved the way for their economies to surpass the West. He used the example of Chinese and Indian children not starting to learn English until they are schoolchildren, while he censured Nigerian parents for not teaching their children to speak in their native tongue. Explaining the social impact of maligning Nigerian culture in favor of the West, he stated, "We don't have to take it hook, line, and sinker without looking at how it impacts us, how does it benefit us, how does it affect us. We have our own way of doing things. What is wrong is now what is right. It's not making us better, we are becoming worse as a people."

The judge then told me a story about a friend of his who had summer plans to vacation in England. He chastised his friend's plans as a waste of money and part of the "mental culture" that looks to foreign goods and destinations as better than African ones. The judge asked his friend why he couldn't travel around Nigeria suggesting specific sites like the Obudu Cattle Ranch or Yankari Game reserve or other parts of Africa like Morocco or Kenya instead. I was intrigued by the parallels between Judge Abayomi's recommendations to his friend to support domestic sightseeing and Nigerian pageant supporters' campaign to develop the country as a global tourist destination, though they stemmed from different perspectives. The judge's suggestions were primarily framed around a broader appreciation of Nigerian culture, while Nigerian supporters sought to augment the country's economic profit. He ended our conversation by reiterating the need to refocus on Nigerian values, which, he explained, would allow "every other thing to fall into place."

Another of the judge's grievances was the contest's public funding, which he lampooned as a "bloody waste of time and resources," adding that the government's involvement distracted it from more pressing concerns facing ordinary Nigerians such as the erratic power supply, poor roads, and public health problems. Sheikh Dauda Abdurahman had similar sentiments stating, "our money was being spent recklessly and scandalously." Alhaji Akanni also shared this view. Sitting in the backseat of his white Honda Civic, he described Miss World as a private venture, and took issue with its government financing. Indicting the first lady and the president, he talked about how their assurances that the logistical assistance the government would provide through a number of federal agencies would not cost the public coffers rang hollow. Nigerian opponents viewed the involvement of the first lady's charity as evidence of the president's, and by extension the government's, tacit approval of the contest.

Citing the government's misplaced priorities, Alhaji Akanni said he regarded hosting the pageant as failing to benefit average Nigerians. He disputed the way in which Nigerian supporters depicted their position as patriotic and having a widespread national impact, a narrative that they boldly championed in the local press. Repeating his point about the contest's negative consequences on the moral fabric of the nation, he stated:

> So it is now projecting nudity that is going to develop Nigeria? I have said it now that we are sending a wrong signal to our female folks that selling their body, going nude, that they can make some money, that they can be famous, be popular throughout the world if they win a beauty pageant. But the long-term consequences are just worse than the profits they are going to get out of it.

Nigerian opponents critiqued the self-interested, profit-driven motives of individual private investors. They underscored that the state had an ethical obligation to be sensitive to the diverse perspectives of Nigeria's populace and stressed that while they were against beauty pageants in their entirety, their decision to actively organize against the Miss World Pageant was due to the state's failure to fulfill its moral responsibilities to the Nigerian nation as whole. They maintained that the federal government had to be especially vigilant about not appearing to be supportive of any one group over the other. They felt that the pageant would not better the socioeconomic position or well-being of ordinary Nigerians and would in fact lead to a corrupting force that would render vulnerable Nigeria's higher moral standing in the global landscape. Opponents interpreted state support of the pageant as a value-laden stance that neglected the moral concerns of the populace. They made a distinction between Nigerian national pageants, which were entirely private affairs without obligations to account for religious or moral concerns, and the Miss World contest, which were supported in part by state resources. When I asked Alhaji Akanni why he did not target his opposition toward the growing crop of Nigerian pageants, he focused again on state support, firing back:

> [Local pageants] have the right [to organize] because not all of them are Muslims, and they are not using government money. Blue chip companies like STV, UAC, and the rest of them put their money [up] because they are going to get a lot of benefits from the publicity stunt. But the Miss World was being organized with government funds, that is the immoral part of it! It was immoral to use government funds that belong to Muslims, Christians and even the pagans to organize something that is not of any benefit to the average Nigerian.

Alhaji Akanni participated in demonstrations in Abuja after Friday prayers, where he claimed there were as many as 10,000 protestors, some traveling from nearby cities such as Kano and Kaduna, who gathered to distribute leaflets that catalogued their reasons for opposing Miss World.[31] Characterizing the Abuja protests as peaceful, he distanced this group from the riots in Kaduna, stating, "They were protesting against a statement, we were protesting against a concept," which suggested that the protests in Abuja would have gone forward whether or not the offensive *ThisDay* article had been published. Picking up on the narrative of embodied protection as a key reason for the cancelation of the contest, Alhaji Akanni explained:

Because the girls themselves that came from all over the world felt threatened, nobody was going to harm them but they thought they were going
to be harmed, especially when we were going closer to the Hilton hotel
where they were camped. They were calling their boyfriends. Their parents were also sending signals to the federal government that they should
allow their daughters to go back home.

Alhaji Akanni's disapproval also hinged on the pageant's international
scope. As he continued to answer my question about why he and others did not
aim their protests at Nigerian pageants, he offered the following reasoning:

You know all those ones are more or less localized, you know, if they want
to do Miss Oyo [a state in the Southwest] for instance, it's something that
is localized, it doesn't have the kind of effect that we are going to have
if the whole world is watching. . . . All of them [international pageants]
could take Nigeria by storm, you know, with all their negative repercus-
sions. The local ones do not have effects like the international one[s].

Alhaji Akanni asserted that international pageants remained a central
target because they had deeper negative effects that could contaminate
the national body through corruptive forces. His perspective was in stark
contrast to Nigerian supporters who sought to use the international contest
to pivot positive attention toward Nigeria. While he was critical of international beauty contests, he also savored the international media attention
that their protests generated. Nigerian opponents realized that their actions
had worldwide reach. With a sly smile on his face, Alhaji Akanni recalled
his interview with CNN:

Oh yes, it was fantastic, it was a world event, the whole world was
aware. . . . The whole media world was already in Nigeria to cover [the
pageant]. They covered the demonstration and it was being viewed by
the whole world as it was going on and that was why it had immediate
impact. It got adequate publicity. If publicity was localized within Nigeria, the event would have been staged [in Nigeria].

He couched his group's efforts as being tied in part to the global awareness
of his group's concerns and ability to publicize their voices on the world

stage, a feat that would be impossible to realize if the event only received local media attention.

While Nigerian entrepreneurs who organized the competition conveyed that beauty pageants elevated women and directed their energies toward defending foreign female contestants from possible external threats, Nigerian opponents viewed the pageant itself as a threatening force from which all women needed protection. They highlighted how the beauty pageant's support of the public exposure of women's bodies violated spiritual respect. By opposing the pageant, they sought to restore the appropriate revered spiritual position of women and also expressed that the Nigerian nation should uphold a high moral standard. By stressing the spiritual dimension of protecting women's bodies from commodification and cautioning against Westernization, opposition groups within Nigeria promoted a vision of the nation as a pious protective force for women, responsible for preserving the authentic cultural elements of the country. The international hue of the pageant played a profound role in stoking demonstrations against the event since it was seen as having greater negative national consequences in terms of violating the dignity of women.

I met Sheikh Abdurahman and Alhaji Ahmad Suleiman in an Abuja mosque about two hours before Asr (afternoon) prayers. Tightening the scarf around my neck and removing my shoes, I headed upstairs to one of the meeting rooms, where they were both waiting for me. Greeting me as I stepped through the door, Sheikh Abdurahman said, "*Salam Alaikum,*" a common Arabic salutation among Muslims that means "Peace be upon you." When I replied, "*Wa Alaikum Salam*" ("And unto you, peace"), Alhaji Suleiman spoke up, "Are you a Muslim? You should give the full greeting." I then gave the extended response: "*Wa alaikum salam wa rahmatullahi wa barakatuh.*" as I took a seat in the chair that Sheikh Abdurahman had gestured toward with his prayer beads in hand. As they were well aware of my status as a Nigerian-American, I understood Alhaji Suleiman's request for the full Arabic greeting as a basic appraisal of my Muslim background. In the course of our conversation, they discussed a topic that by now I had expected. Bringing up my upbringing in the United States, Sheikh Abdul-Rahman explained the West's immorality:

> I presume that Western nations always oppose any tendency towards decency and morality because they want to corrupt the whole world.

Ethically, anything of a high moral standard they don't like it because it will affect their markets. No rules, no morality, no decency, no shame, no restraint. This is how they want the world to be because it is suits them.

But his words turned to an unexpected target of his scorn. He aimed it at women's rights campaigns like the Beijing UN World Conference on Women, where in 1995 member governments passed the Platform for Action, a resolution promoting gender equity for women, and where Hillary Clinton gave her famous "Women's Rights Are Human Rights" speech. He also discussed the Child Rights Act, a Nigerian law that was passed in 2003 to set the minimum marriage age at eighteen, which was primarily aimed at underage girls. According to him these unnecessary policies and laws, which had been passed in the name of women's rights, were actually ratified due to bribery from foreign entities seeking to implement delinquency and a baseless Nigerian society. He viewed the law as an example of Western encroachment under the guise of human rights. His words matched some of Mr. Abe's thoughts about how human rights discourses are used to generate revenue, but the sheikh's words suggested another motive—that of dragging the country into moral disrepute.

Human Rights, Advocacy, and Civic Protection

Human rights organizations such as Amnesty International supported a boycott of the pageant because of Nigeria's hosting and issued urgent appeals against Amina Lawal's sentence.[32] These international nongovernmental organizations (INGOs) became the public face of this international boycott, which included a broad group of constituents, such as other beauty contestants and politicians, who jointly relied on an *advocacy* discourse to assist the most vulnerable women in Nigerian society. The ruling, which condemned Lawal to death by stoning for alleged extramarital sexual relations, became connected to the pageant because the massive attention the Miss World contest brought to Nigeria provided leverage for these organizations to highlight human rights abuses that were routinely ignored in Nigeria. In response, the pageant organizers worked closely with state representatives to deal with the controversy. In spite of assurances by the organizers that the case would follow due process in Nigeria and justice would prevail for Lawal, the boycott proceeded, and several contestants threatened to, and did, drop out. These groups focused on the need to protect the civic needs of defenseless women in Nigeria, stressing the legal responsibility of the Nigerian nation-state to adhere to international universal regulations and protocols on human rights. I use the term *civic protection* to describe the mobilization of legal instruments, demand for government intervention, and the focus on political citizenship—the rights that individuals are entitled to as members of political communities that the protection of women's bodies entailed.

These groups organized under the banner of "saving Amina" and other potentially vulnerable Nigerian women from being stoned to death.[33] Amnesty International launched a global letter-writing campaign and organized fundraisers, demonstrations, and an electronic petition campaign asking people to write letters to the president of Nigeria, the Minister of Justice, and ambassadors and high commissioners in their countries, as well as local representatives. Emails with photos of Lawal wrapped in a purple veil, cradling her infant daughter with eyes downcast, were forwarded throughout the world and urgent pleas for support were posted on various websites. The campaign against Amina Lawal's sentencing became one of the most successful viral Internet awareness campaigns of its time, drawing the support of public figures and celebrities such as Bill Clinton and Oprah Winfrey. As a college student at the time, who was an active member of the on-campus Women's Union (WU) as a work-study student, I recall getting a flurry of emails on the Lawal case from classmates and other WU workers about a mounting legal and activist campaign to reverse Amina Lawal's death sentence. The email stated:

> As many of you may have heard, a Nigerian woman was recently sentenced to death—for having a child out of wedlock. Amina Lawal has been sentenced to death by STONING—she is to be buried up to her neck in the ground, after which her punishers will surround her and throw rocks at her head until her skull is crushed and she dies a painful and horrible death. I am sure you will feel equal parts shock and disgust at this sentence, and I want you to know that she has only thirty days to appeal her trial. Please go to the Amnesty International site, htttp:// mertonai.org/amina and sign the letter addressed to the President of Nigeria. It literally takes only a minute and could help save her life, as well as help put an end to this kind of cruel and disgraceful judgement

in a country that calls itself as a democracy. Please copy and forward this letter to others in your address book as well. Please help her!

The Amnesty International site encouraged people to take action, writing not only to denounce Lawal's case but to also use the opportunity to voice their support for abolishing the death penalty and the "cruel and degrading punishment in Nigeria." Their instructions also requested that readers contact their state representatives to cosponsor U.S. House Resolution 351, a resolution passed in the House International Operations and Human Rights Subcommittee that condemned stoning as a "gross violation of human rights."[34]

The email I received was just one of thousands, if not millions, of emails forwarded throughout the world. The campaign focused on Lawal as a victim of poverty and unjust gender discrimination whose fundamental human rights were violated. As such, they organized around the internationally recognized mantra of "women's rights are human rights." For instance, an Amnesty International website set up to bring awareness to the case stated:

> Women's and human rights organisations in Nigeria have already highlighted the emerging pattern of people from poor backgrounds—particularly women—being the victims of cruel, inhumane and discriminatory sentences introduced by regional laws in the states of northern Nigeria . . . . Under Federal Nigerian law, Amina has the right to have her life and personal dignity respected. This right is enshrined in the 1999 Nigerian Constitution, which confirms the sanctity of human life. This right is also recognized by all the international and regional human rights declarations and conventions to which Nigeria is a signatory.[35]

Lawal's "personal dignity" needed to be fully safeguarded through the recognition of legal regulatory instruments like declarations, conventions, and constitutions. As such, they established that the protection of women, especially those from poor backgrounds, could primarily be guaranteed through the enactment of civic protocols—established and agreed-upon procedures that included international and domestic endorsements and regulations.

Through signature campaigns that targeted government authorities in countries around the world, international human rights organizations directly aimed their efforts at the state and tried to put pressure on the Nigerian court system by pointing out Nigeria's obligation to international conventions and its own constitution. By focusing on the administration's commitment to follow international treaties as ratified by the Nigerian government, human rights organizations focused on the protection of women through the legal branch of the state. The organizations also admonished the potentially coercive reach of the state government as a violator of standardized human rights, particularly through its adoption of sharia law and its codification of the poor treatment of women and other marginalized groups.

Amnesty International, for example, was careful to stress that it was not against sharia laws per se, but rather against the penal code's violation of Nigeria's constitution and international law. For example, one spokesperson for the organization wrote:

> We have continually asked the Nigerian authorities not to introduce punishments which amount to ill-treatment and torture under new laws based on Sharia. The new Sharia Penal Codes as they are currently enacted and practised puts Nigerian citizens at risk of discrimination on grounds of gender, religious belief and social status. The Nigerian authorities at [the] state and federal level have the responsibility to ensure that international human rights standards prohibiting the death penalty, cruel, inhuman and degrading punishments are respected in any legislation enacted in Nigeria. We are puzzled by the response of the Nigerian officials; the Federal Minister of Justice himself has declared these sentences unconstitutional yet no practical action is taken to end what must be a prolonged psychological torture for Amina Lawal who still faces an agonising death. The danger of human rights becoming victim of politics is real.[36]

Amnesty International expressed frustration at the Nigerian federal authorities' lack of active interference in the judicial process and doubted that the execution could be stayed without international intervention. They viewed the Lawal case as tied to broader political concerns wrapped in the legal authority of the Nigerian nation-state, which was accountable for ratifying legislation to protect human rights, especially those deemed at risk, such as women, the poor, and religious minorities.

International NGOs focused the bulk of their attention, not only on raising public awareness, but also on demanding that political officials intervene. Foreign politicians, whom groups like Amnesty International directly lobbied, were thus involved in denouncing the Miss World contest, even after it moved to London. Member of Parliament Glenda Jackson (Labour) declared, "They should call the whole thing off as a mark of respect to the people who died in Nigeria. What's the point of such a contest anyway? It's such an antediluvian concept. Miss World has become utterly irrelevant."[37] In calling attention to the idea that the Miss World Pageant was archaic, she drew a deep contrast with Nigerian organizers' hopes of using the event to display the country as innovative and forward-thinking. The European Parliament passed a resolution condemning the Lawal sentence, and the Commission of the European Union resolved to provide financial aid to strengthen Nigeria's legal and democratic structures.

The European Parliament's committee on women's rights unanimously voted in favor of boycotting Miss World, and the chair, Anna Karamanu of Greece, remarked that Nigeria "treats women in a totally unacceptable way." The Amina Lawal case became a rallying point to underscore Nigeria's mistreatment of women, which was viewed as invalidating support for the contest. In the United Kingdom, the Tory international development spokeswoman, Caroline Spelman, added: "There is a degree of responsibility on the part of those who organise international events like this," meaning that Miss World should be held responsible for embroiling the contest in political matters and should have known better than to host it in a volatile nation like Nigeria.[38] She noted that she would press the British International Development secretary to review British-Nigerian diplomatic ties in order to prevent a similar incident from recurring.[39] Nigeria's mistreatment of women constituted a rallying point to validate international opposition to the pageant. International boycotters focused on the need to regulate Nigeria through international legal and political structures like democratic systems, international law, parliamentary procedures, and court systems. They viewed their opposition as a means of advocating for victimized women through legal and political procedures both in and outside Nigeria.

A group of ten British Members of the European Parliament wrote an open letter to the newly crowned Miss England, urging her to condemn the scheduled sentencing of Amina Lawal for its "horror and inhumanity" and to use her position to compel organizers to move the venue away from Nigeria. The letter stated in part, "For beauty queens to celebrate in shimmering clothes, while offstage a Nigerian woman's most basic right to life is violated, drags the whole competition into disrepute."[40] They buttressed their intervention with universalized regulations that were globally sanctioned. Miss England declined the request, responding that her presence in Nigeria would bring additional attention to the plight of women in the country and that she felt reassured that the Nigerian government would intervene as necessary. In doing so, she positioned herself as an advocate for women's rights in Nigeria with clout that could place political pressure on Nigeria and other countries to intervene. This created a gulf between different groups of women who were in need of protection. Politicians, the international press, human rights organizations, and boycotting beauty contestants jointly gave primacy to advocacy, transnational legal intervention, and universal human rights in targeting vulnerable Nigerian women. They defended their intervention through the need to protect "basic" human rights, which drew on universalized global expectations.

In contrast to Miss England's decision to attend the contest, Miss Denmark, Masja Juel, was the most outspoken beauty contestant in favor of an outright boycott. In a news article interview, she admitted that she was initially excited to take part in Miss World, hoping that she would ink a modeling contract through her participation. But her elation quickly turned to horror when she heard of Lawal's plight. Admitting that she was not very politically aware but did have a budding interest in learning more about current world affairs, she bewailed, "I was told about the case of Amina Lawal and that she would be stoned to death in Nigeria simply for having sex outside marriage. I just couldn't believe it. How can this kind of thing happen in 2002? What kind of country would do such a terrible thing?" Confirming the reality of the sentence sealed her final decision. She pronounced that she "could no longer take part in the competition if this atrocity was going to happen. You cannot have a show celebrating beautiful women in a country that is stoning a woman to death." Like others, she contrasted the attractiveness of foreign contestants with Lawal's grotesque sentence. Refusing to identify as a feminist because she did not buy into the presupposition that it was degrading for women to wear bathing suits on stage, she noted that it was not just Lawal's gender that bothered her but that she was "a poor oppressed person who [was] being treated dreadfully." She blasted the Miss

World Organization as caring more about money than they do women and proclaimed her desire to shift her attention to politics, starting with organizing a petition to the European Parliament to advocate in Lawal's case.[41] Together, INGOs, foreign politicians, and boycotting beauty contestants advocated for justified civic interventions to protect the vulnerable bodies of Nigerian women like Amina Lawal.

CONCLUSION

This chapter documented how multiple groups produced narratives that relied on gendered, embodied protection filtered through a critical world event. I found that diverse institutional actors similarly leaned on the need to protect women, as premised on the moral constitution of their bodies. However, they relied on diverse interpretations of the responsibilities of the nation-state and the consequences of globalization to reinforce their claims, a process that I link to global-nationalism. Nigerian entrepreneurs' sponsorship of the pageant sought to legitimize a militarized security state that focused on increasing Nigeria's standing in the global political economy through making efforts to signal wealth and political order by providing adequate protection for elite beauty delegates. The aspirations of the Nigerian pageant supporters to present a modern, rising Nigeria were ultimately crushed. Nigerian opponents, on the other hand, perceived the contest as one of bending to Western influence rather than a triumphant entry onto the global stage. While supporters of Miss World sought to further align Nigeria with a global community, opposition groups interpreted this as a signal of Westernization rather than internationalization. Nigerian Muslim protestors encouraged the state to focus on their ethical obligation to shield women's bodies and maintain a neutral position that acknowledged diverse perspectives that would prevent the intrusion of a Western-dominated globalized culture. Nigerian supporters and opponents relied on different rhetorical strategies, but both viewed the matter of sharia as separate from their positions on the pageants and also remained critical of narratives that presupposed Western superiority. International NGOs advanced the need for the Nigerian nation-state to focus on legal rights that guaranteed women's protection through international civic responsibilities and legal structures in compliance with regulated global universal human rights.

The protests occurred amid the mounting of Obasanjo's reelection campaign, five months before the turbulent elections of 2003. Regional jostling among political factions came into play. Considerations of Abuja as the host city increased opposition to the planned location of the pageant. These protests left an indelible blemish on the international pageant's history as well as constituting a national embarrassment. The long-term legacy of these events remains; Nigerians still see it as a blot on their reputation and a setback to the goal of elevating and reviving Nigeria's image. Joy, who competed in international beauty pageants, admitted in an interview with me that she felt that the event had become so entangled with Nigeria's broader national narrative that it affected her chances at world contests. She felt others looked at her with disdain and pity, but never respect. Mr. Abe vowed to stage a "comeback" of Miss World to again play host to the international community and secure Nigeria's position as a global leader. The fissures that so dramatically emerged in 2002, filtered through the world of beauty pageants, shape the two dominant national orientations—cultural-nationalism and cosmopolitan-nationalism—that exist in Nigeria today. The events of 2002 were a culmination of the nation's attempts to stage itself internally and externally as a cohesive nation. They illustrate how nation-states are defined in part through embodied debates about globalization and the cultural politics of nation-building.

7 | AFTER THE SPOTLIGHT

DURING MY LAST VISIT TO NIGERIA in 2018, nearly ten years after I first began this project, I caught up with Will at a lunchtime business meeting with his client Teresa, about a beauty competition that needed his services. He was now an owner of his own video production company. In the meeting Will and Teresa discussed how there were now over three thousand pageants in Nigeria. Teresa interjected that there were so many pageants starting up that they were running out of names to differentiate themselves, and they were now making use of strange names like "Miss Peculiar." Their discussions echoed Basketmouth's joke about the deluge of pageants in the country. It was clear to me that the industry's growth had shown no signs of slowing down. Social media has become increasingly important to the industry, as beauty queens use Instagram to grow a following and brand themselves as influencers. There have also been signs of further professionalizing of the industry—such as having award shows and nonprofit registration for pageants. In a news article discussing Miss Nigeria in 2017, the Minister of Information and Culture, Alhaji Lai Mohammed, said the state should make pageantry a "national asset" and put it on a pedestal.[1] His ringing endorsement spoke volumes. While, to my knowledge, he has yet to follow up on this statement through an action plan, it highlights the degree to which beauty diplomacy still plays out today.

In my follow-up interviews with contestants, I observed, post-pageant, that they had taken different paths. Some took a professional route, becoming doctors, lawyers, or bankers. Others opened up their own beauty-related businesses, selling skin-care products, handbags, or hair extensions. Still others pursued a career in entertainment as singers, actresses, and television or radio show hosts. Another group was made up of housewives who had a side business for additional cash to supplement their household incomes or to keep in their own personal accounts. The one key difference I saw, regardless of the chosen path, was between those who played up their status as an ex–beauty queen and those who actively hid it, wanting to completely distance themselves from the negative perceptions the label entailed. Among the latter was yet another group, which Lota, an ex-beauty queen, called "the vanished"—those who took care to hide out from the public eye.

These differences highlight the continued set of contradictions that beauty pageants navigate. Beauty queens must showcase that they possess aesthetic capital but not act elitist. They are elevated as upwardly mobile role models, but contend with stereotypes as uneducated and sexually promiscuous. Beauty pageants give women a voice with which to be heard through specific platforms, yet beauty queens still recognize that they are embedded in a larger system, often out of their control, which constrain their bodies, behavior, and mobility.

Contestants were expected to have skills traditionally associated with Nigerian women, which suggested an "authentic" African context by showing competence in traditional cooking or wearing traditional outfits, for example. At the same time, however, they were not to be *wholly of that context*. This shows how an ambivalent stance toward "tradition" may figure into modernity. Embracing "traditions" may symbolize region and identity, while rejecting the actual way of life.[2] Other ironies include the fact that the bodies prized in Nigerian contests—thin and with a tall stature—are not seen as traditionally ideal. Nigerian beauty pageants use cultural events that are viewed as out of fashion and a lower-class activity in some areas of the Global North as trendy, elite markers of status, with the aim of using these activities to redeem the country's national image. The same pageants that are viewed as bringing class and respectability to Nigeria are accused of being backward and passé in countries such as the United

States. Beauty pageants are linked to a global machinery that enriches those already in positions of power, yet Nigerian beauty pageant participants hoped to use the beauty diplomacy narrative as a response to perceived inequalities around aesthetics that ignored or undervalued the country. These are paradoxes that lead to more complex questions about power, belonging, and difference.

Nigeria is now the largest economy in Africa, surpassing South Africa according to recent statistical figures (as of 2014), which showed the country's gross domestic product (GDP) as having doubled in one year.[3] While economists and financial analysts interpret these figures as mainly having symbolic effects, since they improve confidence in the country's economic trajectory rather than reflecting structural changes, the period of my fieldwork in 2009–10, before they were released, likely captured a moment at which anxiety about Nigeria's political economic future was especially heightened. While oil and gas have typically dominated foreign exchange earnings and government revenues, the industry is becoming less important to Nigeria's GDP, with many analysts pointing to the rise of service sectors as driving future economic growth for the country. These include sectors such as consumer goods and retail as well as the media and entertainment industry. The latest figures show that the services sector accounts for 50 percent of GDP. The arts, entertainment, and recreation sector in particular accounts for nearly 2 percent of GDP and has grown thirteen-fold since 2010.[4] This exponential growth in recent years is in many ways integral to the Nigerian beauty pageant industry because of corporate sponsorship, the contestants' endorsement of merchandise, and the career aspirations of the beauty queens, who often pursue careers in these fields.

These larger shifts in the political economy provide the needed context to understand how material conditions impact the broader efforts to highlight Nigeria's competitiveness on the global stage while appealing to a broad and diverse domestic population. As I have shown throughout this book, Nigeria's beauty pageant industry is a site where ideas about the nation are created yet also challenged. While these circumstances are uniquely Nigerian, with conditions specific to this national context shaping its trajectory from postindependence to an emerging nation, there are many ways in which this argument is applicable to other contexts.

This book advances three core theoretical arguments. First, *I contend that national logics work through multilayered orientations.* Emerging nations such as Nigeria simultaneously seek to unify the country within their borders while positioning themselves as major global players to the outside world. This process is especially heightened within the context of Nigeria due to the high stakes involved; if these logics are not reconciled, this emerging nation will be at risk of internal disintegration, as well as the loss of its foothold in the international political economy. Foreign nations also influence Nigeria's national trajectory because the country's international reputation often comes to bear on its sense of national identity. The dynamics of national belonging and global achievement can alternately validate or threaten each other, as they are shaped by articulated processes related to class, gender, and ethnoreligion. These processes are also historically contingent. In the case of Nigeria, the rise of religious fundamentalism fuses together religion and politics. Nigeria's specific form of emergent nationalism also embeds tensions between its federal system and the forces of indigeneity that influence understandings of ethnicity, culture, and nation, as well as those stemming from its economic status as an oil-rich nation with the accompanying contradictions between state and market.

My second line of argument *highlights a shifting direction of globalization, evident in the rise of emerging nations that are on the cusp of cementing their positions as countries successfully following in the footsteps of countries such as China and India.* Since Nigeria is still in the middle of this transition and has been lauded for its high potential, it is an especially fruitful location for analyzing this shift. I argue that paying close attention to emerging nations is critical to understanding the next phase of globalization, as a range of nations seek to dominate the international political economy and the cultural marketplace. Middle-stage countries such as Nigeria and other countries such as Vietnam and Indonesia seek to shift the global center toward their own nations by helping to create a new world order that challenges yet recognizes Westernization and the hybridity of cultures. While the globalization literature tends to ignore Africa or only focus on the region as a victim of globalization,[5] I highlight Nigeria, which is a regional powerhouse, as a prominent national actor in this process.

Countries such as China, India, and Brazil have emerged as economic leaders in the global marketplace. These governments and their people on the ground are actively working to assert themselves on the global stage through terms that acknowledge Western influence, but also account for their own circumstances on their own terms. Emerging nations, such as Nigeria, that are new centers for rising wealth and population growth see the opportunity to become global powerhouses setting new international standards. Nigeria's position in the global political economy exists within a broader "Africa rising" narrative. As Nigerians strive for global recognition, they also seek to preserve their country's uniqueness. Past scholarship on globalization assumes that either cultural homogeneity through Western dominance or cultural heterogeneity through mixture will prevail in nations such as Nigeria. While I do not entirely discount these processes, I also note another possibility, which is that previously marginalized nations struggle to assert themselves as pivotal members of the international political economy. My focus on Nigeria, which is currently in the middle of transitioning into the status of a newly emerging nation, allows for a deeper understanding of the motivations underlying this evolution.

Finally, *I analyze relationships between globalization and nationalism by examining connections among economy, politics, and culture.* I challenge the dominant perspectives in scholarship on nationalism and globalization, both of which open inquiry by highlighting the growth of economic capital or the influence of the state, and assume that the ideological dimensions of both processes are filtered through arrangements between the state and capital. These literatures assume that cultural changes are merely a consequence of economic and political conditions. However, while acknowledging the importance of Nigeria's political economy, I emphasize the importance of culture as a key way in which people position themselves as members of the international political economy and guide the trajectories of their nations. In this way, I show how symbolic changes in and of themselves can influence the economy and politics. Cultural shifts are not only shaped by the political economy, but also influence the direction that it may take, informed by global and national formations. I examine these relationships at both the macro and micro levels by showing how the Nigerian beauty pageant industry attempts to connect everyday understandings of national and global belonging on the ground to macro shifts in the Nigerian political economy through the state and private enterprise. These forms of nationalism are historically situated, predicated on Nigeria's shift from postindependence to its current "emerging nation" status. I defined emerging nationalism in two ways: (1) emerging onto the international political economy during a period of economic growth and reform; and (2) settling into more concrete definitions of national identity that promote both solidarity and heterogeneity. This book shows the importance of culture in linking material and symbolic dimensions of nationalism, globalization, and ethnoreligion. That is, this type of civic-cultural work filters the larger ideas that influence how we understand the interactions between political and economic dynamics. These symbolic moves, which center on Nigeria's rich and vibrant culture, open up new possibilities of imagining the world and Nigeria's place within it.[6] A rising-realist approach recognizes the aspirations for accession but also acknowledges the structural realities that limit these ambitions, such as class divides, ethnoreligious cleavages, and international appraisals.

The themes of this book can also be extended in other directions outside of beauty pageants. The core idea of *gendered diplomacy* could be focused on other instances in which women are positioned as working in ways that promote cultural ambassadorship, such as by examining the political and cultural influence of first ladies. The comparison between beauty contestants and first ladies remained a consistent theme throughout my research. Dr. Musa Rasheed, a professor I interviewed about his opposition to the Miss World Pageant, directly compared beauty queens to first ladies through the lens of embodiment and cultural representation. I sat across from him in his office, with a desk separating us, and a shelf stuffed with books to our left. He had described hosting Miss World as a "bad omen" for the country. When I asked why he used that term, he responded:

> Ladies these days want to copy beauty queens [like] the way [they dress]. Before you know it, you will be promoting the culture of nakedness in our society. The late Stella Obasanjo was known for a particular dress, the one that leaves her chest open and while she was the First Lady of Nigeria that became in vogue. Every other lady wanted to dress the way

she dresses. That was not a good legacy, one for the wife of the Head of State to be exposing her beauty like the way she did. Worst still because she was supposed to be a role model. . . . Her carriage must be done with all caution and decorum.

Dr. Rasheed's easy transition from condemning beauty queens to criticizing first ladies shows the similar focus on the necessity of decorum and positions as national exemplars. These expectations, which transcend beauty queens to also focus on the impact of first ladies and other sociopolitical positions, draw in public performance and gendered diplomacy.

The book's analysis could also be extended to examine the hosting of other political and cultural events that are used as a form of destination-branding, including sporting events, such as the Olympics and the World Cup, and major conferences, such as the World Economic Forum and the G-20 summits. There are also other industries that highlight how Nigeria tries to compete and gain recognition on the global stage. For example, the prolific Nollywood film industry is consumed all around the world. Since 2009, Nollywood has surfaced as the second largest film industry in the world when measured by volume and per capita revenue.[7] Recent attention to the #BringBackOurGirls social movement, a political campaign organized to demand state intervention on over two hundred schoolgirls kidnapped by Boko Haram, a militant group in Northeast Nigeria, highlights the tensions between the image of Nigeria rising and the continued challenges to that image. Shifting discourses of effacement and aggrandizement persist. Taken together, these sites can further deepen our understandings of how countries around the world are negotiating internal sensibilities while laying claims for global recognition. Beauty pageants include a heterogeneous set of actors and are an especially highly charged site for the production and reception of nationalism through negotiations of belonging as well as exclusion.

Notes

CHAPTER 1

1. There are many royal families in Nigeria who reign over specific areas or regions of the country. Though stripped of their constitutional power as a result of colonialism and largely relegated to a ceremonial status, traditional rulers continue to wield significant economic, cultural and political power in Nigerian society. For more on the historical relationship between indigenous rulers and state power, see Vaughn (2006).

2. "Government Congratulates Darego, Miss World," *ThisDay*, November 22, 2001.

3. "You Are a Pride of the Black Race, Tinubu Tells Darego," *ThisDay*, December 10, 2001.

4. Muyiwa Adeyemi, Joseph Ollor-Obari, and Oghogho Obayuwana, "I Know Agbani Will Go Places, Says Father," *Guardian*, November 24, 2001.

5. "Darego, Be Good Ambassador," *ThisDay*, December 7, 2001.

6. Joseph (2008).

7. Scholars use other acronyms in reference to emerging markets, including BRICET (BRIC + Eastern Europe and Turkey), BRICS (BRIC + South Africa), BRICM (BRIC + Mexico), and BRICK (BRIC + South Korea).

8. World Bank (2018).

9. These financial organizations include Morgan Stanley Capital International (MSCI), the Financial Times / London Stock Exchange (FTLE), and Goldman Sachs (which also coined the term BRIC to refer to the fastest growing economies in the world).

10. Haub and Kaneda (2015); Kaneda and Bietsch (2016).

11. Adelani Adepegba, "₦13bn Ikoyi Cash: EFCC Declares ex-NIA DG, Oke, Wife Wanted," *Punch*, March 25, 2019.

12. In 1993, the U.S. Federal Aviation Administration suspended commercial air service between Lagos and the United States (Rokita 1994). Direct flights between the two countries were unavailable until 2001, when they reopened for major foreign carriers (Nigerian-owned airlines could not fly into or out of the United States until 2009).

13. Transparency International (2001); Transparency International (2018). There has been a slight improvement over the years, but CPI figures for the last fifteen years have been mostly stagnant.

14. D. Smith (2007). See also Pierce's (2016) exhaustive historical account on corruption in Nigeria.

15. Falola and Heaton (2008).

16. Adunbi (2015); Okonta (2008); Ukiwo (2003).

17. Yates (1996).

18. Falola and Heaton (2008, 217–21); Lewis (1996).

19. Apter (2005); Lewis (1996); Watts (2004).

20. Anthropologist Andrew Apter's (2005) work on FESTAC77 (the Second World Black and African Festival of Arts and Culture) vividly captures a moment of the petro-state's self-assurance as a global cultural, political, and economic epicenter during the late 1970s. Apter documents how the economic boom of the 1970s and the financial bust of the 1980s shaped changes in the political economy that directly impacted cultural spectacle and reputational politics.

21. I've used pseudonyms for all interviewees.

22. "Agbani Lifts Abuja Tourism in Germany," *Daily Trust*, July 18, 2002.

23. As further evidence for my point about emerging nations and using aesthetics as a means of changing the global hierarchy, when the United States won the Miss World Pageant in 2010 and hosted it in 2016, there was not nearly as much media attention or framing of the event as reorienting an American

national trajectory as in Nigeria. Since the United States is already considered a cultural hegemon, this same degree of framing is not as necessary.

24. Adeyemi, Ollor-Obari, and Obayuwana, "I Know Agbani Will Go Places."

25. This program was linked to First Lady Patience Jonathan's "Women for Change" initiative.

26. The exact breakdown of religious groups is disputed. Moreover, there is also a minority population that subscribes to indigenous and syncretic spiritual beliefs.

27. In 2004, Silverbird Productions, the owners of MBGN, hosted the "Miss Silverbird International Pageant" in Lagos, with organizers hoping to have the event serve as a reset after the disastrous 2002 Miss World hosting. Redoubling their efforts, they also devised a strategy of sending multiple winners to different types of international pageants to further maximize their chances.

28. During the inauguration of the program, Dora Akunyili, the Minister of Information and Communication, noted that the program would serve to "develop a sense of pride and authority through [the] process of national renaissance. We want to inspire a rebirth in our belief system, [to] repackage Nigeria and represent her to the world in a more acceptable manner." Nosike Ogbuenyi, "Why We Are Re-branding Country, by Akunyili," *ThisDay*, February 9, 2009.

29. Dittmer (2017); McConnell, Moreau, and Dittmer (2012).

30. World Bank (2019).

31. Sarah Banet-Weiser (1999) shared similar responses to her research on Miss America.

32. Oyěwùmí (1997).

33. Banet-Weiser (1999); Tice (2012).

34. See, for example, Bartky (1997); Bordo (1993); Wolf (1991).

35. See, for example Bobel and Kwan (2019); Casanova and Jafar (2016); Chapkis (1986); hooks (1992); Miller-Young (2014).

36. Cohen, Wilk, and Stoeltje (1996, 2).

37. Stanfield (2013, 2).

38. Craig (2002, 14).

39. See Levey (2007). The 2019 Miss America slipped to a record low with 4.3 million viewers.

Viewership of the Miss America pageant has been in decline since the 2014 Miss America pageant when the contest hit its best ratings since 2004 with a viewership of 9.8 million people. At its height in 1960, an estimated 85 million people tuned in. Toni Fitzgerald, "Miss America 2019 Ratings: Viewership Falls Again for Revamped Pageant," *Forbes*, September 10, 2018; Patt Morrison, "There She . . . Well . . . Isn't," *Los Angeles Times*, September 14, 2005; "ABC's 'Miss America Pageant' Surges to Its Best Ratings Since 2004," TV by the Numbers, September 16, 2013, online at https://tvbythenumbers.zap2it.com/network-press-releases/abcs-miss-america-pageant-surges-to-its-best-ratings-since-2004/.

40. See Ahmed-Ghosh (2003); Dewey (2008); Gilbert (2015); Ochoa (2014). There is no television-rating system in Nigeria, so there is no way of tracking audience numbers. However, organizers described a marked increase in the attendance at auditions, from a few dozen to several hundred, since Agbani Darego's crowning in 2001.

41. National Bureau of Statistics (2018).

42. Alegi (2010).

43. Alegi and Bolsmann (2013).

44. Boykoff (2014); Schimmel (2012); Tomlinson and Young (2006).

45. Lenskyj (2014).

46. Price and Dayan (2008).

47. Banet-Weiser (1999); Craig (2002).

48. Brockett (1992).

49. Oza (2001); Parameswaran (2001).

50. See, for example, Saavedra (2003); Thangaraj (2015).

51. Charmaz (2014); Weiss (1994).

52. Reyes (2018).

CHAPTER 2

1. Mougoué (2019).

2. Obafemi Awolowo's (1947) opinion is crystalized in the following quote: "Nigeria is not a nation. It is a mere geographical expression. There are no 'Nigerians' in the same sense as there are 'English,' 'Welsh,' or 'French.' The word 'Nigerian' is merely a distinctive appellation to distinguish those who live within the boundaries of Nigeria and those who do not" (47–48).

3. Three of these states (Kaduna, Niger, and Gombe) have limited versions of the code that only apply to parts of the state with large Muslim populations. See Eltantawi (2017) and Imam (2005) for more on the implementation of sharia in Northern Nigeria.

4. These image campaigns have continued. The 2016 Buhari presidency restored War Against Indiscipline brigades, task forces focused on clean streets, punctuality, and orderly queues, as well as the "Change Begins with Me" operation, which advocated civic engagement and personal responsibility. For more on these image campaigns from a historical perspective, see Falola and Heaton (2008).

5. See Obadare (2004); Rotberg (2004); Suberu (2001).

6. See Alegi (2010); Bowen and Gaytán (2012); DeSoucey (2010).

7. Griswold (2000); Spillman (1997).

8. Adams (2010); Gellner (2006); Hobsbawm (1992); A. Smith (2010).

9. Billig (1995); Bonikowski (2013); Brubaker et al. (2008); Surak (2013).

10. Mayer (2004); McClintock (1995); Yuval-Davis (1997).

11. Enloe (1990); Moallem (2005); Nagel (1998).

12. Burke (1996); Cole (2010); Mojola (2014); Thomas (2009).

13. See George (2014) for a historical account of how elite women in Lagos took up the helm of social reform during the colonial era.

14. Edmonds (2010, 30).

15. See Hoang (2015); Kim-Puri (2005); Radhakrishnan and Solari (2015); Salzinger (2003).

16. From 1950 to 1959, daily circulation rates increased from 25,000 to 95,000.

17. The *DTN* was incorporated on June 6, 1925, as the Nigerian Printing and Publishing Company Ltd. by Richard Barrow, L. A. Archer, Adeyemo Alakija, and V. R. Osborne; see *Daily Times Nigeria*, online at https://dailytimes.ng/about-us-dailytimes/.

18. This was following the Nigerian Enterprises Promotion Decree, which promoted the indigenizing of foreign enterprises.

19. For more on the history of the *Daily Times*, see Oso (1991).

20. In 1966, the year of Nigeria's first military coup, the Miss Nigeria Pageant was not held for the first time in its nine-year history, but it returned the following year. In 1967, the Nigerian Civil War began, with Biafra and other southeastern provinces seeking to secede from Nigeria to become a self-governed republic.

Although the movement received some sympathy from international sources, only five countries (Gabon, Haiti, Ivory Coast, Tanzania, and Zambia) officially recognized the new republic. The civil war ended in 1970. There was no pageant held in 1971. There was a pageant in 1972, but there were no pageants held between 1973 and 1976. There was also an extended gap between 2004 and 2010 when there was no contest.

21. "Sir James Leaves for UK," *Daily Times Nigeria*, May 19, 1957, 8.

22. Adeyemi, Muyiwa, "My Reign as First Miss Nigeria," *Guardian*, December 7, 2002.

23. "Miss Nigeria Competitors Proudly Show Off Their Wins," *Daily Times Nigeria*, April 7, 1957, 12.

24. *Daily Times Nigeria*, July 18, 1957, 11; *Daily Times Nigeria*, January 31, 1959, 6.

25. *Daily Times Nigeria*, September 14, 1959, 8.

26. "Singer Sewing Machines News," *Daily Times Nigeria*, April 14, 1957, 7.

27. *Daily Times Nigeria*, July 10, 1957, 10.

28. Larkin (2008).

29. The *Daily Times Nigeria* later spotlighted Oyelude in 1963 after she returned from an extended nurse-training course in London and returned to practice nursing in Nigeria.

30. "Miss Nigeria 1957 Selected," *Daily Times Nigeria*, April 7, 1957, 8–9.

31. *Daily Times Nigeria*, July 20, 1957, 11.

32. "Miss Nigeria Sees Brighton, Leaves for UK," *Daily Times Nigeria*, May 19, 1957, 8.

33. "My Visit to England—by Miss Nigeria," *Daily Times Nigeria*, May 20, 1957, 6–7.

34. *Daily Times Nigeria*, April 14, 1957, 7.

35. "My Visit to England—by Miss Nigeria."

36. This was in 1975.

37. Incidentally, this was the same year that FESTAC, the Festival of Black African Culture, began. FESTAC was a celebration of Pan-African culture, which included Black nations throughout the world. Andrew Apter (2005) observes that this time period was a phase of massive oil production for the country, which sought to announce itself as the center of the Black world.

38. While MBGN organizers claimed that due to the military regime, less money circulated in the marketplace, which made finding sponsorship difficult,

the organization was able to weather the economic downturn despite these hardships. However, the military regime did have an impact for MBGN on the international stage. In 1993, MBGN's representative, Toyin Raji, was forced to exit the Miss World competition held in South Africa due to political pressures from international human rights organizations protesting the Abacha military regime, which had just executed Ken Saro-Wiwa, a prominent activist. This example further demonstrates the entangling of beauty competitions with national and global politics.

39. Chris Agabi, "Miss Nigeria Returns after 6 Years, without Swim Wear Segment," *Daily Trust*, June 27, 2010.

40. Ibid.

41. B. Anderson (1991).

42. Adebanwi (2016, 8).

43. Unless otherwise noted, I use the $1 = ₦150 conversion rate which was the average value of the Nigerian naira when I conducted primary fieldwork in 2009–10.

44. Despite recent political turmoil, Miss Venezuela remains popular. In 2018, Miss Venezuela was postponed, not because of escalating political unrest in the country, but due to corruption and prostitution scandals that plagued the contest. The pageant was reorganized under new leadership, which included ex–beauty queens.

45. Jha (2015); King-O'Riain (2006).

46. Banet-Weiser (1999); Craig (2002).

47. Forrest (1994) profiles the family in his book on entrepreneurs and Nigeria's political economy.

48. Silverbird Productions also organizes the Mr. Nigeria competition.

49. The Miss International Pageant is headquartered in Tokyo, Japan. It initially started in 1960 in Long Beach, California, and then moved to Japan in the 1970s. The Miss Earth Pageant is based in Manila, Philippines, and was started in 2001.

50. Calhoun (2008).

51. Otis (2016).

52. Diouf (2000); Landau and Freemantle (2010); Werbner (2006).

53. Surak (2013).

CHAPTER 3

1. Tice (2012) defines platforming as "the deliberate and ongoing process/ project of self-making, sculpting, and performing normative class, race, and gender competencies—on stage and off" (15–16). She examines platforming in the context of campus pageantry.

2. Bourdieu (1973, 1984, 1986).

3. Shilling (2003).

4. Giddens (1991).

5. Warhurst and Nickson (2001), 13. See also Elias, Gill, and Scharff (2017); Otis (2011); Williams and Connell (2010).

6. Mears and Connell (2016, 335).

7. Gimlin (2007).

8. T. Anderson et al. (2010, 566).

9. Entwistle and Wissinger (2006); Holla and Kuipers (2015).

10. Based on research on fashion models, Wissinger (2015) calls this type of work "glamour labor."

11. For more on aesthetic capital see T. Anderson et al. (2010); Holla and Kuipers (2015).

12. Robertson, Ndebele, and Mhango (2011).

13. Sociologist Maxine Craig (2009) examined the Miss Bronze Pageant's emphasis on charm school and etiquette classes that specifically targeted working-class and dark-skinned contestants as a way of showcasing the purposeful training of Black middle-class femininity, an ideal that all members of the community should and could strive toward.

14. Balogun and Hoang (2018).

15. Mears (2011).

16. Lagos is an emerging epicenter for Nigeria's rapidly growing yet underrated fashion industry, whose members have hopes to rival established fashion capitals such as New York, Paris, and Milan (Pool 2016).

17. See Sabrina Billings (2014) for an analysis of the language politics of pageants in Tanzania.

18. Ochoa (2014).

19. Casanova (2004).

20. Juliet Gilbert (2015) has shown how Nigerian beauty contestants justify their participation on religious grounds in ways that reconcile their desire to

perform service for themselves, the nation, and God. They use their personal fame for spiritual ends to court God's grace and fuse the sacred and spiritual with body-centered transformations and personal empowerment.

21. This was a follow-up interview that took place in 2018, after the naira sharply fell in 2016. I use the $1-to-₦360 conversion rate here.

22. Mojola (2014, 35).

23. See Hinojosa and Carle (2016).

24. Stutern (2017).

25. Ami Sedhi and Mark Anderson, "Africa Wealth Report 2015: Rich Get Richer Even as Poverty and Inequality Deepen," *Guardian*, July 31, 2015.

26. Nuruddeen M. Abdallah, "74 Percent of Applicants Don't Get University Admission," *Daily Trust*, August 28, 2017; Dayo Adesulu, "JAMB Admission Shortfall—Nigeria Needs 1M Varsity Spaces," *Vanguard*, May 3, 2018.

27. Byfield (2002); Clark (1994).

28. In general, armored cars are not common in Nigeria, but are popular among business executives and especially politicians.

29. See Pierre (2008) for a discussion of skin tone and class in Ghana.

30. Ochoa (2014).

31. Ibid., 110.

CHAPTER 4

1. For more on this debate, see Glenn (2008); Hunter (2011); Lee (2008); Tate (2017).

2. Dosekun (2017); Ogunyankin (2018). For more on the decentralization of power, see Alarcón, Kaplan, and Moallem (1999); Grewal and Kaplan (1994).

3. Saraswati (2013).

4. World Health Organization (2011). Some dispute the reliability of these figures as over-estimates.

5. Dewey (2008).

6. Dosekun (2015).

7. Robb Young, "African Wealth and African Style at a Glamourous Juncture," *New York Times*, October 4, 2009.

8. For more on the abject position of Black women's bodies, see K. Ford (2008); Hobson (2005); Magubane (2001). See Craig (2002) for the history of the "Black Is Beautiful" discourse in the United States; Thomas (2009) for its history

in South Africa; and T. Ford (2015) for a diasporic perspective. The investment in centering Whiteness in understanding beauty in the Global South is so deep that Darego has erroneously been described as light skinned in academic and popular publications.

9. See Faludi (1991); Wolf (1991).

10. See Oloruntoba-Oju (2007); Norimitsu Onishi, "Globalization of Beauty Makes Slimness Trendy," *New York Times*, October 3, 2002.

11. Brink (1989).

12. Scholars and journalists have documented similar practices among specific ethnic groups in other African contexts, such as in Niger, Uganda, and Tanzania (Popenoe 2004).

13. T. Ford (2015).

14. Human Rights Watch (2001); Scacco (2010).

15. Adams (2010); Comaroff and Comaroff (2009).

16. Hobsbawm and Ranger (1983). See Ranger (1983) on the invention of tradition in colonial Africa. For more on invented traditions in postcolonial Nigeria, see Apter (2005). For more on performing the nation in Africa, see Askew (2002); Gilman (2009); and Shauert (2015).

17. See Balogun (2019).

18. Dowry practices vary widely across Nigeria, dependent upon the religious, ethnic, and class backgrounds of families. Dowry payments range from a token amount and symbolic items to larger sums of money and lavish gifts.

19. See Rodriguez (2013) for more on coming-of-age rituals in the context of Filipino and Mexican immigrant communities in the United States. She theorizes the importance of these special occasions in understanding intersections of gender, ethnicity, class, and age.

20. See Agberia (2006).

21. Deeb (2006); Mahmood (2005).

22. The National Broadcasting Commission banned cinemas from showing the film *Fifty Shades of Gray* due to its explicit content. The popular cable television reality competition, *Big Brother Naija*, is a spinoff of the original Dutch version, which involves contestants in their twenties who are filmed around the clock living together in a custom-built home. The show has faced rising criticism from politicians, opinion writers, and religious leaders for its depiction of sexual activity among contestants who pair off, and for the "indecent dressing"

of the female contestants in particular, who wear shorts, spaghetti-strap tank tops, and midriff tops.

23. See Bakare-Yusuf (2009); Tamale (2016).

24. This example speaks more broadly to how the commodification of skin color can be viewed as a form of exoticism. These differences map onto the different niches in the modeling industry that Mears (2011) points out. Commercial models tend to be more racially diverse and less thin relative to high-end editorial models. Tastemakers exoticize dark skin as a marker of an edgy appeal.

25. In some instances, contestants who win an independent state-level contest prior to MBGN get priority in representing that state. MBGN organizers saw this as a way of encouraging young women to enter these contests, which they believe will prime contestants and ultimately help MBGN, although anyone can qualify to audition.

26. Mamdani (2001, 661). For more on indigeneity and state politics, see Kraxberger (2005).

27. "Poll Respondents Seek Equal Rights for Settlers, Indigenes," *ThisDay*, February 16, 2009. For more on federalism and indigeneity in Nigeria, see Bach (1997); Human Rights Watch (2006).

CHAPTER 5

1. The latest figures from the World Bank's "Ease of Doing Business" index have ranked Nigeria as 146th out of 190 nations in the world (Doing Business 2019). The index includes measures of business regulations, investor protections, and credit access.

2. Hoang (2015); Mears (2015).

3. Cole (2010); Cornwall (2002); D. Smith (2017).

4. For scholarship on embodiment and masculinity, see Barber (2016); Bridges (2009).

5. For more on sports diplomacy, see Murray (2012); Ndlovu (2010).

6. Iyabo Lawal, "23 States Owing Workers, Says Labour," *Guardian*, June 16, 2015.

7. Chabal and Daloz (1999); Joseph (1987).

8. Apter (2005) argues that the petro-naira heightened corruption in Nigeria due to the inflated value of currency as tied to oil revenue.

9. Mbembe (2001, 110).

10. Page (2018).

11. Okafor (2011).

12. Bayelsa State Tourism Development Agency (2013).

13. Mama (1995).

14. In international contests, there's a tacit expectation that the delegate from the host country will make the top ten because of a home-court advantage, but to win is unlikely and would likely raise suspicions of an unfair process.

CHAPTER 6

1. This term was coined by Nassim Taleb (2007).

2. See Adesina Abiodun, "Agbani Daregold," *Tempo*, November 29, 2001.

3. "Nigeria to Host Miss World Pageant?," *Tempo*, June 20, 2000.

4. "Miss World 2001: The Well-Connected Pageant," *Pageantry*, 2002, https://www.pageantrymagazine.com/magazine/features/2002/a02/a02missworldwebed.html.

5. Sklair (2001).

6. Eltantawi (2017); Parvez (2017).

7. Ferree and Tripp (2006); Kardam (2004).

8. Mama (1998); Nguyen (2011); Puri (1999).

9. "'Miss World 2002 Will Be the Most Lavish and Spectacular Production That We've Ever Undertaken': Now There Are 220 People Dead, 1000 Injured, and 8000 Homeless from the Miss World Riots in Nigeria," Democracy Now, November 27, 2002, https://www.democracynow.org/2002/11/27/miss_world_2002_will_be_the.

10. These statistics are from the International Olympic Committee (IOC) and the International Federation of Football Association (FIFA) and are likely to be inflated.

11. The decree met with some disagreement over its validity from Islamic scholars within Nigeria and other Muslim countries around the world since Daniel had issued an apology and was also not subject to Islamic rulings since she was not a Muslim.

12. "An Apology to All Muslims," *ThisDay*, November 22, 2002.

13. There is estimated to be almost an even split between Christians and Muslims in Kaduna city. In Kaduna, Muslims dominate the Northern part and Christians are concentrated in the Southern part. Kaduna state is estimated

to be about 60 percent Muslim, but because of the sensitivity of religion and the politics of demography in the state and Nigeria as a whole, the census does not collect statistics on religious identification, so the exact breakdown remains in dispute.

14. James Astill, "Miss World's Nigerian Odyssey Abandoned After Three Days of Rioting Leave 100 Dead," *Guardian*, November 23, 2002.

15. "Nigeria Calls Off Miss World Show," *BBC News*, November 23, 2002, http://news.bbc.co.uk/2/hi/africa/2505353.stm.

16. For more on the complex religious and legal history of the Amina Lawal case, see Eltantawi (2017). Ayesha Imam and Sindi Medar-Gould, members of BAOBAB for Women's Human Rights, a Nigerian NGO, denounced the international letter writing campaign as misguided, misinformed, and damaging to Lawal's case. In their open letter, they noted that international pressure could exacerbate the injustices, and that local mechanisms to appeal Lawal's case remained the priority. They requested resources like money and information from experts in similar contexts, in lieu of petitions. Ayesha Imam and Sindi Medar-Gould, "Please Stop the International Amina Lawal Protest Letter Campaigns—for Now," BAOBOB for Women's Human Rights, 2003, http://www.wluml.org/node/1025. Eltantawi argues that while Lawal's case benefited from Western financial assistance to Nigerian political organizations like Women's Rights Advancement and Protection Alternative (WRAPA), the case relied on legal arguments based on sharia and the Nigerian constitution and not international arguments based on human rights. Lawal's lawyers used an argument based in sharia about "extended pregnancy" in which a woman can carry a child for up to five years after conception before giving birth. Since she would have been still married to her ex-husband, given that timing, her case was successfully overturned.

17. Contestants from Denmark, Switzerland, Austria, Iceland, Mauritius, Sri Lanka, and Costa Rica formally decided to boycott and did not participate in any pageant-sponsored activities. The Korean representative withdrew from the pageant while it was still in Nigeria. Delegates from Panama, South Africa, Spain, and Tahiti initially boycotted but reversed their decisions once the pageant was moved to London. See www.pageantopolis.com, which is a leading archive of beauty pageant material from around the world.

18. There are some discrepancies in the number of contestants reported in the media. These numbers were reported on http://www.pageantopolis.com.

19. For some interesting parallels to the polio crisis in Nigeria, see Obadare (2005).

20. Das (1995).

21. For more on sharia in Northern Nigeria, see Eltantawi (2017); Imam (2005); Kendhammer (2013).

22. Kendhammer (2013).

23. Mr. Abe's statement, in part, makes reference to the North's desire to disrupt the unwritten "gentleman's agreement" of the PDP (Nigeria's then-ruling national party) that party nominations and presidential politics would be based on a rotational formula, with Northern and Southern candidates taking turns at the seat of presidential power.

24. Since the sharia legal system was introduced beginning in November 1999, more than a dozen people have been sentenced to death by stoning. None of these sentences have been meted out because they were reversed on appeal, commuted, or, as Eltantawi (2017) states, are stagnant, as between a dozen to several hundred people languish in "legal purgatory" in prison awaiting trial (10).

25. In fact, in 2005, Silverbird organized an international pageant named "Miss Silverbird International" in Lagos including fourteen contestants from around the world that hardly made a blip on the media's radar.

26. "Nigeria and Miss World 2002," *ThisDay*, December 17, 2002.

27. Jagger was invited to be a judge for the Miss World Pageant but declined and wrote an editorial for a British newspaper which called for a boycott of the contest due to the Lawal case. Bianca Jagger, "All Miss World Contestants Must Quit Now; Only a Complete Boycott Can Bring Nigeria to Its Senses," *Evening Standard* (London), November 29, 2002, 11.

28. Abu-Lughod (2002); Mohanty (1988); Spivak (1988).

29. "Nigeria's Boko Haram Militants Claim ThisDay Attacks," *BBC News*, May 2, 2012.

30. There is a great deal of scholarship that documents the feminist backlash against beauty pageants. See, for example, Wolf (1991).

31. I was not able to verify the number of protestors. Most of the coverage of Abuja focused on rioting youth that numbered in the hundreds. There was reportedly an internal dispute between the chief imam of Abuja's central mosque (who had written a letter to the president in protest against Miss World) and youths who disagreed with his advice to take a peaceful approach. See Human Rights Watch (2003).

32. These groups had participated in a similar campaign for Safiyatu Hussaini, the first woman to receive the death penalty for adultery in Nigeria. Hussaini's sentence was reversed just four days prior to Lawal's verdict. For more information on this case, see Kalu (2003).

33. Jaggar (2005).

34. In response to Safiyatu Hussaini's stoning sentence on March 14, 2002, Betty McCollum of Minnesota introduced House Resolution 351 to the U.S. House of Representatives, which stated that "execution by stoning is an exceptionally cruel form of punishment that violates internationally accepted standards of human rights. . . . Women around the world continue to be targeted for discriminatory, inhuman, and cruel punishments by governments who refuse to protect the rights of all of their citizens equally." The resolution makes mention of death by stoning punishments in Afghanistan under the Taliban, Saudi Arabia, Sudan, Somalia, Iran, and Yemen, framing stoning as a world-wide violation imposed by Islamic fundamentalism. Expressing the Sense of Congress that the United States Should Condemn the Practice of Execution by Stoning as a Gross Violation of Human Rights, and for Other Purposes, H.R. 351, 107th Cong., 2d Sess., introduced in House March 14, 2002, https://www.congress.gov/107/bills/hconres351/BILLS-107hconres351ih.pdf.

35. The website no longer exists, but an archive of the statement is posted here: Amnesty International, "Amina Lawal—Another Woman Facing Death by Stoning," September 15, 2002, http://www.onlineopinion.com.au/view.asp?article=1559.

36. Amnesty International (2002).

37. Patrick Hennessy, Humfrey Hunter, and Elaine Galloway, "Calls to Scrap Miss World over Riot Death." *Evening Standard* (London), November 25, 2002, 5.

38. Ibid.

39. Ibid., 5.

40. "Letter: Boycott Miss World," *Guardian*, September 25, 2002, 19.

41. Hadley Freeman, "Why I Quit Miss World," *Guardian*, November 6, 2002.

CHAPTER 7

1. "I Want Miss Nigeria Pageantry Elevated to National Asset," *Vanguard*, February 17, 2017, https://www.vanguardngr.com/2017/02/want-miss-nigeria-pageantry-elevated-national-asset-lai-mohammed/.

2. See Collier (1997).

3. John O'Sullivan, "How Nigeria's Economy Grew by 89% Overnight," *Economist*, April 8, 2014, https://www.economist.com/the-economist-explains/2014/04 /07/how-nigerias-economy-grew-by-89-overnight.

4. National Bureau of Statistics (2019). Prior to 2014, GDP figures were based on outdated statistics from 1990 that did not account for the growth of industries such as banking, telecommunications, or entertainment. In 1990, oil accounted for 33 percent of GDP; it now accounts for 9 percent.

5. Ferguson (2006).

6. Scholars such as William A. Callahan (2006) have developed the idea of "culture-driven development" to discuss how cultural activities promote the nation's political economy. Melissa Aronczyk's (2013) research shows how national governments rely on public relations firms, marketing consultants, and communication experts to brand their nations. Through the concept of "cultural wealth," cultural and economic sociologists have established how a nation's reputation is a key component of attracting foreign investment, building tourism, and driving economic growth. Taken together, these scholars establish how culture matters to both politics and the economy (Reyes 2014; Rivera 2008; Wherry 2006; Wherry and Bandelj 2011).

7. For more on the Nollywood industry, see Haynes (2016); Krings and Okome (2013); Tsika (2015).

Works Cited

Abu-Lughod, Lila. 2002. "Do Muslim Women Really Need Saving? Anthropological Reflections on Cultural Relativism and Its Others." *American Anthropologist* 104, no. 3: 783–90.

Adams, Laura L. 2010. *The Spectacular State: Culture and National Identity in Uzbekistan*. Durham, NC: Duke University Press.

Adebanwi, Wale. 2016. *Nation as Grand Narrative: The Nigerian Press and the Politics of Meaning*. Rochester, NY: University of Rochester Press.

Adunbi, Omolade. 2015. *Oil Wealth and Insurgency in Nigeria*. Bloomington: Indiana University Press.

Agberia, John Tokpabere. 2006. "Aesthetics and Rituals of the Opha Ceremony Among the Urhobo People." *Journal of Asian and African Studies* 41, no. 3: 249–60.

Ahmed-Ghosh, Huma. 2003. "Writing the Nation on the Beauty Queen's Body: Implications for a 'Hindu Nation.'" *Meridians: Feminism, Race, Transnationalism* 4, no. 1: 205–27.

Alarcón, Norma, Caren Kaplan, and Minoo Moallem. 1999. "Introduction: Between Woman and Nation." In *Between Woman and Nation: Nationalisms, Transnational Feminisms, and the State*, edited by Caren Kaplan, Norma Alarcón, and Minoo Moallem, 1–17. Durham, NC: Duke University Press.

Alegi, Peter. 2010. *African Soccerscapes: How a Continent Changed the World's Game.* Athens: Ohio University Press.

Alegi, Peter, and Chris Bolsmann, eds. 2013. *Africa's World Cup: Critical Reflections on Patriotism, Play, Spectatorship, and Space.* Ann Arbor: University of Michigan Press.

Amnesty International. 2002. "Nigeria: Amina Lawal Must Not Face Death by Stoning." Press release. Amnesty International UK. Online at https://www.amnesty.org.uk/press-releases/nigeria-amina-lawal-must-not-face-death-stoning-0.

Anderson, Benedict R. 1991. *Imagined Communities: Reflections on the Origin and Spread of Nationalism.* London: Verso.

Anderson, Tammy L., Catherine Grunert, Arielle Katz, and Samantha Lovascio. 2010. "Aesthetic Capital: A Research Review on Beauty Perks and Penalties." *Sociology Compass* 4, no. 8: 564–75.

Apter, Andrew H. 2005. *The Pan-African Nation: Oil and the Spectacle of Culture in Nigeria.* Chicago: University of Chicago Press.

Aronczyk, Melissa. 2013. *Branding the Nation: The Global Business of National Identity.* Oxford: Oxford University Press.

Askew, Kelly. 2002. *Performing the Nation: Swahili Music and Cultural Politics in Tanzania.* Chicago: University of Chicago Press.

Awolowo, Obafemi. 1947. *Path to Nigerian Freedom.* London: Faber and Faber.

Bach, Daniel. 1997. "Indigeneity, Ethnicity, and Federalism." In *Transition Without End: Nigerian Politics and Civil Society Under Babangida*, edited by Larry Jay Diamond, Anthony Hamilton, Millard Kirk-Greene, and Oyeleye Oyediran, 333–49. Boulder, CO: Lynne Rienner Publishers.

Bakare-Yusuf, Bibi. 2009. "Nudity and Morality: Legislating Women's Bodies and Dress in Nigeria." *East African Journal of Peace and Rights* 15, no. 1: 53–68.

Balogun, Oluwakemi M. 2019. "Beauty and the Bikini: Embodied Respectability in Nigerian Beauty Pageants." *African Studies Review* 62, no. 2: 80–102.

Balogun, Oluwakemi M., and Kimberly Kay Hoang. 2018. "Political Economy of Embodiment: Capitalizing on Globally Staged Bodies in Nigerian Beauty Pageants and Vietnamese Sex Work." *Sociological Perspectives* 61, no. 6: 953–72.

Banet-Weiser, Sarah. 1999. *The Most Beautiful Girl in the World: Beauty Pageants and National Identity.* Berkeley: University of California Press, 1999.

Barber, Kristen. 2016. *Styling Masculinity: Gender, Class, and Inequality in the Men's Grooming Industry*. New Brunswick, NJ: Rutgers University Press.

Bartky, Sandra Lee. 1997. "Foucault, Femininity, and the Modernization of Patriarchal Power." In *Writing on the Body: Female Embodiment and Feminist Theory*, edited by Katie Conboy, Nadia Medina, and Sarah Stanbury, 129–54. New York: Columbia University Press.

Bayelsa State Tourism Development Agency. 2013. "Most Beautiful Girl in Nigeria Pageant Comes to Bayelsa." Press Release. Yanagoa. Online at http://tourbayelsa.com.ng/news.

Billig, Michael. 1995. *Banal Nationalism*. London: Sage.

Billings, Sabrina. 2014. *Language, Globalization, and the Making of a Tanzanian Beauty Queen*. Bristol, UK: Multilingual Affairs.

Bobel, Chris, and Samantha Kwan, eds. 2019. *Body Battlegrounds: Transgressions, Tensions, and Transformations*. Nashville: Vanderbilt University Press.

Bonikowski, Bart. 2013. *Varieties of Popular Nationalism in Modern Democracies: An Inductive Approach to Comparative Research on Political Culture*. Cambridge: Weatherhead Center for International Affairs.

Bordo, Susan. 1993. *Unbearable Weight: Feminism, Western Culture, and the Body*. Berkeley: University of California Press.

Bourdieu, Pierre. 1973. "Cultural Reproduction and Social Production." In *Knowledge, Education, and Social Change*, edited by Richard Brown, 71–112. London: Taylor and Francis.

Bourdieu, Pierre. 1984. *Distinction: A Social Critique of the Judgment of Taste*. London: Routledge.

Bourdieu, Pierre. 1986. "The Forms of Capital." In *Handbook of Theory and Research for the Sociology of Education*, edited by John G. Richardson, 46–58. New York: Greenwood.

Bowen, Sarah, and Marie Sarita Gaytán. 2012. "The Paradox of Protection: National Identity, Global Commodity Chains, and the Tequila Industry." *Social Problems* 59, no. 1: 70–93.

Boykoff, Jules. 2014. *Activism and the Olympics: Dissent at the Games in Vancouver and London*. New Brunswick, NJ: Rutgers University Press.

Bridges, Tristan. 2009. "Gender Capital and Male Bodybuilders." *Body & Society* 15, no. 1: 83–107.

Brink, Pamela J. 1989. "The Fattening Room Among the Annang of Nigeria." *Medical Anthropology* 12, no. 1: 131–43.

Brockett, Charles D. 1992. "Measuring Political Violence and Land Inequality in Central America." *American Political Science Review* 86, no. 1: 169–76.

Brubaker, Rogers, Margit Feischmidt, Jon Fox, and Liana Grancea. 2008. *Nationalist Politics and Everyday Ethnicity in a Transylvanian Town*. Princeton, NJ: Princeton University Press.

Burke, Timothy. 1996. *Lifebuoy Men, Lux Women: Commodification, Consumption, and Cleanliness in Modern Zimbabwe*. Durham, NC: Duke University Press.

Byfield, Judith. 2002. *A Social and Economic History of Women Dyers in Abeokuta (Nigeria), 1890–1940*. Portsmouth, NH: Heinemann.

Calhoun, Craig. 2008. "Cosmopolitanism and Nationalism." *Nations and Nationalism* 14, no. 3: 427.

Callahan, William A. 2006. *Cultural Governance and Resistance in Pacific Asia*. London: Routledge.

Casanova, Erynn Masi de. 2004. "'No Ugly Women': Concepts of Race and Beauty Among Adolescent Women in Ecuador." *Gender & Society* 18, no. 3: 287–308.

Casanova, Erynn Masi de, and Afshan Jafar. 2016. "The Body as a Site of Resistance." In *The SAGE Handbook of Resistance*, edited by David Courpasson and Steven Vallas, 139–55. London: Sage.

Chabal, Patrick, and Jean-Pascal Daloz. 1999. *Africa Works: Disorder as Political Instrument*. Bloomington: Indiana University Press.

Chapkis, Wendy. 1986. *Beauty Secrets: Women and the Politics of Appearance*. Boston: South End Press.

Charmaz, Kathy. 2014. *Constructing Grounded Theory*. London: Sage Publications.

Clark, Gracia. 1994. *Onions Are My Husband: Survival and Accumulation by West African Market Women*. Chicago: University of Chicago Press.

Cohen, Colleen Ballerino, Richard R. Wilk, and Beverly Stoeltje. 1996. *Beauty Queens on the Global Stage: Gender, Contests, and Power*. New York: Routledge.

Cole, Jennifer. 2010. *Sex and Salvation: Imagining the Future in Madagascar*. Chicago: University of Chicago Press.

Collier, Jane Fishburne. 1997. *From Duty to Desire: Remaking Families in a Spanish Village*. Princeton, NJ: Princeton University Press.

Comaroff, John, and Jean Comaroff. 2009. *Ethnicity Inc*. Chicago: University of Chicago Press.

Cornwall, Andrea. 2002. "Spending Power: Love, Money, and the Reconfiguration of Gender Relations in Ado-Odo, Southwestern Nigeria." *American Ethnologist* 29, no. 4: 963–80.

Craig, Maxine Leeds. 2002. *Ain't I a Beauty Queen? Black Women, Beauty, and the Politics of Race*. New York: Oxford University Press.

Craig, Maxine Leeds. 2009. "The Color of an Ideal Negro Beauty Queen: Miss Bronze 1961–1968." In *Shades of Difference: Why Skin Color Matters*, edited by Evelyn Nakano Glenn, 81–94. Stanford, CA: Stanford University Press.

Das, Veena.1995. *Critical Events: An Anthropological Perspective on Contemporary India: Delhi*. New York: Oxford University Press.

Deeb, Lara. 2006. *An Enchanted Modern: Gender and Public Piety in Shi'i Lebanon*. Princeton, NJ: Princeton University Press.

DeSoucey, Michaela. 2010. "Gastronationalism." *American Sociological Review* 75, no. 3: 432–55.

Dewey, Susan. 2008. *Making Miss India Miss World: Constructing Gender, Power, and the Nation in Post-Liberalization India*. Syracuse, NY: Syracuse University Press.

Diouf, Mamadou. 2000. "The Senegalese Murid Trade Diaspora and the Making of a Vernacular Cosmopolitanism." *Public Culture* 12, no. 3: 679–702.

Dittmer, Jason. 2017. *Diplomatic Material: Affect, Assemblage, and Foreign Policy*. Durham, NC: Duke University Press.

Doing Business. 2019. "Training for Reform. Economic Profile—Nigeria." Report. World Bank, Washington, DC. Online at https://www.doingbusiness.org /content/dam/ doingBusiness/country/n/nigeria/NGA.pdf.

Dosekun, Simidele. 2015. "For Western Girls Only? Postfeminism as Transnational Culture." *Feminist Media Studies* 15, no. 6: 960–75.

Dosekun, Simidele. 2017. "The Risky Business of Postfeminist Beauty." In *Aesthetic Labour: Rethinking Beauty Politics in Neoliberalism*, edited by Ana Sofia Elias, Rosalind Gill, and Christina Scharff, 167–81. London: Palgrave Macmillan.

Edmonds, Alexander. 2010. *Pretty Modern: Beauty, Sex, and Plastic Surgery in Brazil*. Durham, NC: Duke University Press.

Elias, Ana Sofia, Rosalind Gill, and Christina Scharff. 2017. *Aesthetic Labour: Beauty Politics in Neoliberalism*. London: Palgrave Macmillan.

Eltantawi, Sarah. 2017. *Shari'ah on Trial: Northern Nigeria's Islamic Revolution*. Berkeley: University of California Press.

Enloe, Cynthia H. 1990. *Bananas, Beaches and Bases: Making Feminist Sense of International Politics*. Berkeley: University of California Press.

Entwistle, Joanne, and Elizabeth Wissinger. 2006. "Keeping up Appearances: Aesthetic Labour in the Fashion Modelling Industries of London and New York." *Sociological Review* 54, no. 4: 774–94.

Falola, Toyin, and Matthew M. Heaton. 2008. *A History of Nigeria*. New York: Cambridge University Press.

Faludi, Susan. 1991. *Backlash: The Undeclared War Against American Women*. New York: Anchor Books.

Ferguson, James. 2006. *Global Shadows: Africa in the Neoliberal World Order*. Durham, NC: Duke University Press.

Ferree, Myra, and Aili Tripp. 2006. *Global Feminism: Transnational Women's Activism, Organizing, and Human Rights*. New York: New York University Press.

Ford, Kristie A. 2008. "Gazing into a Distorted Looking Glass: Masculinity, Femininity, Appearance Ideals, and the Black Body." *Sociology Compass* 2, no. 3: 1096–114.

Ford, Tanisha C. 2015. *Liberated Threads: Black Women, Style, and the Global Politics of Soul*. Chapel Hill: University of North Carolina Press.

Forrest, Tom. 1994. *The Advance of African Capital: The Growth of Nigerian Private Enterprise*. Charlottesville: University of Virginia Press.

Gellner, Ernest. 2006. *Nations and Nationalism*. Malden, MA: Blackwell.

George, Abosede A. 2014. *Making Modern Girls: A History of Girlhood, Labor, and Social Development in Colonial Lagos*. Athens: Ohio University Press.

Giddens, Anthony. 1991. *Modernity and Self Identity*. Stanford, CA: Stanford University Press.

Gilbert, Juliet. 2015. "'Be Graceful, Patient, Ever Prayerful': Negotiating Femininity, Respect and the Religious Self in Nigerian Beauty Pageant." *Africa* 85, no. 3: 501–20.

Gilman, Lisa. 2009. *The Dance of Politics: Gender, Performance, and Democratization in Malawi*. Philadelphia: Temple University Press.

Gimlin, Debra. 2007. "What Is 'Body Work'? A Review of the Literature." *Sociology Compass* 1, no. 1: 353–70.

Glenn, Evelyn Nakano. 2008. "Yearning for Lightness: Transnational Circuits in the Marketing and Consumption of Skin Lighteners." *Gender & Society* 22, no. 3: 281–302.

Grewal, Inderpal, and Caren Kaplan. 1994. "Transnational Feminist Practices and Questions of Postmodernity." In *Scattered Hegemonies: Postmodernity and Transnational Feminist Practices*, edited by Inderpal Grewal and Caren Kaplan, 1–36. Minneapolis: University of Minnesota Press.

Griswold, Wendy. 2000. *Bearing Witness: Readers, Writers, and the Novel in Nigeria*. Princeton, NJ: Princeton University Press.

Haub, Carl, and Toshiko Kaneda. 2015. "2014 World Population Data Sheet." Report. Population Reference Bureau, Washington, DC. Online at https://www.prb.org/2014-world-population-data-sheet/.

Haynes, Jonathan. 2016. *Nollywood: The Creation of Nigerian Film Genres*. Chicago: University of Chicago Press.

Hinojosa, Magda, and Jill Carle. 2016. "From Miss World to World Leader: Beauty Queens, Paths to Power, and Political Representations." *Journal of Women, Politics & Policy* 37, no. 1: 24–46.

Hoang, Kimberly Kay. 2015. *Dealing in Desire: Asian Ascendancy, Western Decline, and the Hidden Currencies of Global Sex Work*. Oakland: University of California Press.

Hobsbawm, Eric J. 1992. *Nations and Nationalism Since 1780*. Cambridge: Cambridge University Press.

Hobsbawm, Eric J., and Terence Ranger, eds. 1983. *The Invention of Tradition*. Cambridge: Cambridge University Press.

Hobson, Janell. 2005. *Venus in the Dark: Blackness and Beauty in Popular Culture*. New York: Routledge.

Holla, Sylvia, and Giselinde Kuipers. 2015. "Aesthetic Capital." In *International Handbook for the Sociology of Art and Culture*, edited by Laurie Hanquinet and Mike Savage, 290–304. London: Routledge.

hooks, bell. 1992. *Black Looks: Race and Representation*. Boston: South End Press.

Human Rights Watch. 2001. "Jos: A City Torn Apart." Report. New York. Online at https://www.hrw.org/reports/2001/nigeria/.

Human Rights Watch. 2003. "The Miss World Riots: Continued Impunity for Killings in Kaduna." Report. New York. Online at https://www.hrw.org /report/2003/07/22/miss-world-riots/continued-impunity-killings-kaduna.

Human Rights Watch. 2006. "'They Do Not Own This Place': Government Discrimination Against 'Non-Indigenes' in Nigeria." Report. New York. Online at https://www.hrw.org/report/2006/04/25/they-do-not-own-place /government-discrimination-against-non-indigenes-nigeria.

Hunter, Margaret L. 2011. "Buying Racial Capital: Skin Bleaching and Cosmetic Surgery in a Globalized World." *Journal of Pan African Studies* 4, no. 4: 142–64.

Imam, Ayesha. 2005. "Women's Reproductive and Sexual Rights and the Offence of Zina in Muslim Laws in Nigeria." In *Where Human Rights Begin: Health, Sexuality, and Women in the New Millennium,* edited by Wendy Chavkin and Elle Chesler, 65–94. New Brunswick, NJ: Rutgers University Press.

Jaggar, Alison. 2005. "'Saving Amina': Global Justice for Women and Intercultural Dialogue." *Ethics and International Affairs* 19, no. 3: 55–75.

Jha, Meeta Rani. 2015. *The Global Beauty Industry: Colorism, Racism, and the National Body.* London: Routledge.

Joseph, Richard. 2008. "Progress and Retreat in Africa: Challenges of a 'Frontier' Region." *Journal of Democracy* 19, no. 2: 94–108.

Joseph, Richard A. 1987. *Democracy and Prebendal Politics in Nigeria: The Rise and Fall of the Second Republic.* New York: Cambridge University Press.

Kalu, Ogbu. 2003. "Safiyya and Adamah: Punishing Adultery with Sharia Stones in Twenty-First-Century Nigeria." *African Affairs* 102, no. 408: 389–408.

Kaneda, Toshiko, and Kristin Bietsch. 2016. "2016 World Population Data Sheet." Report. Population Reference Bureau, Washington, DC. Online at https:// www.prb.org/2016-world-population-data-sheet/.

Kardam, Nüket. 2004. "The Emerging Global Gender Equality Regime from Neoliberal and Constructivist Perspectives in International Relations." *International Feminist Journal of Politics* 6, no. 1: 85–109.

Kendhammer, Brandon. 2013. "The Sharia Controversy in Northern Nigeria and the Politics of Islamic Law in New and Uncertain Democracies." *Comparative Politics* 45, no. 3: 291–311.

Kim-Puri, H. J. 2005. "Conceptualizing Gender-Sexuality-State-Nation." *Gender & Society* 19, no. 2: 137–59.

King-O'Riain, Rebecca Chiyoko. 2006. *Pure Beauty: Judging Race in Japanese American Beauty Pageants*. Minneapolis: University of Minnesota Press.

Kraxberger, Brennan. 2005. "Strangers, Indigenes and Settlers: Contested Geographies of Citizenship in Nigeria." *Space and Polity* 9, no. 1: 9–27.

Krings, Matthias, and Onookome Okome, eds. 2013. *Global Nollywood: The Transnational Dimensions of an African Video Film Industry*. Bloomington: University of Indiana Press.

Landau, Loren B., and Iriann Freemantle. 2010. "Tactical Cosmopolitanism and Idioms of Belonging: Insertion and Self-Exclusion in Johannesburg." *Journal of Ethnic and Migration Studies* 36, no. 3: 375–90.

Larkin, Brian. 2008. *Signal and Noise: Media, Infrastructure, and Urban Culture in Nigeria*. Durham, NC: Duke University Press.

Lee, Sharon Heijin. 2008. "'Around the World with Oprah': Neoliberalism, Race, and the (Geo)politics of Beauty." *Women & Performance: A Journal of Feminist Theory* 18, no. 1: 25–41.

Lenskyj, Helen Jefferson. 2014. *Sexual Diversity and the Sochi 2014 Olympics*. London: Palgrave Macmillan.

Levey, Hilary. 2007. "Here She Is . . . There She Goes?" *Contexts* 6, no. 3: 70–72.

Lewis, Peter. 1996. "From Prebendalism to Predation: The Political Economy of Decline in Nigeria." *Journal of Modern African Studies* 34, no. 1: 79–103.

Magubane, Zine. 2001. "Which Bodies Matter? Feminism, Poststructuralism, Race, and the Curious Theoretical Odyssey of the 'Hottentot Venus.'" *Gender & Society* 15, no. 6: 816–34.

Mahmood, Saba. 2005. *Politics of Piety: The Islamic Revival and the Feminist Subject*. Princeton, NJ: Princeton University Press.

Mama, Amina. 1995. "Feminism or Femocracy? State Feminism and Democratisation in Nigeria." *Africa Development/Afrique et Développement* 20, no. 1: 37–58.

Mama, Amina. 1998. "Khaki in the Family: Gender Discourses and Militarism in Nigeria." *African Studies Review* 41, no. 2: 1–18.

Mamdani, Mahmood. 2001. "Beyond Settler and Native as Political Identities: Overcoming the Political Legacy of Colonialism." *Comparative Studies in Society and History* 43, no. 4: 651–64.

Mayer, Tamar. 2004. "Embodied Nationalisms." In *Mapping Women, Making Politics: Feminist Perspectives on Political Geography*, edited by Lynn A. Staeheli, Eleonore Kofman, and Linda Peake, 153–67. New York: Routledge.

Mbembe, Achille. 2001. *On the Postcolony*. Berkeley: University of California Press.

McClintock, Anne. 1995. *Imperial Leather: Race, Gender, and Sexuality in the Colonial Contest*. New York: Routledge.

McConnell, Fiona, Terri Moreau, and Jason Dittmer. 2012. "Mimicking State Diplomacy: The Legitimizing Strategies of Unofficial Diplomacies." *Geoforum* 43, no. 4: 804–14.

Mears, Ashley. 2011. *Pricing Beauty: The Making of a Fashion Model*. Oakland: University of California Press.

Mears, Ashley. 2015. "Girls as Elite Distinction: The Appropriation of Bodily Capital." *Poetics* 53: 22–37.

Mears, Ashley, and Catherine Connell. 2016. "The Paradoxical Value of Deviant Cases: Toward a Gendered Theory of Display Work." *Signs: Journal of Women in Culture and Society* 41, no. 2: 333–59.

Miller-Young, Mireille. 2014. *A Taste for Brown Sugar: Black Women in Pornography*. Durham, NC: Duke University Press.

Moallem, Minoo. 2005. *Between Warrior Brother and Veiled Sister: Islamic Fundamentalism and the Politics of Patriarchy in Iran*. Berkeley: University of California Press.

Mohanty, Chandra Talpade. 1988. "Under Western Eyes: Feminist Scholarship and Colonial Discourses." *Feminist Review* 30, no. 1: 61–88.

Mojola, Sanyu. 2014. *Love, Money, and HIV: Becoming a Modern African Woman in the Age of AIDS*. Oakland: University of California Press.

Mougoué, Jacqueline-Bethel Tchouta. 2019. *Gender, Separatist Politics and Embodied Nationalism in Cameroon*. Ann Arbor: University of Michigan Press.

Murray, Stuart. 2012. "The Two Halves of Sports-Diplomacy." *Diplomacy & Statecraft* 23: 576–92.

Nagel, Joane. 1998. "Masculinity and Nationalism: Gender and Sexuality in the Making of Nations." *Ethnic and Racial Studies* 21, no. 2: 242–69.

National Bureau of Statistics. 2018. "Labor Force Statistics—Volume 1: Unemployment and Underemployment Report." Report. Abuja.

National Bureau of Statistics. 2019. "Nigerian Gross Domestic Product Report Q12019." Report. Abuja.

Ndlovu, Sifiso Mxolisi. 2010. "Sports as Cultural Diplomacy: The 2010 FIFA World Cup in South Africa's Foreign Policy." *Soccer & Society* 11, nos. 1–2: 144–53.

Nguyen, Mimi. 2011. "The Biopower of Beauty: Humanitarian Imperialisms and Global Feminisms in an Age of Terror." *Signs: Journal of Women in Culture and Society* 36, no. 2: 359–83.

Obadare, Ebenezer. 2004. "In Search of a Public Sphere: The Fundamentalist Challenge to Civil Society in Nigeria." *Patterns of Prejudice* 38, no. 2: 177–98.

Obadare, Ebenezer. 2005. "A Crisis of Trust: History, Politics, Religion and the Polio Controversy in Northern Nigeria." *Patterns of Prejudice* 39, no. 3: 265–84.

Ochoa, Marcia. 2014. *Queen for a Day: Transformistas, Beauty Queens, and the Performance of Femininity in Venezuela.* Durham, NC: Duke University Press.

Ogunyankin, Grace Adeniyi. 2018. "A 'Scented Declaration of Progress': Globalisation, Afropolitan Imagineering and Familiar Orientations." *Antipode* 50, no. 5: 1145–65.

Okafor, Emeka Emmanuel. 2011. "Youth Unemployment and Implications for Stability of Democracy in Nigeria." *Journal of Sustainable Development in Africa* 13, no.1: 358–73.

Okonta, Ike. 2008. *When Citizens Revolt: Nigerian Elites, Big Oil, and the Ogoni Struggle for Self-Determination.* Trenton, NJ: Africa World Press.

Oloruntoba-Oju, Taiwo. 2007. "Body Images, Beauty Culture and Language in the Nigeria, African Context." Understanding Human Sexuality Seminar Series. African Regional Sexuality Resource Centre, Lagos, Nigeria.

Oso, Lai. 1991. "The Commercialization of the Nigerian Press: Development and Implications." *Africa Media Review* 5, no. 3: 41–51.

Otis, Eileen M. 2011. *Markets and Bodies: Women, Service Work, and the Making of Inequality in China.* Stanford, CA: Stanford University Press.

Otis, Eileen M. 2016. "Bridgework: Globalization, Gender, and Service Labor at a Luxury Hotel." *Gender & Society* 30, no. 6: 912–34.

Oyěwùmí, Oyèrónké. 1997. *The Invention of Women: Making an African Sense of Western Gender Discourses.* Minneapolis: University of Minnesota Press.

Oza, Rupal. 2001. "Showcasing India: Gender, Geography, and Globalization." *Signs* 26, no. 4: 1067–95.

Page, Matthew T. 2018. *A New Taxonomy for Corruption in Nigeria.* Washington, DC: Carnegie Endowment for International Peace.

Parameswaran, Radhika. 2001. "Global Media Events in India: Contests over Beauty, Gender and Nation." *Journalism & Communication Monographs* 3, no. 2: 51–105.

Parvez, Fareen. 2017. *Politicizing Islam: The Islamic Revival in France and India.* Oxford, UK: Oxford University Press.

Pierce, Steven. 2016. *Moral Economies of Corruption: State Formation and Political Culture in Nigeria.* Durham, NC: Duke University Press.

Pierre, Jemima. 2008. "'I Like Your Colour!' Skin Bleaching and Geographies of Race in Urban Ghana." *Feminist Review* 90, no. 1: 9–29.

Pool, Hannah Azieb, ed. 2016. *Fashion Cities Africa.* Bristol, UK: Intellect.

Popenoe, Rebecca. 2004. *Feeding Desire: Fatness, Beauty, and Sexuality Among a Saharan People.* New York: Routledge.

Price, Monroe E., and Daniel Dayan, eds. 2008. *Owning the Olympics: Narratives of the New China.* Ann Arbor: University of Michigan Press.

Puri, Jyoti. 1999. *Woman, Body, Desire in Post-Colonial India: Narratives of Gender and Sexuality.* New York: Routledge.

Radhakrishnan, Smitha, and Cinzia Solari. 2015. "Empowered Women, Failed Patriarchs: Neoliberalism and Global Gender Anxieties." *Sociology Compass* 9, no. 9: 784–802.

Ranger, Terrence. 1983. "The Invention of Tradition in Colonial Africa." In *The Invention of Tradition*, edited by Terrence Ranger and Eric Hobsbawm, 211–62. Cambridge: Cambridge University Press.

Reyes, Victoria. 2014. "The Production of Cultural and Natural Wealth: An Examination of World Heritage Sites." *Poetics* 44: 42–63.

Reyes, Victoria. 2018. "Ethnographic Toolkit: Strategic Positionality and Researchers' Visible and Invisible Tools in Field Research." *Ethnography*, October 25. Online at https://doi.org/10.1177/1466138118805121.

Rivera, Lauren A. 2008. "Managing 'Spoiled' National Identity: War, Tourism, and Memory in Croatia." *American Sociological Review* 73, no. 4: 613–34.

Robertson, Charles, Nothando Ndebele, and Yvonne Mhango. 2011. "A Survey of the Nigerian Middle Class." Renaissance Capital. Online at http://www.fastestbillion.com/res/Research/Survey_Nigerian_middle_class-260911.pdf.

Rodriguez, Evelyn Ibatan. 2013. *Celebrating Debutantes and Quinceañeras: Coming of Age in American Ethnic Communities.* Philadelphia: Temple University Press.

Rokita, Theodore Edward. 1994. "Why U.S.-Enforced International Flight Suspension Due to Deficient Foreign Airport Security Should Be a No-Go." *Indiana International and Comparative Law Review* 5, no. 1: 205–36.

Rotberg, Robert I. 2004. *Crafting the New Nigeria: Confronting the Challenges.* Boulder, CO: Lynne Rienner.

Saavedra, Martha. 2003. "Football Feminine—Development of the African Game: Senegal, Nigeria and South Africa." *Soccer & Society* 4, nos. 2–3: 225–53.

Salzinger, Leslie. 2003. *Genders in Production: Making Workers in Mexico's Global Factories.* Berkeley: University of California Press.

Saraswati, L. Ayu. 2013. *Seeing Beauty, Sensing Race in Transnational Indonesia.* Honolulu: University of Hawai'i Press.

Scacco, Alexandra. 2010. "Who Riots? Explaining Individual Participation in Ethnic Violence in Nigeria." PhD dissertation, Columbia University.

Schimmel, Kimberly S. 2012. "Neoliberal Redevelopment, Sport Infrastructure, and the Militarization of US Urban Terrain." In *Sport and Neoliberalism: Politics, Consumption, and Culture*, edited by Michael L Silk and David L. Andrews, 160–76. Philadelphia: Temple University Press.

Shauert, Paul. 2015. *Staging Ghana: Artistry and Nationalism in State Dance Ensemble.* Bloomington: Indiana University Press.

Shilling, Chris. 2003. *The Body and Social Theory.* London: Sage Publications.

Sklair, Leslie. 2001. *The Transnational Capitalist Class.* Oxford: Blackwell Publishers.

Smith, Anthony D. 2010. *Nationalism.* Cambridge: Polity Press.

Smith, Daniel Jordan. 2007. *A Culture of Corruption: Everyday Deception and Popular Discontent in Nigeria.* Princeton, NJ: Princeton University Press.

Smith, Daniel Jordan. 2017. *To Be a Man Is Not a One-Day Job: Masculinity, Money, and Intimacy in Nigeria.* Chicago: University of Chicago Press.

Spillman, Lyn. 1997. *Nation and Commemoration: Creating National Identities in the United States and Australia.* Cambridge: Cambridge University Press.

Spivak, Gayatri Chakravorty. 1988. "Can the Subaltern Speak?" In *Marxism and the Interpretation of Culture*, edited by Cary Nelson and Lawrence Grossberg, 271–313. Urbana: University of Illinois Press.

Stanfield, Michael Edward. 2013. *Of Beasts and Beauty: Gender, Race, and Identity in Colombia.* Austin: University of Texas Press.

Stutern. 2017. "The Nigerian Graduate Report 2016." Report. Lagos. Online at https://app.stutern.com/whitepapers/nigerian_graduate_report.

Suberu, Rotimi T. 2001. *Federalism and Ethnic Conflict in Nigeria*. Washington, DC: United States Institute of Peace Press.

Surak, Kristin. 2013. *Making Tea, Making Japan: Cultural Nationalism in Practice*. Stanford, CA: Stanford University Press.

Taleb, Nassim. 2007. *The Black Swan: The Impact of the Highly Improbable*. New York: Random House.

Tamale, Sylvia. 2016. "Nudity, Protest and the Law in Uganda." Lecture at Makerere University School of Law, Kampala, Uganda. Online at http://www.searcwl.ac.zw/downloads/Tamale_Inaugural_Lecture.pdf.

Tate, Shirley. 2017. "Skin: Postfeminist Bleaching Culture and the Political Vulnerability of Blackness." In *Aesthetic Labour: Rethinking Beauty Politics in Neoliberalism*, edited by Ana Sofia Elias, Rosalind Gill, and Christina Scharff, 199–213. London: Palgrave Macmillan.

Thangaraj, Stanley I. 2015. *Desi Hoop Dreams: Pickup Basketball and the Making of Asian American Masculinity*. New York: New York University Press.

Thomas, Lynn. 2009. "Skin Lighteners in South Africa: Transnational Entanglements and Technologies of the Self." In *Shades of Difference: Why Skin Color Matters*, edited by Evelyn Nakano Glenn, 188–210. Stanford, CA: Stanford University Press.

Tice, Karen Whitney. 2012. *Queens of Academe: Beauty Pageants and Campus Life*. New York: Oxford University Press.

Tomlinson, Alan, and Christopher Young. 2006. *National Identity and Global Sports Events: Culture, Politics, and Spectacle in the Olympics and the Football World Cup*. New York: State University of New York Press.

Transparency International. 2001. "Corruption Perceptions Index 2001." Report. Berlin. Online at https://www.transparency.org/research/cpi/cpi_2001/0.

Transparency International. 2018. "Corruption Perceptions Index 2018." Report. Berlin. Online at https://www.transparency.org/cpi2018.

Tsika, Noah A. 2015. *Nollywood Stars: Media and Migration in West Africa and the Diaspora*. Bloomington: Indiana University Press.

Ukiwo, Ukoha. 2003. "Politics, Ethno-Religious Conflicts and Democratic Consolidation in Nigeria." *Journal of Modern African Studies* 41, no. 1: 115–38.

Vaughn, Olufemi. 2006. *Nigerian Chiefs: Traditional Power in Modern Politics, 1890s–1990s*. Rochester, NY: University of Rochester Press.

Warhurst, Chris, and Dennis Nickson. 2001. *Looking Good, Sounding Right*. London: Industrial Society.

Watts, Michael. 2004. "Resource Curse? Governmentality, Oil and Power in the Niger Delta, Nigeria." *Geopolitics* 9, no. 1: 50–80.

Weiss, Robert S. 1994. *Learning from Strangers: The Art and Method of Qualitative Interview Studies*. New York: Free Press.

Werbner, Pnina. 2006. "Vernacular Cosmopolitanism." *Theory, Culture & Society* 23, nos. 2–3: 496–98.

Wherry, Frederick F. 2006. "The Nation-State, Identity Management, and Indigenous Crafts: Constructing Markets and Opportunities in Northwest Costa Rica." *Ethnic and Racial Studies* 29, no. 1: 124–52.

Wherry, Frederick F., and Nina Bandelj. 2011. *The Cultural Wealth of Nations*. Stanford, CA: Stanford University Press.

Williams, Christine L., and Catherine Connell. 2010. "'Looking Good and Sounding Right': Aesthetic Labor and Social Inequality in the Retail Industry." *Work and Occupations* 37, no. 3: 349–77.

Wissinger, Elizabeth. 2015. *This Year's Model: Fashion, Media, and the Making of Glamour*. New York: New York University Press.

Wolf, Naomi. 1991. *The Beauty Myth: How Images of Beauty Are Used Against Women*. New York: William Morrow.

World Bank. 2018. "The World Bank in Nigeria—Overview." Report. Washington, DC. Online at https://www.worldbank.org/en/country/nigeria/overview.

World Bank. 2019. "Washington Development Indicators." Database. Washington, DC. Online at https://databank.worldbank.org/source/world-development-indicators.

World Health Organization. 2011. "Preventing Skin Disease Through Healthy Environments: Mercury in Skin Lightening Products." Press release. World Health Organization.

Yates, Douglas A. 1996. *The Rentier State in Africa: Oil Rent Dependency and Neocolonialism in the Republic of Gabon*. Trenton, NJ: Africa World Press.

Yuval-Davis, Nira. 1997. *Gender and Nation*. Thousand Oaks, CA: Sage Publications.

Index

Page references in italics refer to figures.

idealized femininity. *See* femininity

Igbo (ethnic group), 4, 42, 83, 148–49, 150

image campaigns, 7, 10–12, 17, 40, 78, 241n4, 252n6

India, 4–5, 25, 28, 112, 200, 232–33

Indonesia, 54, 112, 232

International Civil Aviation Organization, 7

international human rights. *See* human rights

invented tradition, 121–22, 134, 148–49. *See also* traditional segment of pageants

IQ segment of pageants, 83

Islam. *See* Muslim communities

Jackson, Glenda, 225

Jagger, Bianca, 210, 250n27

Jamaica, 62

Jewel by Lisa fashion brand, 5

Jonathan, Patience, 239n25

Juel, Masja, 226–27

Kaduna riots (2002), 14, 197, 218

Karamanu, Anna, 225

Kebede, Liya, 114

Kenya, 90

Lagos, description of, 96–97, 152–53, 202, 203, 244n16

Lagos International Airport, 6–7, *8*

Lagos Island Club, 45

language, 83–84

Larkin, Brian, 48

Lawal, Amina, 14, 197–98, 201–2, 221–27, 249n16

Little Miss Nigeria, 23

local *vs.* classy girls, distinction of, 96

magazine industry, 114

makeup, 73, 74, 99, 139

male beauty pageants, 23, 160, 243n48

male gaze, 102–3, 169. *See also* gender inequality

Mamdani, Mahmood, 149

market women, 94, 95

marriageability, 101–2, 130

masculinity, 158, 161

Mass Mobilization for Self-Reliance, Social Justice, and Economic Recovery (MAMSER), 40

Mayer, Tamar, 42

Mbembe, Achille, 179

MBGN (Most Beautiful Girl in Nigeria) Pageant, 13, 182; desired contestant types for, 94–97; on international beauty standards, 128–29; invented ethnic tradition and, 121–22; media industry and, 55–58, 163–67, 190; modeling segment in, 139–41; operations of, 58–63, 242n38; program of, *111*; regional representation in, 146–53; rise of, 53–54; swimwear segment in, 63, 132, 143–46; tactical cosmopolitan-nationalism in, 63, 110–11, 119, 138–39, 153; traditional segment of, 119–21, 147; winning prizes of, 74

redemptive politics in, 9–15; royal
families of, 237n1; sharia law in, 14,
15, 40, 150, 197, 200–201. *See also*
national identity
"Nigerian factor," 7, 15, 104, 179
Nigerian Labour Congress, 168
Nigerian Postal Service (NIPOST), 12
Nigerian Television Authority (NTA),
64, 66. *See also* TV Enterprises
(TVE)
Nigerian Tourism Development Cor-
poration (NTDC), 10
Nivea, 111–12
Nnaji, Genevieve, 114
Nollywood film industry, 5, 114, 235
nostalgic-nationalism strategy,
37, 39
"No Woman, No Nation" slogan, 43
nudity, 132, 195, 212–21. *See also* bikini
segment in pageants

oba, 1, 237n1
Obasanjo, Olusegun: on Darego's pag-
eant win, 1, 7; image campaign of,
40; reelection of, 201–2, 203, 228
Obasanjo, Stella, 193, 196, 234
Ochoa, Marcia, 85, 102
Ogunyankin, Grace Adeniyi, 112
oil and gas industry, 7–9, 178–79, 231,
247n8
Okorafor, Nnedi, 5
Olympic Games, 10, 27, 28, 196, 235
Onweagba, Oluchi, 114
Otis, Eileen, 63
Ovaltine, 47

Oyekan, Adeyinka, 1
Oyelude, Grace Tinuke, 45–50,
242n29
Oyěwùmí, Oyèrónkẹ́, 23

pageant owners, 162–70. See also
names of specific owners
pageantry. *See* beauty pageant industry, overview
People's Democratic Party (PDP),
184–86, 250n23
personal sponsorships, 85, 89–90, 103,
170–72
pet projects. *See* charitable work
picture queens, 82
piety, 212–21
plastic surgery, 113–14, 145
Plateau (state), 118, 184
Platform for Action, 221
platforming, as concept, 244n1
platform of pageantry, 199; for careers
of contestants, 13, 20, 24, 68–69,
78–79, 90–91, 168–69; cultural
and economic mobility from,
92–102; cultural capital from, 70,
72, 252n6; economic capital from,
70, 72, 157; for national and global
promotion, 43, 60, 69, 165–67,
175–76; social capital from, 70, 72,
85–91, 157, 171–72. *See also* business
of pageants
postcolonial feminism, 42, 112
poverty, 92–93. *See also* unemployment
prizes for pageant winners, 24, 45, 48,
51–52, 73, 147, 155–56, 167, 187–88

GLOBALIZATION
IN EVERYDAY LIFE

As global forces undeniably continue to change the politics and econo-mies of the world, we need a more nuanced understanding of what these changes mean in our daily lives. Significant theories and studies have broadened and deepened our knowledge on globalization, yet we need to think about how these macro processes manifest on the ground and how they are maintained through daily actions.

Globalization in Everyday Life foregrounds ethnographic examina-tion of daily life to address issues that will bring tangibility to previously abstract assertions about the global order. This series employs three central approaches: (1) the examination of local negotiations of global forces; (2) the mapping of everyday operations of the institutions, systems, and spaces of globalization; and (3) the analysis of various mediums of global exchanges. Moving beyond mere illustrations of global trends, books in this series should underscore mutually constitu-tive processes of the local and global by finding unique and informative ways to bridge macro- and microanalyses. We seek books that combine rich theoretical and empirical treatments, and that can speak across various disciplines including anthropology, communications, cultural studies, environmental studies, political science, and sociology. This series will be a high-profile outlet for books that offer accessible reader-ship, innovative approaches, instructive models, and analytic insights to our understanding of globalization.